SERVING LESBIAN, GAY, BISEXUAL, TRANSGENDER, AND QUESTIONING TEENS

A How-To-Do-It Manual for Librarians

HILLIAS J. MARTIN, JR.
JAMES R. MURDOCK

HOW-TO-DO-IT MANUALS FOR LIBRARIANS

NUMBER 151

NEAL-SCHUMAN PUBLISHERS, INC.
New York   London

Published by Neal-Schuman Publishers, Inc.
100 William St., Suite 2004
New York, NY 10038

Printed and bound in the United States of America.

The paper used in this publication meets the minimum requirements of American National Standard for Information Sciences—Permanence of Paper for Printed Library Materials, ANSI Z39.48-1992.

ISBN-13: 978-1-55570-566-4
ISBN-10: 1-55570-566-9

Library of Congress Cataloging-in-Publication Data

Martin, Hillias J.
   Serving lesbian, gay, bisexual, transgender, and questioning teens: a how-to-do-it manual for librarians / Hillias J. Martin, Jr., James R. Murdock.
        p. cm. — (How-to-do-it manuals ; no. 151)
   Includes bibliographical references and index.
   ISBN-13: 978-1-55570-566-4 (alk. paper)
   ISBN-10: 1-55570-566-9 (alk. paper)
   1. Libraries and sexual minorities. 2. Libraries and teenagers. 3. Sexual minority youth—Bibliography. 4. Libraries—Special collections—Sexual minorities. 5. Libraries—Special collections—Young adult literature. I. Murdock, James R. II. Title.
   Z711.92.S49M37 2007
   027.6'3—dc22
                                                          20066039469

Serving Lesbian, Gay, Bisexual, Transgender, and Questioning Teens: A How-To-Do-It Manual for Librarians is a long overdue resource, an extremely positive addition to the canon of materials available to young adult librarians. The work is truly eye-opening and energizing to read. The authors have put their heart and soul into making sure this is a useful and meaningful tool. They do an excellent job of conveying their passion for serving queer teens, pointing out the various inequalities these patrons face in public libraries.

I unequivocally recommend this book to other young adult librarians. They are desperate for resources on LGBTQ teens, and this one certainly fills the gap. The bibliographies, booktalks, and programming sections are gold mines of ideas for collection development and of roads for librarians to take in making this population feel more comfortable in the library. The authors raise important concerns on how central libraries often collect LGBTQ materials yet don't pay attention to what's happening in the branches. This book shows how *all* libraries can improve their service to LGBTQ teens and train staff members to become more tolerant and understanding.

Amelia J. Shelley
Manager, Youth and Outreach Services
Laramie County Library System
Laramie, Wyoming

Serving Lesbian, Gay, Bisexual, Transgender, and Questioning Teens: A How-To-Do-It Manual for Librarians is fulfilling, immediately useful, and engaging. It takes a sorely undertreated topic and applies both readily accessible theory and practical advice that should be welcome in any contemporary library setting in which there is the potential to serve LGBTQ youth. Indeed, I am already talking up this resource with both my peers and the youth staff whom I supervise.

This is an excellent resource on several fronts: its original approach to discussing library services for queer youth; its grounded discussions of collection development, booktalking, program planning, and other library tasks that are pertinent to serving anyone and everyone, including but not limited to queer youth; the amiable tone assumed by the authors; the intellectual rigor with which they discuss both sociopolitical and professional matters; and the inclusion of voices from their peers in other communities to present a balanced presentation.

The book is well organized and accessible, inviting exploration by both library students and seasoned practitioners. The authors demonstrate how to use life experience on the job without stumbling into setting up a cult of a particular personality. The choices of materials to include in collections, booktalks, and programs are all spot-on. Not only would I encourage YA librarians to buy and use this book, but I would call it to the attention of library administrators and paraprofessional staff working in any library where queer youth have the potential to be served.

Francisca Goldsmith
Library Services Manager
Berkeley Public Library
Berkeley, California

We dedicate this book to our grandmothers.

CONTENTS

FOREWORD
BY DAVID LEVITHAN

Shortly before my novel *Boy Meets Boy* was published in 2003, I went to see Brent Hartinger in Tacoma, Washington. Brent's gay-themed teen novel *Geography Club* had been published a few months before, and we joked that we were newly minted members of the Gay Teen Lit Club— active population, single digits. But growing. Hopefully growing. We talked about what it was like to be published, and then Brent said something that has become, for me, one the most significant parts of being an author.

"Wait till you get the e-mails," he said.

I knew what he meant. As an editor, I'd seen how willing teen readers were to write to authors and tell them about how they'd connected to what they'd just read. And as an author, I knew that my book would probably inspire some reaction.

But really, I had no idea.

It's not like the old days, when a teenager had to pick up a pen, find a stamp and envelope, procure an address, and, most likely, write a return address in the upper left corner. No—now the reaction is instantaneous, the access complete. "I just finished reading your book five minutes ago." "I had to write you." "You probably get this all the time, but your book meant so much to me." "I know you're writing about me."

We members of the Gay Teen Lit Club (there are more than a dozen of us now) get thousands of these e-mails. They are inspiring and humbling and gratifying and heartbreaking and mind-blowing. I can remember so many of them so clearly: the girl who carried a copy of my book in her backpack at all times for when she started to doubt herself; the boy, age twelve, who didn't have a problem with being gay, but definitely had a problem with the fact that he couldn't find a boyfriend; the fourteen-year-old girl who thanked me because my book made her realize that "homosexuals are really human beings"; the straight boy who wrote because his girlfriend asked him to read the book, and he loved it so much he wanted to get a signed copy for her; the eighty-year-old who wrote to say that "things sure have changed since I was a high school student in the 1940s!" Kids and adults. Girls and boys. Gay kids and straight kids. So many different things said, but all of them pointing to the same thing: Books matter.

It's true. I've seen it. I've read the e-mails. I've met some of the kids. I've seen how it works. The right book at the right time can make such a difference. Books do not create identities, but they can affirm identities. A single book cannot make a reader at home in the world, but it can make that reader know that she or he is not alone.

Sometimes words aren't enough. One of the most sobering experiences I've ever had was coming across a Myspace profile of a gay kid who had killed himself; *Boy Meets Boy* was listed as one of his favorite books. But for every time when words aren't enough—times when there are too many obstacles for someone to overcome—there are dozens where words have helped. As adults, it is our responsibility to make sure that teens navigate the course of their identities as safely as possible. So many things depend on it.

We authors are the lucky ones—we're the ones the readers thank. But really, when they thank us, they are also thanking the people who helped get the book into their hands. Not just the publisher and editor who made the book possible, but also the bookseller and, more often than not, the librarian who made the book visible to them, who decided that their story should be represented on the shelves. I know that readers would be thankful that a book like this one is available, and that the lessons contained within it have helped make so many of their lives that much better. I wish I could line up all the kids and adults who've written to me and have them say thank you to the librarians who opened the door for them. I wish you could see them, could talk to them, and receive their thanks. I promise that by the twentieth reader you'd be speechless, and by the hundredth you'd be beyond speech. And, mark my words, you would have no doubt: Books matter.

PREFACE

Providing library service to a community begins with identifying the community and understanding its needs. Recognizing the community of lesbian, gay, bisexual, transgendered, and questioning (LGBTQ) teens can sometimes be difficult. The reason is simple: These teens look and act like every other kid in the library. This community, in other words, is often invisible. It is tempting to equate invisibility with nonexistence, but LGBTQ teens are everywhere. They are in neighborhoods, schools, and libraries everywhere. Consider these findings:

▼ according to most estimates, 5 to 6 percent of teenagers in the United States today are lesbian, gay, or bisexual—roughly 2.5 million people (Sell, Wells, and Wypij, 1995);

▼ the number of kids who question their sexuality is astonishingly large—research suggests that many ostensibly heterosexual teens engage in sexual activity with others of the same gender, and some studies even suggest that as many as 20 percent of teens today are not completely heterosexual (Savin-Williams, 2005);

▼ other data show that nearly 80 percent of all teens know someone who is LGBTQ (GLSEN, 2005); and

▼ still other surveys document that today's generation is the most tolerant yet—seven out of ten teens believe that LGBTQ people contribute positively to society. (Hamilton College National Youth Polls, 2006)

While some LGBTQ teens are able to admit confidently to themselves and to others who they really are, many long for the day that they can do so. A big reason is that even though today's generation is more tolerant, studies consistently show that nine out of ten teens witness homophobia in the form of bullying or hate speech directed at LGBTQ people (GLSEN, 2005). Homophobia, in fact, is often labeled the last respectable prejudice. As a result of this prejudice, LGBTQ teens receive unequal treatment. Their emotional and physical health often goes unacknowledged by teachers, school administrators, and parents. And, in many communities, their information needs go underrepresented by libraries (Clyde and Lobban, 2001).

Serving Lesbian, Gay, Bisexual, Transgender, and Questioning Teens: A How-To-Do-It Manual for Librarians is a tool to:

▼ suggest how to provide consistent and sensitive service to all teens in a way that helps them build developmental assets;

▼ help librarians identify excellent LGBTQ materials for their YA collections;

▼ present LGBTQ-themed programming that will excite and inspire all teens.

Although this book was designed mainly for young adult specialists in public libraries and school librarians, the suggestions that it contains apply equally to all librarians who serve teens. These recommendations are based on personal experience, the experiences of other YA librarians nationwide, expert research in the field, and, most important, on what teens say they want.

Some librarians, considering their workplace an already inclusive space, may feel it is unwise to single out the needs of just one group of teens. In a sense, we could not agree more. The first and best advice when acquiring materials and offering programs is always to present LGBTQ materials alongside everything else that you offer—if you don't single out these materials as taboo, neither will your patrons. But this isn't always as easy as it sounds, which is partly why this book was written. Other librarians may question the need for singling out the LGBTQ community when the library already boasts a proud history of welcoming it. (It is no coincidence that Barbara Gittings, a pioneer of the LGBTQ civil rights movement, is affiliated with the ALA, or that the Minneapolis Public Library's bookmobile rides in that city's annual Pride Month parade, as do other bookmobiles around the country.) But the forces arrayed against open access to LGBTQ materials speak with a loud and unrelenting voice. In 2004, the American Library Association recorded a spike in the number of books challenged due to same-sex content (ALA, 2005a). Just one year later, lawmakers in Tampa Bay, Florida, quashed the county library's Pride Month programming (Alexander, 2005). Efforts to remove LGBTQ content from the library remain potent, and we ignore them at our peril.

Librarians have an obligation to serve all members of their community. LGBTQ teens visit the library to find books and materials containing characters like themselves; for information about how to come out and about safe sex; for entertainment; and to find solace. Many straight kids seek exactly the same thing—because they have LGBTQ friends and family, or because they simply want to be entertained by good stories. The point is that LGBTQ-themed materials are not just meant for a single population; they're meant for everyone. And for many teens, particularly those unable to access these materials at home, the library is a lifeline.

Serving Lesbian, Gay, Bisexual, Transgender, and Questioning Teens: A How-To-Do-It Manual for Librarians contains a plethora of facts about teens and what they want from the library in the way of LGBTQ materials. It's been nearly forty years since the first acknowledged gay character graced the pages of a YA novel. What began with only a trickle of titles has blossomed into a large and successful publishing niche, with a dozen or so new books appearing each year. The LGBTQ segment of the nonfiction YA market is smaller than the LGBTQ fiction segment but also growing. Other bibliographies have detailed every LGBTQ novel and nonfiction title available for YA readers. This guide focuses on current items that teens like, works guaranteed to fly off the shelves. These materials might constitute a core collection that any library, large or small, could contain.

But library service to teens is so much more than simply building a core collection. Accordingly, *Serving Lesbian, Gay, Bisexual, Transgender, and Questioning Teens: A How-To-Do-It Manual for Librarians:*

▼ provides tools to evaluate LGBTQ materials that might be suitable for a YA collection, including adult materials;

▼ suggests useful approaches to handling readers' advisory and reference interviews with teens seeking LGBTQ materials;

▼ presents step-by-step programming instructions for librarians who want to generate interest in LGBTQ materials and involve teens in their libraries; and

▼ offers a model for helping all teens, LGBTQ and straight, realize their potential.

The strategies presented take into account the fact that communities and schools nationwide differ in their receptiveness to the presence of LGBTQ materials in the library—or the degree to which these materials are already there. Suggestions for how fast librarians can move in building and programming their collections are tailored with this information in mind.

Recognizing a Queer Evolution

Teens today increasingly reject traditional labels for sexual identity. Some still use "gay" to refer to themselves and their larger community, but many others use the label "queer" (Savin-Williams, 2005). The word "queer" certainly has a checkered past, but it is no longer considered a slur (Huegel, 2003). By reclaiming a word once used as an insult, LGBTQ people have not only diffused its negative power but turned it into an affirmative expression of self. Indeed, the word "queer" is now the preferred term of group identification. *Serving Lesbian, Gay, Bisexual, Transgender, and Questioning Teens* intentionally uses only the two terms "queer" and "LGBTQ" to describe this population of users. We, the authors, have done so for the simple reason that both terms are as inclusive of the group as possible without prioritizing or omitting any specific element.

(cont'd.)

Recognizing a Queer Evolution *(Continued)*

Teens in your library may or may not use these two terms, nor should you feel obligated to use them. This book is not a manual on political correctness. Rather, it's intended to introduce you to a vibrant community of library users with many different and evolving identities.

Note: Chapter 1 explores in detail the definitions of the many members of the young adult LGBTQ community.

ORGANIZATION

Part I, "Serving LGBTQ Teens in the Library," examines various elements of the important relationship between teens and the library. It begins with Chapter 1, "Understanding the Community," and Chapter 2, "Identifying Teens' LGBTQ Information Needs," which:

▼ explore the current generation of LGBTQ teens and how they see themselves;

▼ differentiate sexual orientation from sexual identity;

▼ highlight challenges that LGBTQ teens still face today;

▼ review several studies of the LGBTQ information needs of teens at the library;

▼ evaluate research into how well public and school libraries, both small and large, have satisfied these needs; and

▼ outline how to assess teens' LGBTQ information needs in your own library.

Chapter 3, "Offering Effective Service and Providing Safe Spaces," and Chapter 4, "Providing Readers' Advisory and Reference Interviews," explore ways to provide excellent service to all teens. These chapters:

▼ demonstrate a service model based on helping teens build developmental assets;

▼ offer a sensitivity-enhancing thought exercise;

▼ outline ground rules for serving LGBTQ and straight teens alike;

▼ address how LGBTQ librarians might integrate their own sexual identity into the library;

▼ detail specific strategies for ways to recognize the tacit signals that teens are searching for LGBTQ materials;

▼ list resources that can help locate these materials in the catalog; and

▼ profile eleven national groups that assist LGBTQ teens, paying special attention to resources that these groups offer on the Internet.

Chapter 5, "Using Guiding Principles to Build an LGBTQ Collection," and Chapter 6, "Identifying and Acquiring Collection Components," outline how to assemble and maintain an LGBTQ-themed YA collection. These chapters:

▼ explore the library's obligation to represent all members of its community;

▼ highlight different threats to the presence of LGBTQ-themed materials in libraries;

▼ offer strategies for combating book challenges and other threats to open access;

▼ cover the mixture of fiction, nonfiction, and non-print items that an excellent LGBTQ teen collection should contain;

▼ survey the history of LGBTQ themes in teen books;

▼ review nonfiction and non-print materials, including biographies, memoirs, poetry, graphic novels, periodicals, online offerings, music, television, and films; and

▼ spotlight methods for locating new YA items, or adult materials suitable for teens, and how to gauge whether or not they will work in your library.

Chapter 7, "Integrating LGBTQ Themes into Everyday Programs and Services," and Chapter 8, "Finding and Implementing the Right Pace for Change," show how to offer great materials and programming. These chapters:

▼ examine how to program materials in the way that best suits your library and your community;

▼ discuss how to booktalk LGBTQ in a way that excites teen interest;

▼ provide useful tips for overcoming the fear of saying "gay" in front of a room crowded with teens;

▼ offer a self-evaluation exercise designed to help you gauge your current service, paired with specific suggestions for how you can offer LGBTQ materials and services in your library; and

▼ detail four customized plans to help determine how quickly you can move in building a collection, programming it, and creating a safe space in a public or school library.

Part II, "Recommended LGBTQ Materials and Programs," contains four chapters that:

▼ review fifty titles—spanning fiction, poetry, biography, memoirs, periodicals, graphic novels, films, and television—that could constitute an ideal core LGBTQ collection for teens;

▼ offer hundreds of additional titles, organized by theme, into a series of lists spanning everything from fiction for boys who like boys and fiction for girls who like girls, to films, materials for the children of gay or lesbian parents, and adult nonfiction suitable for teens, etc.;

▼ include sample LGBTQ-themed booktalks guaranteed to excite teen interest;

▼ supply step-by-step instructions for designing programs guaranteed to encourage teen participation in a wide variety of different library settings; and

▼ give tips on how to customize LGBTQ-themed programs to suit your library's unique circumstances and budget.

The bibliography lists publication details for all of the recommended materials, as well as for the secondary sources used in researching and writing this book.

The growing number of new LGBTQ-themed YA materials suggests new ways of getting teens involved in their library and the community—and so *Serving Lesbian, Gay, Bisexual, Transgender, and Questioning Teens: A How-To-Do-It Manual for Librarians* is mainly a book of ideas designed to spark your creativity. Most of what you will read are suggestions for how to offer exciting materials and programs in your library, plus ways to empower all teens and help them realize their potential. You know your community and your library best, of course, so some of the things suggested may not work or be necessary in your circumstances. The book can serve as a cheerleader for those of you who are already providing superb LGBTQ service and as a coach for those who want to begin. Serving LGBTQ teens is largely a matter of common sense. Expand your collection to include LGBTQ-themed materials, and treat all teens who use your library with the same level of respect, dignity, and attentiveness.

REFERENCES

ALA (American Library Association). 2005a. "Chocolate War Captures Top Spot on Most Challenged List." Press release. Chicago: American Library Association. www.ala.org/al_onlineTemplate.cfm?Section=february2005a& Template=/ContentManagement/ContentDisplay.cfm&ContentID= 87991 (accessed July 29, 2006).

Alexander, Linda. 2005. "Gay Display Controversy: A Threat to Intellectual Freedom." *Florida Libraries* 48, no. 2 (Fall):24–27.

Clyde, Laurel A., and Marjorie Lobban. 2001. "A Door Half Open: Young People's Access to Fiction Related to Homosexuality." *School Libraries Worldwide* 7, no. 2 (July):17–30.

GLSEN (Gay, Lesbian and Straight Education Network). 2005. *From Teasing to Torment: School Climate in America.* New York: Gay, Lesbian and Straight Education Network. www.glsen.org/binary-data/GLSEN_ATTACHMENTS/file/499-1.pdf (accessed November 12, 2005).

Hamilton College National Youth Polls. 2006. *Hot Button Issues Poll: Guns, Gays and Abortion.* Clinton, N.Y.: Hamilton College. www.hamilton.edu/news/polls/HotButtonFinalReport.pdf (accessed January 5, 2006).

Huegel, Kelly. 2003. *GLBTQ: The Survival Guide for Queer and Questioning Teens.* Minneapolis: Free Spirit Publishing.

Savin-Williams, Ritch C. 2005. *The New Gay Teenager.* Cambridge, Mass.: Harvard University Press.

Sell, Randall L.; James A. Wells; and David Wypij. 1995. "The Prevalence of Homosexual Behavior and Attraction in the United States, the United Kingdom and France: Results of National Population-Based Samples." *Archives of Sexual Behavior* 24, no. 3 (June):235–248.

ACKNOWLEDGMENTS

We want to acknowledge a few of the dozens of people who helped as we researched and wrote this book—people who influenced our thinking or lent their support. In alphabetical order they are: Michael Cart, Rachel Cohn, Jason DeRose, David Gale, Beth Gallaway, Francisca Goldsmith, Megan Honig, Christine Jenkins, Melissa Jenvey, David Levithan, Darla Linville, Ellen Loughran, Sandra Payne, Julie Anne Peters, Joanne Rosario, Anne Rouyer, Sara Ryan, Alex Sanchez, Harriet Selverstone, Diane Solway, Heather Ulesoo, and Phyllis Wender.

James Murdock would like to make a special shout-out to his middle school librarian, Lynn de Freitas, to whom he says: "I've still got 'Library Fever.'"

And finally, one person deserves extra-special thanks from both of us, our friend and mentor, without whom this book would not have been possible: Linda Braun.

SERVING LGBTQ TEENS IN THE LIBRARY

1 UNDERSTANDING THE COMMUNITY

INTRODUCTION

Some adults still refer to all people who are not straight as "homosexuals." The word "homosexual," which first came into use during the 1890s, refers to an individual's sexual desire for a person of the same sex (Merriam-Webster, 1988). In this book, this old-fashioned, clinical term will be used as sparingly as possible. The reasoning, quite simply, is that teens don't use it. Teens today are increasingly accepting of diverse sexual orientations. As researcher Paulette Rothbauer noted in a study of young people's catalog search habits, teens almost never use "homosexual"—instead, they use "queer" and other words (Rothbauer, 2004). So, taking a cue from teens, the terms "queer" and "LGBTQ," an acronym for Lesbian, Gay, Bisexual, Transgender, and Questioning, will be used exclusively.

Some readers may bristle when they see the word "queer" appear so casually on the page, given its origins as a homophobic slur. To these readers one can only say: "It's okay." LGBTQ people long ago reclaimed the word for everyday use—reclaiming it diffuses its power to hurt—and queer is now the most all-inclusive, succinct word to describe the community. For evidence of this transformation, one need look no further than the names of television shows such as *Queer Eye for the Straight Guy* and *Queer as Folk*, or universities that feature departments of "queer studies."

Nonetheless, the word retains its power to rankle. For instance, when researching material for this book in early 2005, Jack Martin sent an e-mail to a YALSA listserv asking for programming suggestions suitable for "queer" teens. He received an earful from some people who felt that this word was unprofessional. But many others came to Jack's defense, from a broad range of states that included Indiana, Iowa, Louisiana, and Ohio. One woman even outed herself during the course of explaining why the term was no longer offensive, which prompted Jack to do the same. And Joseph Wilk, a young adult librarian at the Pittsburgh Carnegie Library, humorously recommended that all librarians should lock themselves in a room and repeat aloud the words "gay," "lesbian," "bisexual," "transgender," and "queer" until they're comfortable saying them—at least as comfortable as their teenaged patrons.

All library service starts with understanding the community that the library represents. As one Midwestern librarian observed, "I live in little old Iowa and I didn't think anything of the term [queer]. I think some of it is knowing what's current and knowing your teens/audience in your locale. I have a feeling if I used the word 'queer' here I'd be in for huge trouble." You know your community best and how teens self-identify in your library. Accordingly, "queer" may not be the first or most appropriate word that shoots out of your mouth. Don't worry about terminology. What's important is to recognize simply that LGBTQ teens—regardless of how they self-identify—live in every community. To start you thinking about the lives of these teens, in this chapter we'll review several nationwide studies of teenage sexuality. First, let's begin with a glossary of essential terms.

EXPLORING DEFINITIONS

LESBIAN

Lesbians are women who are sexually and emotionally attracted to other women. The word has its origins in ancient Greece, where the island of Lesbos was home to the poet Sappho, who described love between women (Huegel, 2003).

GAY

Gay primarily refers to men who are sexually and emotionally attracted to other men, although it is also used to refer to both lesbians and gays (Huegel, 2003). Its current usage, which had its origins in the nineteenth century and came into vogue in the mid-twentieth century, stems from the word's original meanings of "carefree" and "licentious": to be gay, in other words, is to disregard conventional sexual roles (Merriam-Webster, 1988).

BISEXUAL

Bisexuals are sexually and emotionally attracted to people of both sexes (Huegel, 2003). There's no set rule for how to be a bisexual. Some choose to partner with people of the opposite sex while at the same time embracing the fact that they are also attracted to the same sex; others alternate between relationships and sexual encounters with both sexes. Many bisexuals say they are first attracted to a person's personality, not his or her sex—akin to being color-blind. Many teens today are sympathetic to bisexuals and think they're cool, perhaps because they perceive bisexuals as having great freedom. Also, while there are a number of truly bisexual people, many young people self-identify as bisexual because they perceive it as the least offensive term to indicate that they are either unsure of their sexual orientation or might in fact be gay or lesbian (Savin-Williams, 2005; Vare and Norton, 1998). Unfortunately this fuels a long-standing misconception of bisexuality: the notion that it's just a phase. Some gays and lesbians, for instance, see bisexuals as double agents, able to shift back and forth between identities whenever convenience dictates; others view bisexuals as homosexuals who refuse to embrace their true gay or lesbian identity. Just as biracial people are often rejected by both people of color and whites, bisexuals often lack full acceptance in both the straight and queer communities.

TRANSGENDER

Transgender people dress or behave in a way that differs from conventional gender expectations (Frankowski, 2004; Huegel, 2003). The word "trans" has gained increased currency in referring to transgender people, but this term can also refer to transsexuals. There is a big difference between the two groups. Unlike transgender people, transsexuals seek hormone therapy and reassignment surgery to change their sex, making their outward anatomy match inward feelings (Frankowski, 2004; Huegel, 2003). Another important point is that neither transgender nor transsexual people are necessarily lesbian, gay, or bisexual, but they face many of the same challenges and inequities. Similarly, another related group, intersexed people, are not necessarily homosexual or heterosexual. Intersex is a term that describes people who are born with sexual organs of both sexes (Intersex Society of North America, undated).

QUESTIONING

Questioning people do just that: they question their sexual orientation and sexual identity. For some, the answer is that they are lesbian, gay, or bisexual; for others, the answer is that they're straight. Research indicates that questioning one's sexual orientation is more universal than ever previously suspected. As a normal part of adolescence, most ostensibly straight teens experience same-sex crushes (Savin-Williams, 2005). To this end, most people are familiar with Dr. Alfred Kinsey's groundbreaking 1940s study of male sexuality, which showed that few people are 100 percent homosexual or heterosexual, and that most fall somewhere in between. Although Kinsey's research methods have since been questioned, subsequent researchers have supported the fluidity and continuum-like nature of human sexuality (Frankowski, 2004). One study published in 1996 suggested that as many as 80 percent of people question their sexual orientation during adolescence (Savin-Williams, 2005). When researchers probed what led to this uncertainty, males responded either that they had had a sexual experience with another male, or that they had been physically aroused by another male. Females, by contrast, said that they questioned their sexual orientation because of a crush they had on another female.

QUEER

Queer traditionally meant someone who was sexually deviant or abnormal, a variation of the word's original use as a synonym for "odd" (Merriam-Webster, 1988). Although the word has long been used as a slur, gays and lesbians began reclaiming it during the 1980s, taking away its power to hurt. As Ellen Greenblatt and others have noted, historically the queer community has used several different terms to refer to itself—including lesbigay, lesbigatr, GLBT—all of which have come in and out of vogue (Greenblatt, 2001). Today, "queer" is considered the most inclusive term to encompass lesbians, gays, bisexuals, and trans people.

GENDER

Gender, also called sexual identity, is a construct that reflects society's expectations for how someone of a given sex should look and behave, and how individuals conform to, modify, or subvert these expectations (Savin-Williams, 2005). Recognizing this, many employers add "gender expression" as a separate category for legal protection against on-the-job harassment—a reflection of the fact that straight and queer people alike express gender in nontraditional ways.

COMING OUT

Coming out is acknowledging or revealing one's sexual orientation, both to oneself and to the larger world (Hamer, 2003). The opposite is remaining "in the closet," or closeted. Many straight people wonder why queer people feel the need to make known the fact they are attracted to the same sex. These straight observers are missing the point. Coming out is not about sex talk; it's about honesty and being able to communicate openly. For many queer people, coming out is among the most important events in their lives because it is often a gigantic relief: an end to secrecy and lying. But coming out is also an emotionally fraught and risky process, given the unknown variable of how family and friends will react (American Psychological Association, undated; Vare and Norton, 1998). The fear of rejection, which is often a very real possibility, is powerful and leads some queer people to remain in the closet. Likewise, it can be painful for some people to admit even to themselves that they are queer, particularly when doing so conflicts with their religious or family upbringing. Although the coming out process can involve several stages, depending on the individual person, it typically begins with a person's internal acknowledgment of sexual and emotional attraction to the same gender. The next step is revealing this attraction to someone else: usually friends first, possibly siblings, and eventually parents and extended family (Savin-Williams, 2005). The fact that parents and extended family come last reflects the generational difference in society's attitudes to queer people. It also reflects the fact that being rejected by a parent is acutely painful—and, sadly, remains a real possibility for many teens today. While kids are all over the map in terms of when they first experience same-sex desires, research suggests that the average age of coming out has dropped. Studies also show that after coming out, it takes roughly two years for most queer people to feel completely comfortable with their sexual identity (Savin-Williams, 2005).

PRIDE

Pride is a concept that began to take shape during the 1960s, within the context of that decade's other civil rights movements. Simply put, queer people grew tired of being targeted for ridicule, violence, and unequal treatment in the eyes of the law. They started to take pride in who they were and began to stand up for equal rights. Although the fight for equality is ongoing, an early victory occurred in 1973, when the American Psychiatric Association declassified homosexuality as a disease, thanks in part to Barbara Gittings, a pioneer of the queer civil rights movement now affiliated with the ALA (*The GLBTQ Encyclopedia*, undated). Another early victory was the 1969 Stonewall uprising, during which a crowd of gay and trans men resisted a police raid at the Stonewall Inn, a bar in New York City's Greenwich Village. This was not the first instance in which queer people stood up for their rights. Four years earlier in Philadelphia, lesbians and gays—including, again, Barbara Gittings—rallied to protest discrimination in federal hiring practices. And, as early as the 1950s, queer people formed consciousness-raising groups such as the Mattachine Society and Daughters of Bilitis.

PINK TRIANGLES

In addition to the rainbow flag, queer people often use the pink triangle as a symbol to represent themselves. The history of this symbol is similar to that of the word "queer" in the sense that LGBTQ people have reclaimed something that was once a marker of hatred. In the late 1930s, as part of Adolf Hitler's campaign to exterminate people he deemed undesirable, the Nazi state forced members of specific religions, ethnicities, and other groups to wear markers on their clothing: Jews wore yellow stars of David;

Jehovah's Witnesses wore purple triangles; Romany people wore black triangles; and gay men wore pink triangles. In the early 1970s, gay men began reclaiming the pink triangle—first as an act of remembrance, and eventually as a symbol for all things queer (*The GLBTQ Encyclopedia*, undated).

SEXUAL ORIENTATION

As Ritch Savin-Williams, a Cornell University psychologist who studies queer youth, has said: "Sexual orientation is the preponderance of erotic feelings, thoughts, and fantasies one person has for members of a particular sex, both sexes, or neither sex." (Savin-Williams, 2005:28). Sexual orientation is widely believed to be the product of mainly biological influences and, as such, resistant to conscious control (Frankowski, 2004).

SEXUAL BEHAVIOR

Sexual behavior refers to physical intimacy. Studies of adolescents have determined that many teenagers lie about their sexual behavior. For instance, one study of high school students showed that when interviewed on multiple occasions, boys gave different calendar dates for when they lost their virginity—generally revising the date to something more recent (Savin-Williams, 2005). Same-sex contact between boys generally occurs a year or two before a boy identifies as gay or bisexual; between girls, same-sex contact generally occurs after a girl identifies as a lesbian or bisexual. Unlike sexual orientation, sexual behavior can change over time.

SEXUAL IDENTITY

As Savin-Williams writes, "Sexual identity is a socially recognized label that names sexual feeling, attraction, and behavior" (Savin-Williams, 2005:34). In other words, it is the product of sexual orientation, sexual behavior, and the cultural influences surrounding an individual. Sexual identity is the most susceptible to change and often acquires nuances over time as individuals adopt new labels for themselves.

GETTING TO KNOW LGBTQ TEENS

What makes a person queer? The jury is still out, but research increasingly suggests a combination of both genetic and social factors, a classic case of nature and nurture working in tandem. While a vocal minority argue that being gay is a choice, most people today realize this is false. In fact, only 11 percent of people in a recent national survey agreed with the statement that "sexual orientation is a conscious choice" (Epstein, 2006).

Although scientists have yet to identify a so-called "gay gene," it's likely that a certain percentage of people are genetically predisposed to same-sex attraction, and that cultural influences play a role in shaping how people express their sexual orientation (Savin-Williams, 2005). The balance of nature versus nurture varies from individual to individual, but adolescence is the time of life when most people acknowledge their sexual orientation. It's beyond the scope of this book to explore the biological underpinnings of homosexuality or to examine religious teachings on homosexuality or the so-called "ex-gay" movement, which purports to help people change their sexual orientation. Rather, the focus here is everyday life for LGBTQ teens.

Regardless of what makes them queer, teens today are coming out at younger and younger ages. Three decades ago, most gays and lesbians came out during their twenties; now, the average age is sixteen (Huegel, 2003; Savin-Williams, 2005). Studies also suggest that the age when teens first become aware of their sexual orientation is skewing younger. During the 1960s, for instance, gay men first recalled same-sex attractions beginning around the age of fourteen and lesbians around the age of seventeen; by the 1990s, the age for gay men had fallen to ten years old and for lesbians it was twelve (Huegel, 2003; Savin-Williams, 2005).

Teens are acknowledging their sexual orientation at younger ages and they are also increasingly resistant to labeling their sexual orientation. Savin-Williams contends that today's teens perceive the terms "gay," "lesbian," and "bisexual" as connoting adult subcultures and political movements that are alien to their daily experience. He writes:

> [Gay and lesbian] don't carry the same meaning for teens that they do for us, the precursors and recipients of gay liberation and lesbian avengers. Some young people have an idea of what a gay person or a lesbian is. To them, being gay or lesbian is primarily an identity commitment, as in: "I'm gay." "It's who I am." "It's what I label myself." Although some may appreciate the historic significance the word "gay" connotes, I believe few young people aspire to it. (Savin-Williams, 2005:6–7)

Given that teens don't aspire to outdated labels, it's no surprise that less than 2 percent of teens self-identify as gay, lesbian, or bisexual (Savin-Williams, 2005). Instead, kids today are more likely to choose neutral words, multiple terms, or invent their own expressions.

Librarians see new and unusual labels for sexuality all the time. Sara Ryan, a YA author and librarian at the Multnomah County Library in

Portland, Oregon, told us in an April 2005 e-mail that she has encountered the term "LGBTQQIAP: Lesbian Gay Bisexual Trans Queer Questioning Intersexed Allies and Pansexuals (pansexuals being people of any gender who have the capacity to be attracted to some individuals of any other gender—because if you say BIsexual you're implying that there are only two genders)." Similarly, Beth Gallaway, a trainer and consultant at the Metrowest Massachusetts Regional Library System, wrote: "I ran a poetry/creative writing group for several years. In one meeting, one girl mentioned she's bi while we were doing introductions. The next month, eight of ten kids came out. Because it was a mixed group of middle and senior high students, all of these high schoolers said they were 'happy': 'Hi, I'm Danny, and I'm, uh, happy!'" And in surveying queer teens at The New York Public Library, former assistant coordinator for young adult services Darla Linville received the following write-in responses to a question about how the teens self-identified: "Genderqueer, punk cool, gender-exploring, open-minded, intersexed, myself, and veronica-sexual" (Linville, 2004:184). These last terms drive home the point. Each teen is unique, figuring out his or her place in the world: How can someone else's label encapsulate who they are?

As Linville noted in a *Voice of Youth Advocates* article about her survey, adults shouldn't mistake teens' resistance to labels as confusion about their orientation or identity. Rather, teens are simply "feeling out their boundaries, and testing their sexual waters" (Linville, 2004:185). Indeed, the main reason why they actively reject traditional labels is that their sexual behavior defies easy categorization. Consider these statistics:

▼ Although few teens self-identify as exclusively gay or lesbian, and indeed counting the number of gay teens is famously difficult, many observers estimate that at least 5 to 6 percent of teens are gay or lesbian (Huegel, 2005; Savin-Williams, 2005; Sell, Wells, and Wypij, 1995).

▼ Between 15 and 20 percent of all teenagers have some degree of same-sex orientation, according to Savin-Williams, but less than half of them are exclusively same-sex oriented. As he writes in *The New Gay Teenager*, "One undeniable, well-substantiated fact is that most individuals with same-sex contact during adolescence claim at the time to be heterosexual" (Savin-Williams, 2005:40).

▼ Half of gay or bisexual self-identified boys and roughly 75 percent of lesbian or bisexual self-identified girls report that they also engage in heterosexual sex (Savin-Williams, 2005).

▼ More teenaged boys than girls report same-sex behavior; however, whereas half of boys say they quit same-sex behavior after adolescence, most girls continue to pursue same-sex behavior as adults (Savin-Williams, 2005).

▼ In one study, 60 percent of young women changed their sexual identity at least once during an eight-year period (Savin-Williams, 2005).

The tapestry of same-sex attraction during the teen years is more complex than ever before imagined. Just about the only conclusion to be drawn is that their behavior defies rigid labels such as gay or lesbian—even the seemingly flexible label of bisexual.

It's also important to note that cultural differences play a significant role in determining how sexual identity is expressed. In many Hispanic and Latino cultures, for instance, a man may pursue sex with other men without jeopardizing his straight identity, providing that he maintains a "highly masculine demeanor" and does not express "tender feelings toward his partner" (Savin-Williams, 2005:47–48). This concept is similar to one in the African American community called the "down low," or DL for short. The DL refers to self-identified straight men who have sex with other men (Savin-Williams, 2005). While the subject of different ethnic and cultural attitudes toward homosexuality is beyond our scope here, you should at least be aware that a diversity of approaches exists. Also, keep in mind that for a teen of color, being LGBTQ can be an added form of stigmatization (Cianciotto and Cahill, 2003). Unfortunately, as many observers have noted, this entire topic has not been given adequate attention (Cianociotto and Cahill, 2003; Savin-Williams, 2005).

APPRECIATING NEW ATTITUDES

Are we moving toward a "post-gay" society, in which sexual orientation and sexual identity no longer matter? Some observers think so. If we are, the credit largely goes to gay-straight alliances in high schools. Known as GSAs, these extracurricular student groups help combat prejudice and violence toward queer people mainly by raising awareness and by sponsoring events such as "No Name Calling Day" and "Day of Silence." At the same time as GSAs are working to make life easier for LGBTQ school students, popular culture increasingly features visible queer people—out celebrities such as Ellen DeGeneres and Sheryl Swoopes, television shows such as *Queer Eye for the Straight Guy*, and lauded films such as *Brokeback Mountain*.

The increased visibility of queer people not only makes it easier for some teens to come out, it also creates a higher level of tolerance among straight teens. In a 2005 study, the Gay, Lesbian and Straight Education

Network (GLSEN) reported that 75 percent of high school and middle school students said they knew someone who was lesbian, gay, or bisexual; 55 percent said they knew a student who was lesbian, gay, or bisexual; and 19 percent said they had a close personal friend who was lesbian, gay, or bisexual. GLSEN also found that 13 percent of students knew someone who was trans; 7 percent knew a trans student; and 1 percent had a close personal trans friend (GLSEN, 2005).

With increased familiarity comes acceptance, and all signs indicate that today's generation of teens is the most accepting yet. In a 2006 survey of high school seniors, researchers at Hamilton College discovered the following attitudes the students had about queer people:

▼ Fully 75 percent of teens approve of either civil unions or marriage for gays and lesbians. (By comparison, only 20 to 27 percent of adults approve.)

▼ More than 50 percent of teens support outright marriage for gays and lesbians.

▼ Only 25 percent support a constitutional amendment banning marriage for gays and lesbians.

▼ Roughly 66 percent support the right of gays and lesbians to adopt children.

▼ Eighty percent support legislation protecting queer people against discrimination in the workplace.

▼ Nearly 80 percent think queer people "should be accepted by society."

▼ Seventy percent agree with the statement, "Gay people contribute in unique and positive ways to society." (Hamilton College National Youth Polls, 2006)

In light of such findings, it's no wonder that Kevin Jennings, founder of GLSEN and a pioneer of the GSA movement, observed in a recent *Time* magazine cover story: "We're gonna win because of what's happening in high schools right now.... This is the generation that gets it" (Cloud, 2005:45).

GAUGING THE IMPACT OF HOMOPHOBIA

Even if this is the most tolerant generation yet, our own admittedly pessimistic opinion is that if history is any yardstick, a truly post-gay world remains a distant possibility. Some fifty years after the start of the civil rights movement, for instance, the United States is not yet color-blind; likewise, some thirty years after women's liberation, female employees still earn less than their male counterparts in the same jobs. Discrimination remains a fact of life in the United States. Indeed, the average day of the average queer teenager is anything but a warm and fuzzy walk through post-gay utopia. This is not just opinion: The cold, hard facts are that the overwhelming majority of LGBTQ teenagers are still harassed by schoolmates because of their sexual identity, either real or perceived. In its 2001 report titled *Hatred in the Hallways*, Human Rights Watch categorized the daily life of queer high school students this way:

> Gay youth spend an inordinate amount of energy plotting how to get safely to and from school, how to avoid the hallways when other students are present so they can avoid slurs and shoves, how to cut gym class to escape being beaten up—in short, how to become invisible so they will not be verbally and physically attacked. Too often, students have little energy left to learn. (Human Rights Watch, 2001)

Several other studies reinforce this conclusion. For instance, the National Mental Health Association found that nearly 80 percent of high school students report that LGBTQ students are bullied in their school (National Mental Health Association, 2002).

GLSEN conducts the most regular and comprehensive studies of queer youth. Surveying high school students in 2005, it found that fully 90 percent of queer teens said they had been verbally or physically harassed within the past year due to "perceived or actual appearance, gender, sexual orientation, gender expression, race/ethnicity, disability or religion" (GLSEN, 2005). And it wasn't just queer teens who were being bullied for perceived or actual sexual orientation. Sixty-two percent of non-LGBTQ teens reported the same thing. Other findings in this report included: 52 percent of teens say that they hear students in their high school or middle school make homophobic remarks; and 69 percent frequently heard students say "that's so gay," or "you're so gay," both expressions in which the term "gay" connoted something bad or devalued. These statistics have remained relatively unchanged since GLSEN began surveying teens in the mid-1990s.

On the whole, GLSEN's findings suggest that despite greater tolerance for homosexuality among most teens, a certain percentage of kids are still out to bully their queer peers—and, more often than not, they hit their mark successfully. To this end, past GLSEN studies have shown that queer teens are more likely to be in fights that require medical treatment (Kosciw, 2003). These findings suggest a culture that still has deeply conflicted attitudes and misconceptions about homosexuality. On the one hand, teens say they respect and tolerate different sexual orientations; at the same time, however, kids equate anything distasteful with being gay without realizing that this in itself is disrespectful. Again, GLSEN has shown that students hear homophobic and sexist remarks used in school more frequently than racist comments or religious slurs; conversely, students list homophobic comments last on a list of hate speech that their school would be better off without (GLSEN, 2005). A similar study conducted by the National Mental Health Association found that only overweight kids were teased more than LGBTQ kids (National Mental Health Association, 2002).

Bullying queer people is commonly labeled "homophobia," but this word fails to convey the scope and complexity of a bigot's prejudice. Etymologically speaking, "homophobia" is defined as the irrational hatred of homosexuals (Huegel, 2003). In reality, though, many homophobes use well-reasoned, sometimes religious justification for hating queer people. For this reason, homophobia is often labeled the last socially respectable prejudice (Baker, 2002; Carmichael and Shontz, 1996). Like other forms of prejudice, homophobia comes in four varieties: verbal, physical, institutional, and societal. The verbal form of homophobia includes everything from expressions such as "that's so gay," in which being gay is equated with something negative, to outright belittling and intimidation, such as calling someone "sissy," "faggot," "fag," or "dyke."

The physical form of homophobia likewise runs the gamut from pushing and shoving to punching, kicking, beating, and far worse. Although gay bashing hasn't made national headlines since the death of Matthew Shepard—the University of Wyoming student who, in 1998, was strapped to a fence rail, beaten to a pulp, and then left to die—it remains a frightening reality for LGBTQ people in communities nationwide. In fact, some queer advocates believe that incidents of gay bashing are underreported and that they are actually on the rise, representing a backlash against the increased visibility of queer people. Following the strong showing of conservative politicians in the 2004 elections, the group Lambda Legal tracked a rise in hostility toward LGBTQ youth. It also identified "hot spots" where these teens are most at risk: Alabama, Iowa, Missouri, Texas, and Utah (Lambda Legal, 2004).

At the institutional level, homophobia exists when gays, lesbians, bisexuals, and trans people lack legal protections against discrimination in the workplace or in finding a home—to say nothing of the right to marry, adopt children, or be at a partner's hospital bedside during times of illness or death. It's important to remember that as recently as 2003, it was illegal in many states for two consenting adults of the same sex to engage in sexual relations; that year, the U.S. Supreme Court struck down sodomy laws nationwide. Even so, roughly forty states have passed so-called "defense of marriage" acts that specifically prohibit marriage for gays and lesbians—and every month, it seems, another state moves closer to adopting similar laws.

Finally, there is homophobia at the societal level, most often expressed by silence: the failure to acknowledge, let alone tolerate, the queer people in our midst. It's one thing to watch five gay fashionistas dish on the cable television program *Queer Eye for the Straight Guy*, which takes place in New York City, where you'd expect to find gay people—but it's quite another thing to recognize the gay men in your own town, let alone in your own family. In addition to outright denial, silence is the failure to speak up when someone uses a homophobic slur or when someone says ignorant and untrue things about LGBTQ people. At root, silence is embodied by the implicit assumption that the entire world is straight: for instance, when an adult asks a teenaged boy if he has a girlfriend, not if he has "someone special." It may seem like semantics, but it's not.

The danger in silence is that it speaks volumes. It allows bigots to get away with spewing hatred and lies. Silence also sends a signal that being queer is something so abnormal and so abhorrent as to be unspeakable. Psychologist Jean M. Baker, who studies the impact of homophobia on child development, notes that silence sends queer children the message that they are "imperfect in some significant and uncorrectable way" (Baker, 2002:10). Worse still, she adds, silence sends the message that queer people *deserve* to be treated unequally and abused.

When the queer community rallied to fight HIV/AIDS in the late 1980s, the slogan "SILENCE = DEATH" appeared on placards and bumper stickers to call attention to the growing health crisis faced by LGBTQ people. The phrase highlighted the fact that by failing to acknowledge the disease, the U.S. government allowed HIV/AIDS to spread rampantly, effectively signing death warrants for hundreds of thousands of people. Today, silence still equals death when it comes to HIV/AIDS—failing to discuss safer sex practices allows the HIV virus to spread—and silence also equals death when people fail to speak openly and positively about homosexuality. When queer children and teens hear only negative messages about LGBTQ people, they feel victimized and often develop internalized homophobia: difficulty in accepting their sexual orientation (Huegel, 2003; Vare and Norton, 1998). Suffering from internalized homophobia is correlated with higher rates of depression, smoking, and substance abuse; it is also a key factor, along with harassment, that leads LGBTQ kids to drop out of high school at a higher rate than do straight kids (Frankowski, 2004).

Homophobia can even lead to suicide. Queer teens are four times more likely to attempt suicide and account for one-third of successful suicides (Frankowski, 2004; Safren and Heimberg, 1999). Being queer is not, in and of itself, the reason why kids contemplate suicide—homophobia is the culprit. "Gay and lesbian teens pose such high [suicide] risk because 'their distress is a direct result of the hatred and prejudice that surround them,' not because of their inherently gay or lesbian identity orientation," researchers Jonatha Vare and Terry Norton write in an article about the health of queer teens (Vare and Norton, 1998). Although some researchers dispute the higher correlation between suicide rates and LGBTQ youth, it would be rash and irresponsible to ignore this danger.

RECOGNIZING THE LIBRARY'S ROLE IN HELPING TEENS

Regardless of a person's sexual orientation, adolescence can be a lonely and isolated time of life. Teenagers want to fit in with everyone else. Any perceived difference they find in themselves can induce feelings of self-loathing and isolation. Homophobia magnifies the isolation and self-consciousness of some queer teens in untold ways. For instance, many queer teens live in constant fear their sexual orientation will be revealed, while others struggle with the thought that coming out might end relationships with friends or family. Savin-Williams notes that LGBTQ teens have smaller social networks than straight teens and are more likely to be alienated from their parents (Savin-Williams, 2005). The fear of encountering homophobia is, in and of itself, enough to paralyze some teens. Judah S. Hamer, who has researched the information needs of gay teens, found that these kids were often petrified of encountering homophobia when they used the library to find and borrow LGBTQ books (Hamer, 2003).

But reading books and magazines, watching films and television shows, and finding online communities can shatter the silence of homophobia. All teenagers, regardless of sexual orientation, want to find characters in books and films and TV who are like themselves: a sign that they are not alone, however awkward and different they may feel inside, and a sign that it is possible to survive adolescence. Sandra Payne, coordinator of young adult services for The New York Public Library system, explained: "Young people are looking to find themselves. They're looking to find stories about their friends. They're looking to find a way of understanding their parents" (Murdock, 2004a:187). Teens read to empathize, literally putting themselves in a character's shoes and wondering what they themselves would do in the same situation. As one teen whom we interviewed at The New York Public Library in July 2004 observed: "I put a book down and I start thinking about it. I try to relate to the characters, for one thing, like, 'Oh, my God, that's exactly how my mom is!' or, 'I hate it when my best friend does that.' . . . I put myself in [the character's] position. I start thinking like, 'Oh, what would I do? What would I do if that happened to me, or if I had a friend like that?'"

Queer teens are particularly eager to find information about themselves in books and other materials at the library. The situation is dramatized in YA novels, such as *Absolutely, Positively Not . . . .* And the authors of these books are inundated with letters from teens who can't thank the authors enough for putting their stories into print (Levithan, 2004b). For many teens, even in a world full of media offerings, books remain the only window onto LGBTQ issues—particularly because reading is such a personal and private activity. Queer and questioning teens are looking for portrayals of what it means to be queer—a way to describe what they feel, to affirm that it is normal, and to know that they are not alone.

Perhaps most important, LGBTQ teens seek role models: a diversity of depictions of what life might look like for them in the future, and evidence that there are myriad ways of being queer (Hamer, 2003). A sixteen-year-old self-identified gay at The New York Public Library told us in a July 2004 interview: "I didn't have a lot of trouble with my parents, coming out to them or with my friends; really, there weren't a lot of problems with that process, but I didn't feel like satisfied enough with my own story and so I wanted to hear other people's experiences. I don't really like support groups or anything like that because I don't feel like I can relate to strangers; I'm not that kind of person who can just go up to people and talk. So reading stories, even if they're not true, kind of changes what I feel." A fourteen-year-old self-identified bisexual girl shared much the same sentiment. "I know there's a lot of [bisexual] people but you just can't find them because there's always that fear. A book is like a substitute for the real thing and it's good enough. Well, for me it is," she said. After conducting this interview, we revealed to the teen that we were gay. The girl's eyes widened and she got very excited. We weren't bisexual, but at that moment we were the next best thing. Indeed, in that moment we were role models: two well-adjusted adults at ease with our sexual orientation.

Until very recently, few LGBTQ teens have benefited from having openly queer role models. Part of the problem has been that queer adults felt reluctant, even scared, to work with children, lest they be accused of "recruiting" them. For instance, in the early 1990s, while Kevin Jennings was building the organization that became GLSEN, he often heard from fellow queer adults: "Why are you working with kids? What are you, f_____ crazy?" (Cloud, 2005:47). Sadly, these fears deprived past generations of role models. While this situation has improved tremendously, thanks to the efforts of Jennings and other educators, in many communities there are no visible queer adults. It is in these locations that the library becomes a lifeline for queer and questioning teens.

2 IDENTIFYING TEENS' LGBTQ INFORMATION NEEDS

INTRODUCTION

Today, when queer teens come to the library or search its catalog online, what do they want to find? In a word: themselves. Historically, the public library was often the first place that queer and questioning teens would go for information about homosexuality. It's no surprise that the obligatory library search remains a feature of queer YA lit, as seen in the 2005 novel *Absolutely, Positively Not . . . .* Researchers Martin Garnar and Paulette Rothbauer have suggested that the library's role for LGBTQ teens has been diminished with the rise of the Internet, but Judah S. Hamer and others point out that the library is often the only place where teens can access the Internet in private (Garnar, 2001; Hamer, 2003; Rothbauer, 2004). In other words, any way you slice it, libraries matter. And it's not enough that libraries carry queer materials and make Internet access available. They must offer these services in a positive way. Queer teens seek a safe, nonjudgmental space in which LGBTQ materials are readily accessible, with friendly service to help them find these items. That's the bare minimum. This chapter reviews several studies of the LGBTQ resources that teens seek in libraries nationwide, beginning, though, by showing how you can gauge these needs in your library.

ASKING THE RIGHT QUESTIONS

How would you evaluate what queer teens in your community want from your library? As with any decision regarding collections and services, talking directly with your community about its needs is the best route. Finding out what LGBTQ teens want should be as easy as identifying the needs of any other user group: offer written surveys, engage in face-to-face conversations at the reference desk, and broach the topic during teen advisory group meetings. Since many queer teens are not ready or able to come out, you may not be able to engage them in direct conversation, and in this case, anonymous surveying will probably be your best route. A survey can be as simple or as detailed as you make it. Allow teens to answer questions on paper in the library, or, if possible, on your library's Web site through an anonymous online mechanism. Your survey can be a queer-specific sheet, or you can simply add a few questions on queer subjects to your standard questionnaires. However you design the survey, reassure teens that their responses will remain anonymous. Also, be sure to publicize your survey by posting flyers in your library and, if you feel confident doing so, in other locations where teenagers hang out in town and in your community's local queer newspapers.

When designing your survey, you might want to include questions similar to the following:

▼ Do teens see the library as a source of information about sexuality and sexual identity?

▼ What information are teens looking for in the library?

▼ Do teens see the library as a safe place to ask for help with their questions about sexuality?

▼ Do teens generally perceive the library as a safe place to hang out?

▼ What do teens want from books, as opposed to other sources?

▼ How could the library better help queer teens in their search for information?

▼ How can the library help teens feel more secure using online resources?

You could also ask if teens prefer fictional accounts of queer teens, or if they want biographies and other nonfiction materials. You might ask teens to list their favorite queer YA titles and authors. And don't forget to ask about non-print items, such as DVDs, and whether or not teens want help finding community groups and online resources.

REVIEWING THE RESEARCH

Only a handful of researchers have studied the information needs of adult gays and lesbians, and even fewer have specifically examined the needs of queer and questioning teens. As Martin Garnar put it, "In the literature of library and information science, the information needs of the lesbian, gay, bisexual, and transgender…community have been discussed infrequently, studied less, and never treated in their totality" (Garnar, 2001). Although as many studies as possible are acknowledged in this chapter, the focus is mainly on the most recent teen-specific study available. In 2003, Darla Linville, former assistant coordinator of young adult services at The New York Public Library, surveyed self-identified queer teenagers to gauge what they wanted from the library. Her findings were published in the August 2004 issue of *Voice of Youth Advocates*. While Linville's study was limited to New York City, unlike previous studies that focused on only a single sexual identity it had the benefit of including teens across the LGBTQ spectrum.

Linville found that despite the seeming ubiquity of queer culture today, teens still have basic questions about what it means to be queer. Moreover, they depend on the library for help in finding answers. In fact, more than 50 percent of respondents said they used the library for answers to their questions about being gay, or questions about gay people they know. When at the library, teens sought the following information, listed here in order of importance:

▼ real stories of real people. (This response got twice as many votes as any other response.)

▼ coming out stories.

▼ how-to information about activism, such as how to start a gay-straight alliance.

▼ stories of fictional characters.

▼ lists of community resources.

▼ books about what it means to be queer, sexuality, queerness, and gayness.

▼ information about safe sex and sexual health.

▼ materials about trans issues, both fiction and nonfiction.

▼ materials about bisexual and questioning issues.

▼ books that discuss what gay sex is, with personal stories. (Linville, 2004:184)

In evaluating these responses, Linville concluded that LGBTQ teens "want to know that we know that gay people live in every neighborhood, not just in that gay neighborhood over there. And they want to know that we welcome queer people to the library" (Linville, 2004:186).

It's important to remember that it's not just queer teens who are seeking LGBTQ resources in their public libraries. As noted in Chapter 1, nearly 80 percent of teens know someone who is gay, lesbian, or bisexual; a further 13 percent know someone who is trans (GLSEN, 2005). Many of the queer people that these teens know are friends, but undoubtedly many are also brothers, sisters, other family members—or parents. In fact, according to the National Adoption Information Clearing House, there are as many as 14 million children nationwide living with gay or lesbian parents (National Adoption Information Clearinghouse, 2000). And as *Time* magazine indicated in its October 10, 2005, cover story on queer teens, self-identified straight kids constitute the majority membership in gay-straight alliances around the country (Cloud, 2005). Whether these straight kids have queer friends and family members, or they're simply empathetic, it's a safe bet that all of these straight teens would appreciate novels and other materials that portray youth like them who share similar circumstances. Like queer teens, in other words, these straight teens also turn to the library for LGBTQ-themed resources.

Before moving to the next section, which examines how well libraries are doing, it should be acknowledged that all teens, queer and straight, aren't using the library just for information. They also seek entertainment in the form of good fiction, graphic novels, films, and music. This simple and obvious fact sometimes gets lost in all the discussion of the psychological, educational, and social reasons why librarians should include LGBTQ materials in their YA collections. The mark of a good book, be it YA or adult, is that it has the power to touch a wide variety of readers and that the sexual orientation of the book's characters makes no difference. The same applies to films, music, and so on. Queer-themed materials hold appeal for people of all ages and sexual identities.

GAUGING THE CURRENT RESPONSE OF PUBLIC LIBRARIES

In the last section we noted that the information needs of queer and questioning teens are "discussed infrequently, studied less, and never treated in their totality" (Garner, 2001). It should be no surprise, therefore, that studies of how well libraries are meeting these needs are also scarce or outdated. Jennifer L. Pecoskie and Pamela J. McKenzie, as well as Thomas L. Kilpatrick, have tracked the availability of material for adult gays and lesbians (Kilpatrick, 1996; Pecoskie and McKenzie, 2004). Alex Spence, meanwhile, has charted the availability of children's picture books (Spence, 2000), and Laurel A. Clyde and Marjorie Lobban have focused on teen readers (Clyde and Lobban, 2001), but all of the aforementioned studies were conducted prior to the current boom in LGBTQ teen books and today's climate of heightened queer visibility.

The little research that has been done on the availability of library materials and services for LGBTQ teen patrons paints a discouraging picture.

Clyde and Lobban, in their meta-analysis of access to queer materials, wrote: "Just as public library collections in general fail to provide sufficient books to meet the needs of gay/lesbian users of all ages or to provide representative coverage of gay/lesbian lifestyles and issues, so collections developed specifically for young users also generally fail in this regard" (Clyde and Lobban, 2001:25). In another study of barriers to access that exist within libraries, Ellen Greenblatt observed that despite a decade of growing national sensitivity to LGBTQ issues, "The biggest obstacles we must contend with continue to be those of misinformation and prejudice. Many librarians have never questioned the heterosexism that pervades library services, policies, and collections" (Greenblatt, 2001).

Since most studies of LGBTQ teen services were conducted some time ago, the findings of Darla Linville's recent study published in *Voice of Youth Advocates* are emphasized here. In addition to asking queer teens what they want from the library, she asked the obvious follow-up question: How well does the library meet your needs? Her findings are striking, given that she studied libraries in the supposedly queer mecca of New York City. Linville uncovered what she characterized as "disturbing" evidence that many queer YA patrons are underserved and often fail to find the materials they need (Linville, 2004:185). If New York City's libraries can do better, it's likely that other library systems nationwide also have room for improvement. In any event, Linville's findings may inspire you to think about your own library and its quality of service.

Linville's central finding was twofold: Queer teens know what the library has to offer them, and they know what its deficiencies are. She wrote, "[LGBTQ teens] were impressed when they found books or Web sites that covered new territory, and clear about where there was a lack of information" (Linville, 2004: 185). And a dismaying number of respondents felt that the library was indeed lacking information. Some of Linville's findings were:

▼ One-third of teens said they could not find the queer-related materials they wanted.

▼ Nearly 25 percent said that people judged them in the library.

▼ Twenty-five percent did not like to ask the librarians questions, either because they were too fearful or they were afraid of being judged. Some even reported that when they asked librarians for queer materials, the librarians snickered or otherwise made them feel uncomfortable.

▼ Only 20 percent felt safe from harassment in the library.

▼ "Some teens felt that the gay books were hidden in the library, as compared to a bookstore, for example, because there were no signs labeling a section as 'Gay and Lesbian'" (Linville, 2004:185).

▼ Some teens didn't see queer-friendly displays, even during Pride Month.

▼ Many teens noted that although the library catalog listed queer titles as being "checked in," the actual books were missing from the shelves, and that queer titles were not replaced when they went missing.

Linville's survey also identified gaps in the library's collection relating to specific resources that teens wanted but could not find. These included:

▼ lesbian novels.

▼ current gay fiction.

▼ lists of queer community groups.

▼ information about disabled rights and empowerment.

▼ information, resources, and titles about trans issues.

▼ information about how to tell if someone is queer.

▼ information about famous queer people and queer people in history.

▼ local queer newspapers and queer community event listings.

▼ frank and realistic portrayals of sex. (In this respect, queer teens are no different than straight teens, who seek frank portrayals of heterosexual sex.)

There is a difference, of course, between what teens claim the library lacks and whether or not the library's collection is actually deficient. As Linville notes, it could well be that the library does not contain the resources that queer teens want. Equally important, however, it could also be the case that the library offers LGBTQ materials but fails to make them accessible to teens. In both instances, Linville concludes, "Libraries need to do a better job of making queer resources visible" (Linville, 2004:185).

Other researchers have reached this same conclusion. In her study of where lesbian young adults locate LGBTQ information, Paulette Rothbauer wrote of library holdings, "The failure to find desired books is a constant theme" (Rothbauer, 2004:94). Rothbauer's view, which is shared by many others, is that LGBTQ materials are poorly classified in library catalogs, making these materials more difficult to locate—regardless of whether or not they happen to be in the library's collection. Similarly, Jennifer L. Pecoskie and Pamela J. McKenzie found that while libraries do a good job of providing LGBTQ materials in communities with highly visible queer populations, patrons in these libraries still perceive the library as lacking helpful materials (Pecoskie and McKenzie, 2004). The perception of inadequacy, they rightly contend, cannot be ignored.

IDENTIFYING PERCEPTIONS OF SCHOOL LIBRARIES

Students who perceive that their school libraries lack LGBTQ resources are probably correct. While the availability of LGBTQ materials in school media centers is not well documented, as Laurel A. Clyde and others have pointed out, the research that exists paints a dim picture (Clyde, 2003; Clyde and Lobban, 2001). Eric Bryant, who studied school library holdings in the mid-1990s, found that most contained only a handful of books with queer characters or themes (Bryant, 2005). Anecdotal evidence reinforces these findings. In January 2006, *The Advocate*, a queer newsmagazine, polled its teenaged readers to see how many gay-themed books their high school libraries carried. Twenty-seven percent of respondents said "none"; 4 percent said "only one"; 36 percent said "maybe two or three"; and 33 percent said "there are many gay titles there" (Advocate, 2006). Similarly, in 2003 the Gay, Lesbian and Straight Education Network asked if high school students knew where to turn for help with LGBTQ issues: 54 percent listed their school's GSA as a resource, 47 percent listed the Internet, only 45 percent listed the school's media center, and a scant 19 percent listed their textbooks as a resource. When students were asked to identify the adults at school with whom they'd feel most comfortable discussing LGBTQ issues, librarians tied with school nurses for last place, at 38.8 percent. For the record, guidance counselors garnered the top spot; teachers came in second; and principals placed third (Kosciw, 2004). Taken together, these findings suggest that students have a dim view of the school media center's potential to help them in their quest for information about LGBTQ issues—and in many cases they might be right.

INVESTIGATING THE AVAILABILITY OF MATERIALS

One of Darla Linville's most revealing findings about public libraries highlighted a disparity between the availability of queer titles in branch libraries as opposed to systemwide holdings. Another way to think of this disparity is the difference between large libraries and small ones. Given the anxiety that many LGBTQ teens have about asking librarians for assistance in locating queer-themed resources, it is critical that branch and small libraries carry a core collection of seminal queer YA materials so that teens can access them unassisted—that is, without needing to approach the reference desk at all, much less file an interlibrary loan request. It's not enough that the larger system contains queer titles; these titles must be present in branches frequented by teen patrons. Linville writes: "Teens want to see a new, broad selection of gay fiction in their local public library, not just the central library. Most libraries can fill patron requests from other branches, but teens want *their own branch* to have at least some of those books" (Linville, 2004:186). Rothbauer found similar results: Queer teens don't want to risk the exposure of requesting interlibrary loans (Rothbauer, 2004).

Intrigued by these findings, we conducted a search of online catalogs in library systems nationwide to see if there was a difference between branch and systemwide, small library versus large library, holdings for six queer YA books. With the exception of one old but still classic title, the lesbian romance *Annie on My Mind*, the search was for new novels that depict a cross-section of the queer community: the gay favorite *Rainbow Boys;* an African American lesbian novel titled *Orphea Proud; Empress of the World*, a bisexual book; *Luna: A Novel*, about a trans teen; and *Boy Meets Boy*, a romance that envisions a homophobia-free world. The search involved a total of fifty catalogs in eleven states, both socially conservative and liberal. While the search was by no means exhaustive (hence the use of the word "search" to distinguish this endeavor from a scientific study), it did provide a good snapshot of queer teen lit holdings nationwide in 2005.

The findings were that while most large libraries and systems offer a big and diverse selection of LGBTQ titles, most individual branches and small libraries generally do not. While nearly all of the library systems examined contained all six of the desired titles—and often possessed multiple copies thereof—these titles were generally unavailable in branches and smaller cities. These findings are admittedly anecdotal, but if corroborated by future studies, they can have important ramifications when it comes to serving LGBTQ teen patrons. As noted earlier, many queer and questioning teens are scared to approach the library desk for help in finding materials, much less request an interlibrary loan, as they would need to do when their local library lacks a desired title. And, again, it's not just LGBTQ teens who seek these books: it's their friends, families, and others who are simply curious or are seeking entertainment.

Interestingly, before conducting the search we expected to find significant differences between the availability of LGBTQ titles in socially conservative states as opposed to liberal ones. Simply put, we anticipated that so-called "red states" would lag behind their "blue" counterparts in the availability of queer YA books. For the most part, however, the findings did not support this assumption, but there were a few nuances. To start, while library systems in liberal states, such as New York, carry multiple copies of all six titles, conservative states such as Arkansas lacked the more diverse books, such as the trans novel *Luna* and the African American lesbian title *Orphea Proud*. Similarly, conservative states tended to carry fewer overall copies of LGBTQ titles.

The biggest difference discovered among libraries was not a red state/blue state divide, but an urban/rural divide. In all the states where the search was conducted, libraries in major cities contained all six of the titles we sought, whereas libraries in smaller cities did not carry these titles. This finding is corroborated, anecdotally, by GLSEN. Its *2003 National School Climate Survey* reported: "Youth in rural schools were less likely to report that LGBT resources were available in the library and that they had access to LGBT Internet sites at school computers" (Kosciw, 2004). The rural/urban divide has also been observed by Alex Spence. In his study of queer-themed children's picture books, he found that library systems in communities with populations of fewer than 100,000 people carried a smaller selection of these titles (Spence, 2000). And James V. Carmichael, Jr., who has written extensively about the availability of queer material in libraries, has observed: "Lesbigay collections in small and medium sized public libraries are underrepresentative, if they exist at all" (Carmichael, 1998).

Given the budget and space limitations of branch and small libraries, it would be impractical for them to acquire a full range of queer YA titles. However, every community in the United States is home to LGBTQ teenagers, many of whom would like to use their local library as a safe space to find queer information. Given the unique concerns and fears that these teens have in approaching the reference desk for assistance, it's critical that branches and small libraries shelve at least a small selection of current, popular queer YA titles so that teens can locate these materials unassisted. It's not good enough that a small library offers LGBTQ titles in its catalog if these materials are shelved in another branch on the other side of town. For many queer and questioning teens, the extra step of requesting an interlibrary loan is an insurmountable, unacceptable barrier to access. The fear of homophobia holds them back.

EVALUATING LIBRARY SERVICE TO LGBTQ TEENS

Assuming that some queer teens are able to overcome their fears and approach the reference desk for help in finding a title, how well are their needs being met during the reference interview? Of all the topics examined in this chapter, this one is the least understood. Among the few existing studies of this question is "If I Ask, Will They Answer? Evaluating Public Library Reference Service to Gay and Lesbian Youth," published in the Fall 2005 issue of *Reference and User Service Quarterly*. Ann Curry, associate professor of the University of British Columbia's library school, recruited a teenager she nicknamed "Angela" to approach reference desks in twenty Canadian libraries and ask for LGBTQ materials, then rate the quality of service she received. Curry chose this method, known as unobtrusive observation, believing it would yield a more accurate picture than simply asking librarians to rate themselves. Curry had Angela ask librarians the following question: "I am planning to start a club at my high school. A gay-straight alliance. What books do you have that could help me out?" (Curry, 2005:69). Angela then made note of whether or not librarians seemed interested in her question, gave her their full attention, made eye contact, and made her feel comfortable during the reference interview.

Curry concluded, quite simply, that librarians can do better. For instance, although half of the librarians reacted positively during the reference interview with Angela, comfortably using the words "gay" and "lesbian," fewer than half expressed positive interest in helping. Distressingly, many librarians were clearly uncomfortable with Angela's question and were unable to conceal this, which translated into poor service. In several instances, Angela detected a clearly negative response to her question; for instance, one librarian referred to gay and lesbian novels as "weird fiction," while another went looking for a children's picture book and, after failing to find it, returned and said to Angela, "Oh, maybe we didn't put them in there, so we wouldn't offend anyone else" (Curry, 2005:71). Hardly a positive message for an LGBTQ teen!

Curry writes that the worst response that Angela received was silence: "No words—just a blank stare. As the silence continued, Angela noted, 'I was tempted to run away!' Only when she repeated the question did the librarian haltingly begin to help" (Curry, 2005:70). And the opposite response, too much noise, proved nearly as distressing. Given the embarrassment and fear that many LGBTQ teens feel when approaching the reference desk, it was discouraging that Angela encountered librarians who she felt compromised her privacy during the reference interview by talking in an unnecessarily loud voice while others were close at hand. Discretion when it comes to seeking queer resources, other researchers have shown, is paramount (Hamer, 2003).

Even when librarians overcame their jitters in talking to queer teens, one of Curry's most revealing findings was that they did not know where to begin a search for queer-themed materials. She observed: "Few librarians seemed to know where to start a catalog or Internet search, or what terms to use. The two subject headings ideal for this inquiry are 'gay teenagers' and 'lesbian teenagers,' but unfortunately, no one used them" (Curry, 2005:71). In fact, three-quarters of the librarians used only the word "gay" in their searches, while just two librarians used the term "lesbian."

Librarians were also generally unable to find age-appropriate titles for Angela. Some gave her adult reading lists, while others offered children's picture books. Only three librarians showed Angela how to use catalogs, the Internet, and other reference sources. Only six librarians took Angela to the stacks to help her find materials they'd located in the catalog—and sadly, in three of these cases the resources they sought were missing. And finally, only half of the librarians bothered to end the reference interview with a requisite closing statement, such as "Please come back to the desk if you don't find what you need." Based on the service she received, it should be no surprise that Angela said she'd return to only 40 percent of the libraries if she needed help in the future.

UNDERSTANDING THE RESEARCH

Why don't libraries provide adequate service to LGBTQ youth? Although there are probably many reasons, some hypotheses include:

▼ fear of book challenges.

▼ fear that if a controversy does arise, the library will lose funding.

▼ assumption that other libraries will pick up any slack in their own collection.

▼ lack of awareness, or outright denial, that LGBTQ teens frequent the library.

▼ lack of knowledge about LGBTQ issues—or fear of them.

▼ homophobia on the librarian's part.

Many of these hypotheses are supported by James V. Carmichael, Jr., and Marilyn L. Shontz, who studied librarians' attitudes toward queer issues. They suggest that despite the library's tradition of inclusiveness, librarians themselves have conflicted views about homosexuality, preferring to grapple with queer issues on a philosophical level rather than a practical, everyday one (Carmichael and Shontz, 1996). They quote a library administrator who observed, no doubt paraphrasing the great gay poet Walt Whitman, "Be gay, but be quietly gay" (Carmichael and Shontz, 1996:25). This hypothesis is echoed by *School Library Journal* writer Debra Lau Whelan, who noted in her article "Out and Ignored" that school media centers, which are particularly keen to avoid controversy, do not acquire LGBTQ-themed titles, hoping, instead, that the local public library will pick up their slack (Whelan, 2006).

Before leaving this subject, take a moment to reflect on your own library and its level of service to queer teens. What would "Angela," the girl in Ann Curry's study, think of your library? The best way to find out what your real patrons think, of course, is to conduct your own survey. Additionally, you might create a self-evaluation checklist that includes some of the following items:

▼ How many queer-themed YA titles can you name off the top of your head?

▼ How many subject headings for a catalog search of these materials can you name off the top of your head?

▼ What organizations in your community can you name that would be of assistance to queer teens? Which national groups?

▼ Make an inventory of LGBTQ titles available in your catalog, and note whether or not these titles are physically present in the stacks of your library branch.

▼ Look at the overall atmosphere in your library—everything from the visibility of LGBTQ titles and displays, to the body language you and your colleagues use when talking with teens who are seeking queer resources.

▼ Are queer librarians out and visible in your library?

A series of detailed self-evaluation exercises, as well as tips for improvement, appear in Chapter 7. And, in regard to Ann Curry's findings about queer search terms, see Chapter 4 for a list of more than eighty possible OCLC keywords.

3 OFFERING EFFECTIVE SERVICE AND PROVIDING SAFE SPACES

INTRODUCTION

Up to this point, much of what has been discussed has relied on prior studies of LGBTQ teens and library service. This chapter and the next one mark a departure point, taking the first step toward envisioning new ways to connect LGBTQ teens and the library. Being a young adult librarian means more than just recommending good books; rather, it means listening to teens, treating them with respect, thinking about the impact that the library can have on their lives, and helping teens contribute to their world. Happily, these responsibilities are all connected. If you greet teens in a friendly manner as they enter the teen area, you'll help ease any fears they may have in approaching you at the information desk. If you are attentive during readers' advisory and reference interviews, you'll be able to recommend the right materials—and you'll also win teens' trust and admiration. And if you provide opportunities for teens to empower themselves, you'll help them contribute to their world. This approach works with straight and queer teens alike, but queer teens' fear of homophobia remains powerful and librarians must always keep it in mind.

HELPING TEENS BUILD DEVELOPMENTAL ASSETS

As a librarian, what do you want your teenaged patrons to achieve when they reach adulthood? Do you want them to be happy, strong, brave, courageous, self-sufficient, accepted, tolerant, politically aware, culturally savvy, critical thinkers, information seekers, lifelong learners, lifelong library users? Do you want the same thing for your LGBTQ patrons? In order to realize their full potential, all teenagers must acquire a series of developmental assets as they mature into healthy adults. These assets, first identified by the Search Institute, a nonprofit group dedicated to improving children's well-being, range from finding appropriate outlets for physical energy, to learning social conventions, to expressing creativity (Jones, 2002a, 2002b).

The Search Institute established as many as forty assets that children need to acquire as they mature into adults, but others have grouped these assets into a smaller number of broad categories. The Young Adult Library Services Association, for instance, identifies seven key assets that form the framework of its Serving the Underserved trainings:

1. Physical Activity
2. Competence and Achievement
3. Self Definition
4. Creative Expression
5. Positive Social Interaction with Peers and Adults
6. Structure and Clear Limits
7. Meaningful Participation (YALSA, 2003b)

The more of these assets that children acquire, the happier and healthier they will be, and they'll also be less likely to engage in risky behavior (Jones, 2003).

The best way for teens to acquire developmental assets is by empowering them to shape the world around them (Hart, 1992). As a librarian, you can empower teens in myriad ways, but the most effective and obvious step is to encourage teen participation in governing how the YA room functions and what its goals are—in other words, form a teen advisory group and seek its input. For instance, you can seek the group's advice in making decisions about the materials that your library collects, or you can encourage it to establish ground rules for behavior in the YA room. Also, you can offer programs that enable teens to contribute to the community and have their voices heard. Teens are bossed around in school and controlled by their parents at home, but they itch to begin asserting control over the world around them—a vital step in maturing into healthy adults. By allowing them to make decisions in the YA room, and helping them contribute to their community, you enable teens to mature and acquire developmental assets.

FORGING A SUCCESSFUL RELATIONSHIP BY LISTENING

The YA librarian's job goes far beyond simply providing books to teens, much less the "best" books according to some awards committee. Teens return to a library not because of the materials they get there—they can get books anywhere and many can go online anywhere—but because you, the librarian, engage them in conversation, respect what they have to say, and provide opportunities for them to empower themselves and contribute to their community. As Patrick Jones wrote in *New Directions for Library Service to Young Adults*, "The question is no longer merely asking what a young adult finds in a school or public library when entering it, but also what happens to that young adult as a result of checking out a book, participating in a book discussion group, spending time as a student assistant, or learning how to locate information on the Internet" (Jones, 2002b:5). In other words, the goal of a YA librarian is, in part, to become a bridge between patrons and the materials in a library, but it is mainly to help teens develop into healthy adults. The best way to do this is to forge a personal connection with teens in all aspects of service.

Librarians increasingly realize that the old intervention model of YA service, which relied on giving teens books to solve problems—if a kid was gloomy, you gave her a book about depression—no longer works. Instead, by providing positive interactions, friendly service, and focusing on a holistic youth-development and asset-building model of customer service, librarians can instill within teens a sense of self-confidence and belonging during these interactions; they can even provide a moment of inner calm to help teens make it through the rest of their day (Jones, 2002b). Not only will teens feel better, and develop a few assets, they will associate this positive experience with the library and come back again. Books will always be in the library. But unless teens have reasons to keep coming back, the teens may not be.

Queer and questioning kids also want their voices to be heard and look for opportunities to empower themselves, so you should treat them no differently than you would any other YA patron—except for one thing. You must take into account the fact that many queer teens fear you will stigmatize them in the same way that others do. In other words, the ubiquity of homophobia means that you have to take the extra step of showing LGBTQ teens that they are welcome in your library and that they will not be judged. As the sixties' saying goes, you can either be a part of the problem or a part of the solution. Even if you are uncomfortable with homosexuality, a possibility that we examine in depth, be aware that your words and actions have a powerful effect on queer teens. As Jami L. Jones has written, "For adults who work with [LGBTQ] teens, it is important to remember that it isn't about agreeing with their lifestyle, but rather helping them realize their potential" (Jones, 2004:39). Striking a similar tone, psychologist Jean M. Baker made this eloquent observation in her book about homophobia and child development:

> If you are an adult in a role that touches the lives of children you will have an impact, whether intentionally or not, on how children struggling with their sexual identity come to view themselves. There is nothing you can do to prevent children from growing up to be gay, but there are many

things you can do and say to help them keep their hopes and dreams alive and to help them grow up to lead happy, fulfilling lives. (Baker, 2002:xiv)

The least we can do as YA librarians is provide a safe, nonjudgmental space where queer and straight teenagers can gather without encountering homophobia. This is not just opinion—it's what kids themselves say they want. In 2005, the Gay, Lesbian and Straight Education Network reported that 63 percent of teens agreed that life in their schools would be better if they heard fewer homophobic comments (GLSEN, 2005).

EXPLORING THE INNER LIFE OF AN LGBTQ TEEN PATRON

Building a new model of library service begins with the concept of immersion: plunging yourself into the cultural, social, psychological, and historical background of the population you are seeking to represent and serve. In YALSA's Serving the Underserved (SUS) workshops, for instance, librarians contemplate the following question: How can you represent the population you serve, even when that population looks different and behaves differently than you do? It's more than just a philosophical question. Can white librarians represent black patrons? Can straight librarians represent queer patrons? The answer to both questions, of course, is "yes"—as long as you've taken the time to understand the population you represent.

To get inside the minds of teenagers, YA librarians read *Seventeen*, *Vibe*, and other YA magazines; we listen to hip-hop; and we play the latest video games. How can we get inside the minds of LGBTQ teens? One starting point is to pick up a copy of a mainstream queer periodical such as *The Advocate*, a newsmagazine that runs a regular department called "Generation Q" that profiles young queer people. By reading it, you'll be on your way to discovering what's happening in the lives of LGBTQ youth: how they operate in their communities and the challenges they face in the world. Better still, visit an online zine such as *Oasis*, at www.oasismag.com, where LGBTQ teens post blogs and other personal reflections on their daily lives. You could also turn to novels such as Alex Sanchez's *Rainbow Boys* or Sharon Dennis Wyeth's *Orphea Proud*, or watch films about queer teens such as *Beautiful Thing* and *The Incredibly True Adventure of Two Girls in Love*. From these you'll discover that while LGBTQ teens are basically just teens, they face some unique, critical moments in their adolescence that can have lifelong repercussions. In the library setting, it's up to the individual librarian to ensure that the outcome of these moments is positive.

This part of the chapter is a thought exercise designed to get you thinking about queer youth and what they go through every day. This is based on a similar exercise, called the "Moment of Truth Rap," which Patrick Jones originally developed and is now used by YALSA in its SUS workshops (YALSA, 2003a). Four areas are examined, through a series of ten questions each on: (1) inner life; (2) home life; (3) school life; and (4) library life. The questions are by no means comprehensive. They're a jumping off point to get you thinking and reflecting on what it's like to be queer. This exercise may be jarring, even painful, for some of you—and that's the point. With an idea of what LGBTQ teens go through every day, you can begin to think about how you can help them become what you want them to be: happy, healthy, well-adjusted, and lifelong library users. How to do this is the central concern throughout the rest of our book.

INNER LIFE

Begin by looking at a queer teenager's inner life and the emotions swirling within him. These questions assume you're looking at a gay male teenager, but think about how different things would be for a lesbian. Also, think about a bisexual teen: Does she feel compelled to choose being straight or gay? Finally, what is it like for a trans teen to feel ill at ease with her own body, and how does she begin to reverse this discomfort?

1. How does the teen self-identify: Does he think of himself as gay, bisexual, questioning, straight; does he have his own unique label; does he not use a label?

2. When did he first realize that he was attracted to other boys and was he honest with himself about this, or did it take time for him to admit it to himself?

3. Has he ever acted on a same-sex infatuation, and, if yes, how did it turn out?

4. Does he tell himself that maybe if he stops thinking "gay" thoughts, the whole thing will eventually go away?

5. Does he want to be "normal," and what does this mean to him?

6. If he's dating a girl, but has same-sex leanings, how hard is it to be with her and to keep his other feelings concealed? Does he feel guilty, stifled, dishonest?

7. What has shaped the teen's perceptions of queer people, i.e., what are his sources of information?

8. Does the teen know anyone who is out? Has he ever seen two people of the same sex holding hands in

public? Does he wish he could hold hands with a boy he likes without fear of being bashed?

9. Does the teen himself want to come out, or would he prefer to keep his sexual identity private? Does the teen think coming out is a safe and affirming possibility?

10. Does he picture a happy future for himself?

HOME LIFE

Now, expand your sphere to the teen's home life: How does the teen's family treat him? For the sake of brevity, we'll use the term "parents," but keep in mind that a teen might not live with two parents, or he might live with other relatives—grandparents, siblings, etc.—or a foster family, and so on. Again, take a moment to think about how the circumstances might differ for a lesbian, bisexual, or trans teen.

1. How easy was it for him to come out to his parents? Did he risk his entire family relationship by coming out? Did his parents kick him out of the house?

2. Does he have siblings and has he come out to them? Did he come out to them first?

3. How did his parents respond when he came out? Did they accept the news warmly, or were they uncomfortable? Angry? Concerned? Did they express warmth and say they loved their son, regardless of his sexual orientation? Did his parents tell him it was "just a phase"?

4. Do the teen's parents want biological grandchildren, and does this impact their relationship with him?

5. Are the teen's parents ashamed to tell the rest of their family? Do they look upon their son's sexual orientation as a failure to parent correctly? Are they afraid that others will see it this way?

6. How do the family's religious views affect whether or not they accept the teen's being gay?

7. Does the teen's family simply ignore the fact that he came out? Do they still ask him about opposite sex attractions? How difficult is this for him to hear?

8. If he's still in the closet, what is it like for him to keep his sexual identity a secret from his family?

9. Does he feel like he's letting his family down because of his sexual orientation?

10. If he's still in the closet, does he play the "pronoun game"—substituting "she" for "he" and trying to avoid pronouns entirely—when describing the boy he likes?

SCHOOL LIFE

Now think about queer teens at school, as they interact with friends. As indicated in Chapter 1, life for LGBTQ teens is better than it was even a decade ago, but they still encounter a tremendous amount of homophobia. How does this affect their ability to learn and to form friendships? All teens desperately want to fit in. Being different is a heavy load for teens to carry, particularly when added to the usual dramas, upsets, and misunderstandings that are part of everyday life for teens. As always, when you ask yourselves the following questions, think about how things would be different for a lesbian, a bisexual, or a trans teen.

1. Is the teen out at school and was this by choice? Is he out to only a few close, trusted friends?

2. When he enters school in the morning, how is he greeted? Do friends approach and ask "what's up?" Or, is he met with taunts like "fag," "faggot," etc.? Does he get shoved into lockers—or worse?

3. How does the teen cope? Does he try to make himself as unobtrusive as possible, a wallflower who attracts no attention? Does he attempt to let the taunting roll off his back? Does he mock himself to get a laugh?

4. Does he have a support network of friends, or a gay-straight alliance?

5. If he's taunted or bullied, does he report it to teachers and administrators? If yes, how have they handled it? Has he been told that he is the cause of the bullying, e.g., "You bring it on yourself"?

6. If he's in the closet, how does he handle it when his male friends talk about girls? Does he try to play along like one of the guys?

7. If he's in the closet, does he stand by and watch as gay classmates, or classmates perceived as gay, are taunted? Does he participate in the bullying, and how does that make him feel about himself?

8. If the teen is out, what was it like to come out? What was it like to walk down the hall that day and know that for once, in fact, the other kids really were talking about him?

9. Can he concentrate in school, or is he constantly distracted by the bullying and thinking of ways to escape it?

10. Does he plan to finish school—or are things so bad he wants to drop out?

LIBRARY LIFE

Finally, think about queer teens in the library. When a queer teen walks into the library, what does he find? What would a lesbian, bisexual, or trans teen find?

1. Are there LGBTQ books on display? What about symbols, such as the rainbow flag or pink triangle?

2. Is there an LGBTQ information section?

3. How many queer YA novels are there in the library? Are there many popular, current titles? Or, are there only a few dusty copies of books written before 1990?

4. Is there information available at the library about queer community groups?

5. Can he connect with other queer teens online at the library in a confidential and safe manner?

6. Does the librarian answer his questions about LGBTQ materials with as much courtesy and thoroughness as possible when he asks for something?

7. Does the librarian let other kids get away with teasing or using homophobic epithets in the library?

8. Does the queer teen feel safe in the library?

9. Does he feel welcomed by the library?

10. Does he find what he wants in the library?

CONCLUSION

This exercise should have helped you gain insight into the daily thoughts and struggles of queer and questioning teens in your community. Now that you've gained this new perspective, the next step is putting it into practice: as you think about how your library represents LGBTQ teens, both in its collections and in its atmosphere; as you provide readers' advisory, reference interviews, and recommend other materials; and as you welcome all teens into the library by offering services and programs. The next few chapters provide a framework and some ground rules that can help you do this.

MAINTAINING OBJECTIVITY AND EQUITY OF SERVICE

The first part of this book examined LGBTQ teens and what they want from the library. Then, this chapter began by envisioning a way of serving these teens that would help them realize their fullest potential—a process that starts with going inside the heads of queer teens to understand their perspective on the world. Now you are ready to delve into specific strategies for serving them. As you'll see, the key to serving queer and questioning teens effectively is twofold: heightening their visibility by integrating LGBTQ materials into regular library collections and services; and, just as important, protecting their right to privacy in a space that is free of harassment. Although the remainder of this chapter offers specific tips for how you can create this welcoming atmosphere, we'll take a moment now to talk about you, the librarian, and your own attitudes. After all, service starts with you, and you are the face of the library.

As we saw in Chapter 2, Darla Linville surveyed queer teens and found that they wanted librarians to be approachable and nonjudgmental when it comes to LGBTQ issues (Linville, 2004). While most people reading this book fit this description, some of you might be uncomfortable dealing with queer subjects—and some of you may even disapprove of homosexuality. If this is the case, take this simple and direct advice: Get over your discomfort. As YA author David Levithan wrote in a *School Library Journal* article, "Being gay is not an *issue*, it is an *identity*. It is not something that you can agree or disagree with. It is a *fact*, and must be defended and represented as a fact" (Levithan, 2004b:44). He went on to ask if librarians would consider it acceptable to treat an African American patron differently than a white patron, or a Jewish patron differently than a Christian one. The answer, of course, is "no"—just as it should be when it comes to serving queer patrons. So, if you're uncomfortable with queer people, we suggest redirecting that energy and instead attempting to empathize with LGBTQ teens. Put yourself in their shoes. Absorb the pain and isolation they often feel—and the courage expressed in the simple act of approaching you for assistance.

A basic tenet of library service is that librarians provide equal access and equal treatment to all patrons. A successful librarian, according to the Reference User Services Association, "maintains objectivity and does not interject value judgments about subject matter or the nature of the question into the transaction" (Reference and User Services Association, 2004). This advice is doubly important when it comes to queer and questioning teens. As Linville wrote:

> Librarians have the power in the library to make the information available or to hide it, to make teens feel welcome

or to make them feel unwanted. Even if librarians feel nervous talking or thinking about queerness, we must remember that searching young people are much more nervous than we are. We are the ones who can make them comfortable in our space. (Linville, 2004:186)

As a librarian, it is your responsibility to put a patron's needs ahead of your own. The library exists to meet the needs of its community, and all communities include queer people. If you give poor service to LGBTQ teens, you'll surely lose them as patrons. Remember that in Anne Curry's study of reference service, "Angela" said that she would avoid 60 percent of the libraries because of the poor service she had received there (Curry, 2005). Can your library risk alienating patrons? Remember, it's not just queer and questioning teens that you'll lose if you fail to provide sensitive LGBTQ service. You'll also alienate the large number of straight teens who want to read about queer people. No library can risk turning away patrons.

If you worry that by helping teens find LGBTQ materials you might somehow be condoning or promoting homosexuality, take a moment to examine the lack of logic implicit in this assumption. Does carrying Adolf Hitler's autobiography *Mein Kampf* mean that you condone anti-Semitism? Of course not. Likewise, carrying a book such as *GLBTQ: The Survival Guide for Queer & Questioning Teens* does not mean that you are actively promoting homosexuality. This is an admittedly extreme analogy. A more realistic parallel pertains to teachers. During the 1970s, a group of social conservatives in California proposed a ballot initiative to bar gays and lesbians from being teachers. Proponents of the measure argued that queer people set a bad example for children. Harvey Milk, an openly gay San Francisco councilman, elegantly destroyed this logic by noting that if teachers held such a powerful sway over students, then given the number of Catholic schools, "there should be a lot more nuns running around" (*The Times of Harvey Milk*, 1982). Kids pay attention to what adults do, to be sure, but sexual orientation is nonnegotiable. Having queer books in the library will not make kids queer—just as having straight books in the library doesn't make kids straight, either.

COMING OUT IN THE YA ROOM— SUGGESTIONS AND RESOURCES FOR LGBTQ LIBRARIANS

Unfortunately, even today a minority of people believe that queers should not be teachers. We can safely assume that they also frown upon queer YA librarians. This brings us to the question: If you yourself are a queer librarian, how out should you be in the library? Should you become an activist for queer rights in the library? Should you acquiesce to being the token queer, the default go-to person for any and all questions regarding LGBTQ issues? What if a colleague or an administrator is homophobic? For many queer YA librarians, these questions are more than hypothetical; they're everyday concerns. In 2003, for instance, a library in Kansas reprimanded a librarian after a coworker alleged that she created a hostile work environment by discussing her gay son (*American Libraries*, 2003). While this extreme example probably represents every queer or queer-friendly librarian's worst fears, pockets of unease and homophobia linger in many libraries across the country.

Deciding whether or not to come out in a library setting is a topic so broad it warrants its own book—and indeed there are a handful available (Kester, 1997; Kissen, 1996). Here the idea will be discussed only as it relates to how, and why, you might come out in the YA room. Queer librarians have a right to keep their sexual identity private if they so choose—indeed, all people have the right to keep their sexuality private—but the authors' viewpoint is that you should come out because, quite simply, it's what LGBTQ teens want from you. Many respondents in Darla Linville's survey, for instance, suggested that queer librarians wear a small rainbow sticker or pink triangle so that teens could immediately tell who was "safe" to approach for help finding LGBTQ materials—although one teen, preferring a more subtle cue, suggested that queer librarians wear corduroy pants (Linville, 2004). Queer teens seek out adult role models, and by coming out in the library, acting as you normally would and going about your daily business, you satisfy that need; you become the proof that it is possible to survive adolescence. It's as simple as that. And remember, it's not just LGBTQ teens who can benefit from role models. You'll also set an example for straight teens. By simply acting normally, you'll help dispel any wrong-headed notions they have about queer people.

On occasion, being out in the YA room will bring its share of awkward moments. As with any interaction that you have with teens, handling these situations tactfully can turn them into teachable moments. For instance, if a homophobic kid walks up to you and demands to know if you're queer, responding "That's none of your business and you shouldn't ask people that," will alienate the teen and show him that you feel uncomfortable talking about homosexuality—which is probably exactly the response he wants because it suggests that being queer is something shameful. Instead, if someone asks you whether or not you're queer, say something like, "Most of the time." This humorous response will give the kid something to think about. Indeed, as noted in Chapter 1, most people are neither 100 percent straight nor 100 percent homosexual. Most fall somewhere in the middle of the spectrum, and you might want to tell this to the kid, turning the situation into a teachable moment. One thing you should avoid doing, however, is exacerbating the situation by accusing the teen of being homophobic or lecturing him about tolerance. While you shouldn't condone homophobia, accusing people of it is unproductive because even homophobes realize that homophobia is bigotry—and no one likes to be called a bigot, especially when it is true.

RESOURCES FOR LGBTQ LIBRARIANS

When it comes to coming out in the workplace, there are no easy answers, but there are some additional resources. The library has a long history of recognizing the needs of queer employees. The American Library Association's Gay, Lesbian, Bisexual, Transgendered Round Table, founded in 1970, was the first queer professional organization in the nation. Today, the Round Table is best known for presenting the annual Stonewall Book Awards, which recognize queer contributions to fiction and nonfiction. On its Web site, www.ala.org/glbtrt, the group posts newsletters as well as book and film reviews. It also sponsors social hours during the annual and midwinter ALA conventions. These events provide an opportunity to meet other queer librarians and discuss shared concerns.

Another excellent resource is the Gay, Lesbian and Straight Education Network (GLSEN). Founded in the early 1990s as a group for teachers, its mission has expanded to making schools safer for students of all sexual orientations by holding awareness events such as "No Name-Calling Week" and "Day of Silence." Its network of forty chapters nationwide provides support to educators, both straight and queer, who are working to combat homophobia and bullying. The group's Web site, www.glsen.org, features a wealth of digital books and discussion forums, as well as a members-only area designed especially for educators. For more on GLSEN, see Chapter 4.

ESTABLISHING GROUND RULES FOR A SAFE SPACE

Queer teens who patronize the library are as varied as are all teens. Sometimes a kid will walk into the YA room wearing a rainbow flag button that says "Here and Queer." Other times she'll blend right in with the other teens until you notice that she hangs back from the rest of the group and attempts to conceal what she is reading—which you then observe is a queer title. Most of the time, LGBTQ teens are difficult, if not impossible, to identify. Instead of wasting energy trying to spot them, concentrate on providing excellent service to all teens in the library. The advantage of this strategy is twofold: By providing consistent and sensitive service to everyone, you'll automatically make LGBTQ teens feel comfortable and you'll also help straight teens become more considerate of the queer teens among them. What follows are a few ground rules for creating a safe space in the YA room so that everyone feels welcome and respected.

VISIBILITY AND INTEGRATION

This important point can't be stressed enough. As YA author Brent Hartinger said during a panel on LGBTQ concerns at the American Library Association's June 2006 conference: If you treat queer material like "plutonium," i.e., something that requires special treatment, so will everybody else. Queer people are not toxic; they are a normal part of everyday life in communities across the United States. This book began by noting that queer teenagers are everywhere. Integrating LGBTQ books and programs into your everyday routine in the library is the best way of showing teens that you understand this fact. Practically speaking, integration means showing queer teens representations of themselves in the YA room. Thus, if you include LGBTQ books in your normal programming—a Valentine's Day display, for instance, or a display of staff picks—you show that they fit naturally alongside everything else. Integration also means including LGBTQ books as an option when you conduct a readers' advisory—slipping a queer book into a stack of titles that you hand to a kid who wants romances—and including an LGBTQ title in your regular lineup of booktalks. Increasing the visibility of these materials and including them within normal contexts goes a long way to ending the isolation and stigma that many queer and questioning teenagers feel. If there's anything you take away from this book, let it be the concept of integration.

DON'T ASSUME ANYTHING

Do you assume a boy is gay because he's effeminate or has a lisp? Do you think a girl's a lesbian because she's a tomboy? These are stereotypes, and acting on them is sure to make teens feel uncomfortable. Moreover, implying that someone is queer or inadvertently outing someone who is not ready to be outed could jeopardize that person's safety. Instead of trying to pigeonhole teens, it's best to accept them for who they are at any given moment: Follow their lead. If a young woman walks into the library and professes herself to be an out, Goth, vegetarian lesbian, don't be surprised if she returns the following week as a straight, meat-eating cheerleader. While it's not necessary for librarians to indulge teenagers' flights of fancy, we should support teens in the best way we can: by helping to connect them with information.

Whether you're conducting a readers' advisory or a reference interview, treat LGBTQ-related questions with the same sensitivity that you would every other kind of question. Be sure to maintain eye contact, keep a relaxed posture, and use an interested tone of voice. The one key difference is to remember that many queer and questioning teens who approach the reference desk are performing a quiet act of courage in overcoming their fear of homophobia. Although today's teens are more at ease with being queer than any previous generation, every person has different circumstances. Some teens feel internalized homophobia and are embarrassed that you'll think they are gay; others will worry about other people within earshot of the desk; and still others will worry that their friends and family might think they're queer. As Judah S. Hamer found in his study of the information needs of gay teens, approaching the reference desk can be terrifying. "I was scared out of my mind," one boy told him; "I'd always sweat when I'd come to the library," said another (Hamer, 2003:81–82). Instead of heightening this anxiety by making false assumptions, put teens at ease by relying on your professionalism. Answer their questions as thoroughly as possible without revealing any of your own personal opinions.

RESPECT TEENS' PRIVACY

The second ground rule in serving LGBTQ teens is that you should never ask them about their sexual orientation; the same goes for straight teens. A person's sexuality is private information. As a representative of the library, your job is to provide patrons with the information they seek and, in the process, protect their privacy. It's not your job to delve into their private lives. If you try to do this, you'll probably make them feel uncomfortable. That said, sometimes teens might want to talk to you about their sexuality. Again, follow their lead. For instance, a teen might confide that he thinks he's bisexual and ask your advice about what to do next. In this case, you can obviously begin connecting the kid with books, Web sites, and other suitable resources. One thing you should avoid doing, however, is counseling teens that being queer is "just a phase." As noted in Chapter 1, sexual orientation is nonnegotiable but sexual identity is exquisitely malleable. But it's exclusively up to teens to decide for themselves who they are. Any pressure you place on them will at the very least be unwelcome, and at worst could be damaging. Let teens figure it out for themselves. Your job as a librarian is to provide them with helpful resources and refrain from judgment.

ESTABLISH A HATE-FREE ZONE

The last ground rule for creating a safe space is that you must prevent other people in the YA room from making homophobic remarks. You want your library to become an oasis of tolerance in an otherwise harsh landscape for LGBTQ teens. Half of high school and middle school students say they hear other students using slurs such as "faggot" and "dyke," and nearly 70 percent say they hear students use the expression "that's so gay," in which the word "gay" is meant as something distasteful (GLSEN, 2005). Use of the expression "that's so gay" is so widespread that it's become rote for many kids—in other words, they don't stop to think about what the words mean and why they are offensive. The library is not immune to this use of language. Beth Gallaway, a trainer and consultant for the Metrowest Massachusetts Regional Library System, observed in an April 2005 e-mail to us, "In nearly every program I have ever run, I have had to ask at least one teen to cease using the words 'gay' or 'queer' in a negative connotation. I think some teachers let it slide in school, and some adults let it slide at home. I told kids I found that use of the word to be offensive and to broaden their vocabularies."

If you hear kids making homophobic remarks in your own library, step in and say something about it—just as you would if kids were using racist, anti-religious, and sexist slurs. This kind of language creates a climate of intolerance in which LGBTQ teens will feel unsafe and unwelcome. Although sometimes you might hear full-on slurs, most of the time your task will be to break the habit of casual homophobia, such as the expression "that's so gay," calling attention to what is being said and illustrating why it is hurtful. How you go about doing this depends on your own personal style, but try to maintain a normal tone of voice when you're talking. Begin by asking the patron to refrain from using offensive language in the library; add that in your library, everybody is friends with everybody else, including gay people, and that those who have a problem with this are welcome to leave. In *GLBTQ: The Survival Guide for Queer and Questioning Teens*, Kelly Huegel advises teens to counteract homophobic comments with remarks such as: "Why would you say something like that?" "Are you aware that sounds homophobic?" "There are a lot of misconceptions about queer people. They are all human beings, and it can really hurt to hear those kinds of things" (Huegel, 2003: 34).

If calling teens on their remarks fails to work and the problem persists, tell the offenders that you'll eject them from the library the next time they say something offensive. Be prepared to follow through on your promise, because if you don't, they'll perceive that they have power over you—as will all the other teens in the room who witness the encounter. We hope you don't have to become a disciplinarian. That's not the point of this discussion. Instead, we hope that you'll help teens learn a new habit: the habit of avoiding homophobic words. Not only will they be learning a lesson in tolerance, but all teens—queer and straight—will feel comfortable that your library is a place where bullying and mocking people does not happen. Teens grow up, of course, so you'll have to be vigilant as new kids begin using your library. But if you are consistent, eventually teens will step up to the plate and the "no name-calling zone" or "hate-free zone" will perpetuate itself. You can, of course, ensure that this happens by enlisting your teen advisory board to take the lead on establishing and enforcing the ground rules for your YA room's hate-free zone.

Before leaving this topic, you should also be alert for LGBTQ teens, or teens perceived as being queer, who are being bullied in the library. At minimum, bullying is harassment; if left unchecked it can escalate to gay-bashing. Twenty-nine states plus the District of Columbia classify gay-bashing—assault based on a victim's sexual orientation or gender identity—as a form of hate crime, which is a more serious charge than assault (Safe Schools Coalition, 2004). And if you work in a school where a queer or perceived-as-queer teen is being bullied, the school can be held liable if it fails to intervene (Cianciotto and Cahill, 2003). Wherever you work, don't ignore the bullying—and certainly don't blame the LGBTQ victim or accuse this person of provoking it. This may sound obvious, but, sadly, research has found that many school officials blame LGBTQ teens for bringing harassment upon themselves (Cianciotto and Cahill, 2003; GLSEN, 2004; Human Rights Watch, 2001). Shifting blame is truly unconscionable.

The "Dos" When Serving Queer Teens

Do treat LGBTQ teens the same way you treat everyone else who comes into the library.

Do increase visibility by including LGBTQ materials in your regular programming.

Do take teens—queer and straight—for who they are and who they claim to be. Even if teens are closeted and claim to be straight, they'll remember that one librarian who accepted them for who they were, no matter what mask they were wearing at the time.

Do follow the lead of queer teens when it comes to how much of their identity they're willing to reveal, and to whom.

Do respect teenagers' right to privacy when it comes to their sexual identity and willingness to discuss LGBTQ materials openly.

Do ask queer teens what kinds of books they like to read.

Do give teens a variety of materials that includes a mix of queer and straight books.

Do let teens know that your library has other kinds of books if they've only asked for one genre.

Do approach LGBTQ teens with open-ended readers' advisory and reference questions, such as, "Can I help you find any specific item in the library today?" and "Let me know if I can help you find anything else."

Do give teens referrals to community groups outside the library when they ask for them.

The "Don'ts" When Serving Queer Teens

Don't allow kids in your library to get away with using homophobic slurs such as "fag" and "dyke," or using the expression "that's so gay."

Don't assume a teen is or is not queer.

Don't ask teens to tell you their sexual orientation. If they want you to know, they'll get around to telling you on their own time.

Don't single out LGBTQ teens or otherwise treat them differently than you would other teens.

Don't discuss LGBTQ materials loudly or in the immediate presence of others if a teen seems uncomfortable; instead, talk quietly or, if it's permitted in your library, devise an online chat or text messaging system that preserves teens' privacy.

Don't discuss a teenager's sexuality with anyone else.

Don't be shy about using the words "gay" and "lesbian" to help teens narrow their search during readers' advisory.

4 PROVIDING READERS' ADVISORY AND REFERENCE INTERVIEWS

INTRODUCTION

Readers' advisory and reference interviews with LGBTQ teens are little different than offering the same services to straight teens, but there are a few key things to remember. For starters, fear of homophobia may prevent many queer or questioning kids from revealing exactly what they want help finding—an extra degree of evasiveness above and beyond teens' usual lack of clarity. Another thing to keep in mind is that you should broaden your own horizon regarding how you search for information: for instance, using more than just the word "gay" when searching in the catalog. Finally, and this is perhaps the most important thing to remember, don't be afraid to give LGBTQ-themed books to all kids, regardless of their sexual orientation. If a teen asks for romances, in other words, make sure to include a queer book in the mix of titles that you hand to her. As we noted in the last chapter, you should never assume anything—your role is simply to give teens a range of materials and let them chose what suits their needs. This chapter offers tips on how to connect LGBTQ materials with all teens in the library, and also explores a wide range of helpful online resources.

LISTENING FOR AND RESPONDING TO CUES

Readers' advisory and reference interviews are two separate things, but given the paucity of young adult services in many libraries, they are often one and the same. Thus, as a YA librarian, you should be prepared to handle both types of questions—and realize that one question may actually be embedded in another. Readers' advisory typically begins when a patron asks the librarian for a "good book" to read. It could be that the patron wants to read a book for pleasure, or needs to read something for a book report at school, but the general area of inquiry tends to be fairly broad. In a reference interview, by contrast, patrons typically seek answers to specific questions, or seek specific kinds of information. Again, it could be that the teen is seeking information to complete a homework assignment, but she might also be seeking information relevant to her personal life, such as tips on how to come out or safe-sex practices. Your job is to keep unpacking questions until you identify what a patron is really seeking.

When dealing with possible LGBTQ-themed questions, be prepared to do an extra bit of detective work since queer topics make teens especially evasive. For this you'll need to read as many different queer YA titles as you can get your hands on, so that you'll be as knowledgeable as possible, and you'll have to be alert to the subtle cues that teens send when they're looking for LGBTQ materials. The following anecdote illustrates the importance of picking up on subtle cues. A female patron, whom we'll call Heather, approaches the reference desk and asks if you have any love stories. "Do you want love stories that are mysteries?" you ask her. "Do want silly love stories? Serious love stories?" Heather replies that she wants "different" types of love stories. After turning this word over in your head a few times, you go to the stacks and hand Heather a variety of "different" love stories. It includes Angela Johnson's *First Part Last*, Sarah Dessen's *This Lullaby*, Sharon Flakes' *Who Am I Without Him?*, David Levithan's *Realm of Possibility*, and Julie Anne Peters' *Keeping You a Secret*. It turns out that *Keeping You a Secret*, a lesbian novel, is exactly the kind of "different" story that Heather wants.

When Heather used the word "different," your "gaydar"—the ability to spot a queer person—might have perked up, but you should never look at a kid like Heather, assess that she is queer, and then say, "Oh, you want lesbian books, right?" Instead, your job is to give her the information she asks for as well as information you think she might like. Thus, you give Heather a variety of books, including two queer titles, *Keeping You a Secret* and *Realm of Possibility*. A broad selection will empower Heather to chose the book she really wants without having to reveal her sexual identity. Also, by giving Heather a stack of five varied books, not exclusively queer ones, you're maintaining her privacy as she walks through the reading room and starts to browse. Discreet and tactful matching of a teen's interest will demonstrate to teens that you, as a librarian, are not prejudging them but instead are listening to what they have to say, attempting to give them the best information possible, and are showing concern for their privacy. The true sign of a successful interaction will come later when a kid like Heather asks for more books like *Keeping You a Secret*.

MATCHING LGBTQ MATERIALS WITH ALL TEEN USERS

Queer books are not just queer books; they're good books that all kids enjoy, finding characters to whom they can relate. YA author Brent Hartinger said in a panel discussion about LGBTQ books at the American Library Association's June 2006 conference that he gets letters from straight boys who read *Geography Club* and can relate to its main character—even though the main character is gay. The reason is that the character is keeping a secret, a scenario that everyone understands.

One of the many goals of a YA librarian is to present teens with a variety of good reading opportunities. This makes giving teens LGBTQ books a no-brainer. As anyone who's worked on a reference desk in a typical teen reading room knows, kids often ask the most open-ended question possible: "I need a good book to read; what do you have?" is a common one. After asking a few questions to narrow this down a bit—"What kinds of books do you like to read? Mysteries, fantasy stories, funny books? Scary books, love stories, books about real life, etc.?"—you head out to the stacks to gather a pile of books that might be suitable. When you do, slip an LGBTQ title into the mix. It's a great way to provide teens with well-rounded reading opportunities and the best resources you have. Again, you're not giving kids LGBTQ books because they're queer books; you're doing it simply because they're good books—which means that you should be giving them to all teens. And remember, whenever you give out books, be sure to ask for kids' feedback and show that you're interested in listening to them. Tell the teens to have a seat and read the books' dust jackets, or the first few pages, to see if they like where things are going—if it looks good, take it, but if it seems like it might not be of interest, leave it on the table. You won't be offended. Give teens complete freedom to tell you that they hate a book. Let them know that you'll try to do better next time.

On occasion, if you embed queer-themed titles amid a stack of books you might encounter a kid who finds these books and says, "Oh, man, I don't want this: I'm not gay!" More likely, you'll just see that kid snickering about it with his friends. If this happens, just say something like, "Well, if the book's not for you, it's not for you." On rare occasions, however, you might find a teen who is especially defensive and belligerent. If this is the case, try to turn the situation into a teachable moment. Explain that you were not making any assumptions about the teen's sexuality and that, in fact, you provide all teens with LGBTQ titles. Hopefully, this will diffuse the teen's immediate upset. If not, you might also make the point that a person does not have to be gay to read a gay book any more than someone needs to be black to read a book about African Americans. Everyone can enjoy reading a good book.

STEALTHY READERS' ADVISORY AND BORROWING ON THE HONOR SYSTEM

Some teens may simply be too scared or too shy to approach you with any LGBTQ-themed readers' advisory questions. If you take steps to ensure that LGBTQ materials are easy to find, these teens can do their own readers' advisory. For starters, you can prominently post bibliographies of queer books in the teen reading room. A more subtle approach, as YA author and librarian Sara Ryan suggested at the ALA's June 2006 conference, is to place copies of this bibliography inside each of the LGBTQ titles in your YA collection. She advised: "When kids sneak these books off the shelves and discover the list they realize, 'Oh my gosh, there's more!'" So long as these books are easily accessible in the YA room, kids will find them. When it comes time for teens to check these books out of the library, you should consider devising ways to protect their privacy. For instance, you might allow teens to borrow LGBTQ titles in different book jackets, or you might disable magnetic tattletale strips and let teens borrow LGBTQ titles on an honor system.

MATCHING DIFFERENT READING LEVELS

If you know a kid is an avid reader and he seemed to enjoy an LGBTQ title that you've previously given him, the next time he's in the library, feel free to load him down with literally ten queer books at once—the same as you'd do, obviously, if he liked fantasy or sci-fi, etc. For reluctant readers, meanwhile, it's usually best to give them only one or two titles from a stack of books that you know appeal to kids who don't read much or who only like a single genre. These books are instant hits with any reader, written in a streamlined style and packing a whopper of a punch within a minimum of pages. Occasionally, you might want to give reluctant readers a handful of books to take home, just in case they don't like the first few titles. In this case, always follow up afterward to ask which ones they liked so you can better match their interests next time. The kids will leave happy because they feel you care about what they think, and you'll be happy because you've just upped your circulation statistics.

Conducting LGBTQ readers' advisory for younger teens is similar, except that you should always be thinking of book content, as you would with all younger audiences. Until very recently, there were no LGBTQ titles specifically published especially for tweens (kids aged ten to fourteen). But as the size of this demographic cohort has grown, so has the number of titles for it. These books may not have happy endings, but they contain age-appropriate levels of violence, language, and sexual situations. That said, tweens are all over the map in terms of their reading levels. While some are still rereading their favorite children's titles, most generally want to read above their recommended reading level, and some have even surpassed YA books altogether and are reading from the adult collection. In the end, it's up to you to gauge a patron's reading habits and find the LGBTQ book that will be the perfect fit. And remember, regardless of how old patrons are, don't forget to ask for feedback when they're done reading the books you've given them. That way, you'll have a leg up next time they ask for your suggestions.

HELPING PARENTS FIND INFORMATION ABOUT LGBTQ TEENS

On occasion, you might be approached by parents who are seeking information about their queer or questioning children. Once again, there is a tremendous support network available for these parents, beginning with the group PFLAG (Parents, Family and Friends of Lesbians and Gays), which is profiled in the last section of this chapter. If parents are seeking nonfiction titles in your YA collection, refer them to any of the titles offered in our special parents' list found in Chapter 10; you might also consider giving them novels about LGBTQ teens, also listed in the same chapter.

CONDUCTING AN EFFECTIVE REFERENCE INTERVIEW

The range of LGBTQ-related questions you might field at the reference desk is as varied as the teens who seek your help, but there are some broad categories that encompass the content of these questions. These categories include:

▼ how to tell if someone is queer, and information about what homosexuality is.

▼ information about trans issues.

▼ how to come out.

▼ information about safe sex.

▼ how to combat homophobia.

▼ how to start a gay-straight alliance.

▼ real-life stories of LGBTQ teenagers.

▼ profiles of famous queer people.

▼ history of the queer equal rights movement.

▼ the morality of homosexuality.

▼ same-sex marriage.

▼ information about same-sex parents.

While there is no set formula for how to conduct a reference interview, your goal is to determine three pieces of information: (1) what the patron really needs; (2) how much information will satisfy this need; and (3) how sophisticated the material should be (Jones 1998; Vaillancourt, 2000). After you've made these assessments, you can then identify specific materials for a patron and ask if these materials are what he or she wants.

As any librarian who has ever sat on a YA reference desk knows, teens rarely ask for exactly what they want in their first question. Conversely, sometimes what they request differs from what they are actually seeking. For instance, a teen might ask you for help finding information about gay-straight alliances, when what she really wants is to find a fiction title to discuss *during* a meeting of a gay-straight alliance. In any case, your job as the librarian is to narrow down the range of possibilities by restating or paraphrasing what the teen has said; keeping track of what a teen says; and asking open-ended questions. Keep in mind, too, that as Renée Vaillancourt has observed, many teens are apt to be "literal and linear" in their requests: for instance, only seeking a monograph that specifically addresses the subject they need and failing to consult general resources that also mention the desired subject (Vaillancourt, 2000:66). You should help teens to begin thinking in larger terms.

DEVELOPING AN EXPANDED SEARCH STRATEGY

The preface to this book explained the choice to use the terms "queer" and "LGBTQ" as often as possible—to be as all-inclusive as possible in referring to people of different sexual orientations. During the course of casual everyday speech, however, many people use the word "gay" to encompass the entire LGBTQ community. The trap that librarians can fall into when conducting reference interviews is that they don't remember to search for other appropriate queer words and subject headings. This much was clear from Ann Curry's study, in which three-quarters of librarians used only the key word "gay" (Curry, 2005). Obviously, the best choice is to use more specific words.

You should also be aware that when it comes to LGBTQ subjects, standard catalog classification schemes often fail to describe LGBTQ materials accurately (Carmichael, 2002). Indeed, Ellen Greenblatt has observed that the Library of Congress's terminology is "outdated, obscure, and socially insensitive" (Greenblatt, 2001). Moreover, patrons themselves often search using terms that library catalogs do not recognize. For instance, Paulette Rothbauer recently studied the information-gathering techniques of lesbian women and found that they preferred to search using the key word "queer" over the word "homosexual"—and usually failed to generate results because catalogs only use the word homosexual (Rothbauer, 2004). Another sign that library classification systems need updating is that the women in Rothbauer's study turned first to online retailers, such as Amazon.com, to find books—because these retailers offer peer recommendations and other features that make finding queer content easier—and then backtracked to see if titles they found were available in a library.

Improvements in classification and cataloging are needed, but it is beyond the scope of this book to enter the fray of this discussion. Instead,

Suggested Search Keys

Bisexual men	Gay games	Gay police	Lesbian librarians
Bisexual parents	Gay heroes	Gay politicians	Lesbian love
Bisexual women	Gay human services	Gay pride day	Lesbian marriage
Bisexual youth	personnel	Gay press	Lesbian mothers
Bisexuality	Gay labor union members	Gay publications	Lesbian rights
Bisexuals	Gay lib	Gay rights	Lesbian teenagers
Children of gay parents	Gay liberation movement	Gay rights movement	Lesbian youth
Coming out	Gay librarians history	Gay sailors	Lesbians
Female-to-male	Gay librarians	Gay students	Lesbianism
transsexuals	Gay libraries	Gay studies	Same-sex marriage
Gay activists	Gay male couples	Gay teachers	Sexual orientation
Gay actors	Gay marriage	Gay teenagers	Social action
Gay adoption	Gay men's writings	Gay youth	Social change
Gay and lesbian studies	Gay motion picture actors	Gays	Transgender people
Gay artists	and actresses	Gender identity	Transgendered people
Gay athletes	Gay motion picture	Heterosexual parents	Transgenderism
Gay clubs	producers and directors	Homophobia	Transgenders
Gay communities	Gay parents	Homosexuality	Transsexual men
Gay conservatives	Gay parents' children	Lesbian artists	Transsexual orientation
Gay composers	Gay people	Lesbian communities	Transsexual parents
Gay consumers	Gay peoples	Lesbian couples	Transsexuality
Gay couples	Gay persons	Lesbian feminism	Transsexuals
Gay fathers	Gay photographers	Lesbian feminist theory	

familiarize yourself with as many different queer terms as possible and then be specific when trolling through the catalog and databases. To help you brainstorm, here is a list of possible OCLC subject headings you might use. This list is by no means comprehensive—it was compiled by searching in The New York Public Library's catalog—but it should help get your mind working. You'll notice that many of the headings can be modified—plural and singular forms, adjectives and nouns—and that the words "gay," "lesbian," "bisexual," and "transsexual" figure in several different, highly specific contexts. Also, terms can be mixed and matched; for instance, you can search for "lesbian communities" or "gay communities," "gay men's writings" or "lesbian writings." You'll also note that the word "gay" might denote the entire queer community or refer exclusively to homosexual men. Thus, to search for materials about homosexual men you should search under both "gay" and "gay men." And finally, if you're looking for LGBTQ fiction titles, try adding the key word "fiction" to a key such as "gay teenagers" or "lesbian teenagers."

UTILIZING SPECIAL DATABASES AND TOOLS

Several online search tools and databases exist to help you find LGBTQ information and resources. To access some of them, your library might need to subscribe and establish a link through its catalog, while others might be available through a consortium of libraries; still others are free for public use. Here are profiles of three queer-specific subscription databases, as well as one queer-specific online encyclopedia, and a discussion of Internet engines. These tools are highly effective; several of them proved invaluable in writing this book. Others who have tested them can also vouch for these databases (Golderman and Connolly, 2004; Greenblatt, 2005).

GENDERWATCH

GenderWatch, by ProQuest, provides full-text access to more than 100,000 articles dating back to 1970, taken from more than 200 academic journals and popular periodicals such as *The Advocate*, *Columbia Journal of Gender and Law*, *Divorce Magazine*, *off our backs*, and *Transitions*. Topics include: sexuality; gay, lesbian, bisexual, and transgender studies; gender studies; women's studies; feminism; societal roles; eating disorders; family studies; day care; the workplace; and religion.

GENDER STUDIES DATABASE

Combining National Information Service Corporation's Women's Studies and Men's Studies databases, this database provides additional coverage of sexual diversity. It contains thousands of indexed, full-text articles and documents on the Internet. Source documents come from professional journals, conference papers, books, book chapters, government reports, discussion and working papers, theses and dissertations, and more. Subject areas include: legislation, rights, and social change; prejudice and gender discrimination; homophobia and monosexism; coming out; psychology and body image; queer studies; gender identity and sexual orientation; language and terminology; masculinities and boyhood/manhood; male sexualities, bodies, and biology; growing up male; men's movements and groups; men's studies and feminist pedagogy; feminist studies, theory, and history; lesbianism; girl studies; sexual practices and techniques; age of consent; substance abuse; suicide and self abuse.

GLBT LIFE

GLBT Life, by Ebsco, contains indexing, abstracts, and full-text articles for more than eighty queer-specific academic journals, popular periodicals, regional publications, newsletters, dissertations, monographs, and reference books. It also features queer items from more 5,000 other select sources. Available titles include: *The Advocate, Bay Area Reporter, Body Politic, Christopher Street, Gay Times, Journal of Bisexuality, Journal of Homosexuality, Journal of Lesbian Studies, Harvard Gay and Lesbian Review, The Ladder, Lesbian News, Mattachine Review, ONE, Washington Blade,* and more. Subject areas covered by GLBT Life include civil liberties, culture, employment, family, history, psychology, religion, sociology, and more. The database also features a proprietary queer-specific thesaurus of 7,000 terms, developed in consultation with a team of queer scholars and advisors such as ONE Institute & Archives, an organization that houses the world's largest research library on gay, lesbian, bisexual, and transgender heritage and concerns.

THE GLBTQ ENCYCLOPEDIA

The free online encyclopedia www.glbtq.com bills itself as the largest educational Web site covering queer culture and society, and it could well be. Reviewed by an editorial board of academics, the encyclopedia's more than 1,200 entries highlight the lives and contributions of queer people in literature, the arts, law, politics, and more. If you're searching for a biography of lesbian WNBA star Sheryl Swoopes, or a detailed discussion of gay characters in Danish literature since Hans Christian Andersen, you've come to the right place for both. The site also features author interviews, suggested book lists, and moderated discussion boards.

INTERNET SEARCH ENGINES AND OTHER DATABASES

In addition to queer-specific databases, which provide reliable and well-indexed results, you might also consider using more general databases, such as Nexis, or Internet search engines, such as Google. As always, using an Internet search engine may yield an unwieldy number of hits, many of which will be irrelevant. For instance, we typed "gay men" into Google and generated roughly 8 million hits (due to the way search technology works, the number of hits number will vary at any given point in time). Surprisingly, the first Web site listed belonged to Gay Men's Health Crisis, a well-respected organization founded in the early 1980s to combat the HIV/AIDS crisis. Other top hits included agencies that provide assistance for gay men in abusive relationships, gay community centers, and a site for gay men of color— all valid, potentially helpful resources. These hits were on Google's "Web" tab. Its "News" and "Groups" tabs also produced potentially helpful, albeit slightly more random, items. Clicking over to the "Images" tab, however, revealed nothing but pornography. The lesson of this example: As with any Web search, the more specific you are with your search key, the better.

To help narrow results, some search engines provide specific directories. Yahoo!, for instance, offers a directory titled "Lesbian, Gay, Bisexual, and Transgendered (LGBT)." To access it, click on the "Directory" tab at the top of the Yahoo! home page and then type lesbian, gay, bisexual, or transgendered. The first results page will contain a list of related categories, including the "Lesbian, Gay, Bisexual, and Transgendered (LGBT)" directory. Click on the link and you'll then see a variety of subheadings such as "African American," "Youth," "Religion," etc. The listings within each of these categories are generally for valid, helpful queer community resources.

Some Web sites, such as www.rainbowquery.com, purport to be queer-only search engines. We cannot vouch for their efficacy as research tools and indeed many of these sites are intended for adults and the online dating community.

FINDING SUPPORT ONLINE AND IN THE LARGER COMMUNITY

As Darla Linville and others have noted, LGBTQ teens come to the library to find information about queer resources in their community (Linville,

2004). Teens also want help finding online LGBTQ resources—for teens in smaller and rural towns, it is often the only available link to the larger queer community. As Sandra Hughes-Hassell and Alissa Hinckley argue, therefore, "Librarians have a particular responsibility to provide LGBT teens with access to virtual communities and other Internet resources designed specifically for them" (Hughes-Hassell and Hinckley, 2001:39).

As a rule, you should familiarize yourself with the local support network for LGBTQ teens: agencies that can help if teens are having trouble at home, or that simply provide a safe space for queer youth to hang out together. You should also familiarize yourself with national resources available online. To help you get started, the remainder of this chapter provides profiles of eleven organizations that work to improve the life of queer youth and their allies. Many of them will also be of help to you, the librarian, in locating new LGBTQ books, or in helping you to combat censorship. Contact details for each one are included as well as a brief synopsis of what the organization does and what kinds of information it offers on its Web site. This list of groups would make an excellent addition to your library's home page, or you could post it somewhere in your YA room.

Before describing these organizations, one observation should be made about the health and safety of LGBTQ teens. When kids are harassed at school or at home for being queer or perceived as queer, learning about the safety net of community groups and online resources is sometimes all the help they need to get out of harm's way. But in cases when a teen refuses to seek help and you suspect that he or she still needs it, you must make a judgment call. This gray area falls into the same category as physical or sexual assault, so check with your library's administrator to see what your institution's policy is for referring a child to outside authorities.

COLAGE (CHILDREN OF LESBIANS AND GAYS EVERYWHERE)

3543 18th Street, #1
San Francisco, CA 94110
415-861-5437 tel.
415-255-8345 fax
www.colage.org

As many as 14 million children in the United States today live with parents who are lesbian, gay, bisexual, or trans; COLAGE exists to support both them and their parents. Its Web site offers a host of resources including bibliographies for young children, teens, and parents, as well as contact information for COLAGE's twenty-seven chapters nationwide. Among the many programs that COLAGE offers is a pen pal service, through which children of queer parents can write to others like themselves worldwide.

GAY, LESBIAN AND STRAIGHT EDUCATION NETWORK (GLSEN)

90 Broad Street, 2nd Floor
New York, NY 10004
212-727-0135 tel.
212-727-0254 fax
www.glsen.org

There's nothing quite like GLSEN—and the world is a better place for it. More than any other organization, GLSEN has helped shape an entire generation's attitudes toward queer people by helping students to start gay-straight alliances (GSAs) in their high schools. When the predecessor to GLSEN was founded in 1990, only two GSAs existed in high schools nationwide. There are now more than 3,000 of them, and GLSEN acts as their clearinghouse. It offers tutorials and support for students who want to start a GSA in their school, as well as advice for how to combat attempts to dissolve GSAs. Also, each year GLSEN sponsors the "National Day of Silence," on which students peacefully protest the homophobia that remains rampant in high schools. The group also cosponsors "No Name-Calling Week," an event inspired by James Howe's novel *The Misfits*, in which a group of kids rid their school of teasing. GLSEN conducts regular surveys of homophobia in schools nationwide, which it then publishes on its Web site, and holds annual conferences for educators who want to promote tolerance. Its resource-rich home page offers toolkits for creating a safe space as well as links to its forty chapters nationwide. Of special interest to librarians, the "Booklink" page offers annotated bibliographies of virtually every LGBTQ title published since 1990.

HUMAN RIGHTS CAMPAIGN

1640 Rhode Island Avenue NW
Washington, DC 20036-3278
202-628-4160 tel.
202-347-5323 fax
www.hrc.org

The Human Rights Campaign is an advocacy group dedicated to attaining equal rights—human rights—for lesbians, gays, bisexual, and transgender people in the United States. Its Web site contains a wealth of information about the perplexing and unequal patchwork of legal protections for queer people in states around the country, as well as information and resources that can be of assistance to librarians and others who are combating attempts to limit open access to LGBTQ-themed materials. Especially helpful is the site's "Publications" page, which contains downloadable reports on everything from how to come out, to a handbook on understanding transgender people, to how to promote diversity in the workplace.

LAMBDA LEGAL DEFENSE AND EDUCATION FUND

120 Wall Street, Suite 1500
New York, NY 10005-3904
212-809-8585 tel.
212-809-0055 fax
www.lambdalegal.org

Although a large part of Lambda Legal's mission is to fight for queer people's civil rights in court, the group is equally dedicated to education and changing public policy. Its Web site offers a special "Youth and Schools" page, with reports on everything from how to make daily life safer for queer students, to what LGBTQ students should know about their legal rights when it comes to bringing a same-sex date to the prom. It also offers a law library of all the relevant court cases that address legal protections for queer youth and student groups, as well as advice on how to combat attempts to censor the presence of queer resources in a school or library.

NATIONAL ASSOCIATION OF LESBIAN, GAY, BISEXUAL, AND TRANSGENDER COMMUNITY CENTERS

1325 Massachusetts Avenue NW, Suite 600
Washington, DC 20005
202-824-0450 tel.
202-393-2241 fax
www.lgbtcenters.org

If you want to find out if your town has a queer community center, this organization is the starting point. Its online, fully searchable database contains the contact information for more than 140 centers nationwide. If you don't find your town listed, though, don't despair—click on the links to a center in a city near you. Queer people are everywhere.

NATIONAL GAY & LESBIAN TASK FORCE

1325 Massachusetts Avenue NW, Suite 600
Washington, DC 20005
202-393-5177 tel.
202-393-2241 fax
www.thetaskforce.org

Founded in 1973, the Task Force bills itself as the nation's oldest lesbian, gay, bisexual, and transgender advocacy group. Like the Human Rights Campaign and Lambda Legal, it combats discrimination against queer people in all its forms. But the Task Force's Web site is distinguished in that its "Youth" pages boast deep resources, including a directory of LGBTQ youth organizations, reports on how to organize GSAs in schools, handbooks for queer teens and their parents, and more. As of this writing, however, these pages are a little difficult to find, since they are located in a "Youth" submenu of "The Issues" tab at www.thetaskforce.org/theissues/issue.cfm?issueID=13.

NATIONAL YOUTH ADVOCACY COALITION

1638 R Street NW, Suite 300
Washington, DC 20009
202-319-7596 tel.
202-319-7365 fax
www.nyacyouth.org

If a teen walks into your library and wants a helpful online LGBTQ resource, the National Youth Advocacy Coalition's home page should be among the first you recommend. It contains general information for kids about how to come out, how to handle problems at school, and how to find a queer community center or support network. It also offers highly specific information for queer youth of color, disabled queer youth, and trans youth, as well as information for substance abusers and even telephone hotline numbers for crisis counseling. The Web site also offers a searchable, hyperlinked database of queer groups nationwide, as well as a searchable database of full-text articles and reports of interest to LGBTQ teens and their allies. Topics include anti-racism, bullying and harassment, gender issues, and health concerns.

OUTPROUD (THE NATIONAL COALITION FOR GAY, LESBIAN, BISEXUAL & TRANSGENDER YOUTH)

369 Third Street, Suite B-362
San Rafael, CA 94901-3581
www.outproud.org

OutProud is a coalition of groups dedicated to helping queer youth come out and live happy, safe lives. Its easy-to-navigate home page boasts a plethora of facts and figures for LGBTQ teens, news about queer youth nationwide, profiles of queer role models, and links to local community groups. Its online library offers a fully annotated bibliography of materials for queer youth. Titles may be searched according to subject, such as biographies, fiction, and religion, as well as by intended audience, such as parents, teens, and transgendered individuals. The site even offers a list of recommendations for libraries.

PFLAG (PARENTS, FAMILIES AND FRIENDS OF LESBIANS AND GAYS)

1726 M Street NW, Suite 400
Washington, DC 20036
202-467-8180 tel.
202-467-8194 fax
www.pflag.org

PFLAG is often the first service organization that springs to mind when the subject of queer youth arises, and this should be no surprise given that PFLAG boasts more than 200,000 members and 500 affiliates nationwide. Its mission, quite simply, is to promote the health and wellness of queer people by creating a dialog around the subject of sexual orientation and gender identity. To this end, PFLAG offers a wealth of resources: everything from its network of support groups for the family and friends of queer people, to information for queer people on how to come out. Its content-rich home page contains links to these resources and more.

SAFE SCHOOLS COALITION

Safe Schools Coalition
Public Health - Seattle & King County
MS: NTH-PH-0100
10501 Meridian Ave. N
Seattle, WA 98133
206-632-0662 ext. 49 tel.
www.safeschoolscoalition.org

This organization's full name is actually the "Safe Schools Coalition: A Public-Private Partnership in Support of Gay, Lesbian, Bisexual and Transgender Youth," which gives you a good sense of the constituencies that it assists. Based in the state of Washington, the coalition has expanded its focus nationally and provides assistance to queer students as well as the educators who work with them. Its detailed, well-organized Web site offers links to support hotlines for kids who are being bullied. It also provides links to full-text articles and reports on everything from same-sex dating to the "ex-gay" movement. Of special interest to educators and librarians, it provides sample lesson plans and classroom resources.

YOUTH RESOURCE/ADVOCATES FOR YOUTH

2000 M Street NW, Suite 750
Washington, DC 20036
202-419-3420 tel.
202-419-1448 fax
www.youthresource.com
www.ambientejoven.org

Youth Resource is an online project created by Advocates for Youth, a group that advocates a holistic and realistic approach to adolescent sexual health. Its Web site, as well as a companion page in Spanish, serves up plenty of facts about safe sex geared specifically toward an LGBTQ teen audience. Well-designed and streamlined, the page contains everything from articles about why lesbians should use protection during sex, to how teens can overcome body image disorders. The Advocates for Youth site, www.advocatesforyouth.org/about/glbtq.htm, offers even more information and publications for the parents of queer youth, educators, and health professionals.

5 USING GUIDING PRINCIPLES TO BUILD AN LGBTQ COLLECTION

INTRODUCTION

Librarians are no strangers to fighting for equity of service for teens. Even today, many public libraries lack YA specialists and separate YA collections—this despite the arrival of "echo boomers," children of the baby boom generation who are themselves a demographic juggernaut. Inadequate service is especially unfortunate, given that echo boomers are big readers, albeit at the same time as they text friends on their cell phones, download MP3s, and play video games. Publishers recognize this generation's clout. So do booksellers, such as Borders and Barnes & Noble, which now prominently feature teen-only areas. But many libraries, given limited budgets, struggle to compete. Nevertheless, they must make their best effort. A librarian's obligation is to represent an entire community, and this includes teenagers. It also includes queer and questioning teens, who are everywhere. This chapter examines the fundamental principles of collection development, as well as how to handle challenges to materials within a collection; the next chapter then explores the specific components of an LGBTQ collection.

WORKING WITH COLLECTION DEVELOPMENT PLANS

In building a collection, regardless of subject, you should first turn to your library's collection development plan for guidance. Most plans are general, written to be adaptable for evolving community needs. Thus, a typical collection development plan does not say: "You must collect books for the African American neighborhood and some for the Hispanic neighborhood." Instead, it will say something like: "Our goal is to build a collection that represents the diversity of the city's neighborhoods and communities." The key word in that sentence, of course, is "diversity": it is liberating, on the one hand, because it gives you wide latitude in what you can collect;

but on the other hand, the word is almost a challenge to you, because it asks that you document the different groups in your community. In any event, this clause should become your mantra—justification for why you collect queer materials.

Many collection development plans also include a clause to the effect that in selecting materials, the library does not discriminate on the basis of race, age, ethnicity, or religion. Some libraries also list sexual orientation and gender expression among these categories. In an interpretation of its "Library Bill of Rights," for instance, the American Library Association advises:

> Librarians have an obligation to protect library collections from removal of materials based on personal bias or prejudice, and to select and support the access to materials on all subjects that meet, as closely as possible, the needs, interests, and abilities of all persons in the community the library serves. This includes materials that reflect political, economic, religious, social, minority, and sexual issues. (ALA, 1982)

If your library's collection development plan has similar language, it should also become part of your mantra. Why do you need a mantra? People may want to challenge the presence of LGBTQ materials in your collection. If they do, show them your mantra—your library's collection development plan. Show them that you have an obligation to represent your entire community, including queer and questioning people. Although we'll discuss book challenges at length in this chapter, it bears mentioning here that the fear of challenges should not deter you from doing your job

---

Diversity Resources Online

The American Library Association has several guiding principles that address the need for diversity in collection development. Most libraries adopt these principles into their own collection development plans. Here are a few URLs for ALA policies and resources that mention diversity and sexual orientation:

Library Bill of Rights:
www.ala.org/ala/oif/statementspols/statementsif/librarybillrights.htm

Access to Library Resources and Services Regardless of Sex, Gender Identity, or Sexual Orientation: An Interpretation of the Library Bill of Rights
www.ala.org/Template.cfm?Section=interpretations&Template=/ContentManagement/ContentDisplay.cfm&ContentID=31878

Diversity in Collection Development: An Interpretation of the Library Bill of Rights:
www.ala.org/Template.cfm?Section=interpretations&Template=/ ContentManagement/ContentDisplay.cfm&ContentID=61833

Diversity toolkit:
www.ala.org/Template.cfm?Section=diversitytools

when building a collection. Ann Symons, a former president of the ALA and a former high school media specialist, recently recommended in a *School Library Journal* article that librarians build the collection they feel they need and then deal with any controversy later (Whelan, 2006).

DOCUMENTING DIVERSE POPULATIONS

Unlike other populations, such as people of color, the queer community is often hidden from view. Unless there are out teens in your YA room, how do you make the case that they are there and that you need to be collecting for them? To document demand for LGBTQ resources, you should follow three basic steps: (1) study the census; (2) ask patrons what they want; and (3) track circulation statistics.

BY THE NUMBERS, BUY THE BOOK

As researchers Jennifer L. Pecoskie and Pamela J. McKenzie have noted, libraries have long used census data to make the case for collecting materials that appeal to specific populations (Pecoskie and McKenzie, 2004). The U.S. Census Bureau only recently began recording the sexual orientation of adults, but not of teens. That said, most conservative estimates suggest that between 5 and 6 percent of people in the United States are gay or lesbian (Savin-Williams, 2005; Sell, Wells, and Wypij, 1995). Thus, one way to calculate a rough estimate of how many queer teens live in your community is to visit the U.S. Census Bureau's home page, www.census.gov, and find data tables for your town. You will need to drill down a bit, but eventually you should find a chart of age groups in your community. Add up the number of teenagers and multiply that result by 0.055—the product will be your rough estimate for how many queer teenagers live near you.

If you live in a small town and after doing this exercise discover that there are fewer than 100 queer teens out there, does that matter? No. The point of this exercise isn't to compare numbers, or to value the needs of 100 teens less than the needs of 10,000 teens. The purpose is solely to show that there are queer teens in your town. For further proof, check out the Yellow Pages or go online to see if there are any queer community groups nearby. If there's a PFLAG chapter or something similar, it clearly exists to fill a need. Also keep in mind that regardless of how many queer teens your calculations yield, straight teens also read LGBTQ books: to learn about their queer friends and family members, or simply to enjoy a well-written story.

As we noted in Chapter 1, nearly 80 percent of teens say they know some-one who is queer, and there are as many as 14 million children in the United States living with gay or lesbian parents (GLSEN, 2005; National Adoption Information Clearinghouse, 2000). These teens also deserve representation in the library. And it's not just them. As Ellen Greenblatt has noted, the list of potential constituencies for queer YA books is limitless: "Professionals dealing with the community (e.g., social workers, attorneys, doctors, teachers, etc.) and students researching papers" (Greenblatt, 2001).

ASK AND YOU SHALL FIND

The best way to gauge interest for bringing LGBTQ materials to your library is, quite simply, to engage your patrons in conversation and ask them—or survey them. A survey could be as informal as handing kids a paper with a range of materials, including LGBTQ titles, and asking them to circle what they want in their library. Or it could be a queer-specific questionnaire. However you decide to poll your teens, make sure they understand that their responses will remain anonymous. To increase everyone's comfort level, create a secure drop box in which kids may deposit completed forms, or create an anonymous online survey. Anonymity ensures better results, because kids will feel free to speak their minds without fear that others will see what they write and mock them.

If you survey and receive only a handful of requests for LGBTQ materials, that doesn't necessarily mean you shouldn't collect these items. You may not be getting an accurate picture because the stigma of homophobia and internalized homophobia can influence a teen's response, even to an anonymous questionnaire. Also keep in mind that a survey is simply an indication of how much you should be collecting, not whether you should be collecting at all. The best library collections are as inclusive as possible, within budgetary limitations. Another tactic you might use to encourage feedback, suggested by YA author and Portland, Oregon-area librarian Sara Ryan at the ALA's June 2006 conference, would be to contact local queer community groups and get them to file formal requests for your library to begin collecting LGBTQ materials for teens. Similarly, you might want to contact school librarians, teachers, school administrators, or parent coordinators in your area to see what interests them.

TRACK YOUR CIRCULATION

The final way to build the case for acquiring queer materials is to track the circulation of the titles you already have, or a small selection of queer titles that you acquire to gauge interest. This may be difficult to do because some libraries fail to separate YA circulation from overall circulation. If this is the case, try to compile anecdotal evidence from children's and adults' librarians who may have assisted teens in finding LGBTQ material; or, devise a way to track how frequently queer titles are on the shelf. Another way to track interest in LGBTQ materials is to keep a record of any readers' advisory or reference questions you receive. Erin Downey Howerton, a school liaison at the Johnson County Library in Overland Park, Kansas, suggested at the ALA's June 2006 conference that you can even check to see how battered the books' spines are—always a good sign that these books are getting read.

However you're able to do it, tracking circulation is crucial. The best way to justify a collection's importance and ongoing existence is not to buy the most popular titles as determined by an awards committee; rather, the best way to advocate for a collection is to acquire titles and document their circulation (Jones, 1998). It's a very persuasive argument if you have circulation statistics that show a 10 percent increase, say, in overall circulation thanks to the debut of several popular new LGBTQ titles. And remember, when building any new collection, it's critical to promote its existence. If you've acquired LGBTQ titles and they're not circulating, perhaps word of their existence hasn't spread yet; maybe you're not booktalking them enough; or perhaps you need different LGBTQ titles that will better match the needs of your readers. Poor circulation could even be a case of once bitten, twice shy. If patrons have grown accustomed to a lack of LGBTQ materials in the past, they may have stopped looking for them. The point is that you need to let kids know that LGBTQ materials are in your library *now*. More important, you have to spread the word that these titles are not just queer—they're entertaining and they're there for everyone. That should get these materials circulating.

DEFENDING CHALLENGED MATERIALS

It's astonishing that in this day and age people burn books, but burn them they do. In 2003, a group of devout Christians in Greenville, Michigan, burned copies of the Harry Potter books, which they said offended their religion; for the same reason, they also tossed the *Book of Mormon* into the flames (Associated Press, 2003). One shudders to think what this group would do with queer books, but perhaps they'd take their cue from protestors in Montgomery County, Texas, who shredded *Perks of Being a Wallflower* and other LGBTQ-themed books outside six libraries in 2005 (Ervin, 2005). Burning and shredding books, thankfully, remains rare. Unfortunately, however, the same cannot be said for other threats to the presence of queer books in libraries. Our advice in this chapter is simple: Stand up for the presence of LGBTQ-themed YA materials in your library. You collect them for a reason: to represent all members of your community.

WHEN BOOKS ARE CHALLENGED

Challenging a book means more than just saying you don't like it. As defined by the American Library Association's Office for Intellectual Freedom, a challenge is a "formal, written complaint, filed with a library or school requesting that materials be removed because of content or appropriateness" (ALA, undated). In 2004, the ALA received 547 challenges, the highest number in a decade (ALA, 2005a). For every reported challenge, moreover, the ALA estimates that four or five additional ones go unreported—so the actual number of complaints is much higher. The reasons that challengers cite for seeking to remove books from a library remained fairly constant during the 1990s and into the 2000s: Sexually explicit content tops the list, with offensive language, and the vague "material unsuited to age group," rounding out the top three categories.

Homosexuality is further down the list of reasons why books are challenged—somewhere between material that people consider racist and materials that feature drug use—but don't let this fool you. Of the ten most challenged books in 2004, three contained queer content; this was the highest number of queer-related challenges in a decade. The offending titles were: *The Perks of Being a Wallflower*, a novel by Stephen Chbosky; *King & King*, a children's picture book by Linda de Haan and Stern Nijland; and *I Know Why the Caged Bird Sings*, a memoir by Maya Angelou. Queer content still raises the hackles of many a challenger and no doubt will continue to do so even as societal attitudes toward homosexuality continue to relax. Indeed, some observers believe that the number of challenges for homosexual content may actually rise, given the growing number of queer YA titles on the market.

We're Here, We're Queer, We're Challenged!

Between 2000 and 2003, 2,067 challenges were reported or recorded to the ALA's Office for Intellectual Freedom (ALA, 2004). Of these, eighty-four were challenges to material with a homosexual theme or "promoting homosexuality." Between 1990 and 2000, 6,364 challenges were reported or recorded (ALA, 2001). Of these, 515 challenges were filed against material with a homosexual theme or "promoting homosexuality." Among the top 100 most challenged between 1990 and 2000 were the following nine queer-themed titles, four of which are intended for YA audiences:

▼ *Daddy's Roommate*, by Michael Willhoite
▼ *I Know Why the Caged Bird Sings*, by Maya Angelou
▼ *Heather Has Two Mommies*, by Leslea Newman
▼ *The Color Purple*, by Alice Walker
▼ *The New Joy of Gay Sex*, by Charles Silverstein
▼ *Annie on My Mind*, by Nancy Garden
▼ *Jack*, by A.M. Homes
▼ *Arizona Kid*, by Ron Koertge
▼ *The Drowning of Stephen Jones*, by Bette Greene

Some books that make the most challenged list never seem to leave it, such as the 1982 teen novel *Annie on My Mind*, by Nancy Garden. The reason why these books hang on so long provides a revealing insight into the psychology of challengers. Garden's book follows a pair of high school girls who fall in love with each other. You might think that it is challenged because the novel mentions the girls' physical intimacy. In terms of its sexual content, though, *Annie on My Mind* is far more chaste than newer titles. Yet Garden's book is still challenged. Why? In part, people challenge it simply because they know about it—*Annie* was the subject of a 1994 federal court case—and they read it. "If you look at the most challenged books they're usually the books that are the most read," David Gale, the editorial director of Simon & Schuster Books for Young Readers, told us in a July 2004 interview. "*Harry Potter* is challenged because millions of people have read it. Other books that get challenged might not have as many readers, but they stand out more so people think to challenge them. *King & King*, which is a gay-themed picture book, has just gotten a lot of media attention and so people think to challenge it."

Homosexuality is a separate category that people may use as a reason why they are challenging a book, but many queer-themed books are challenged on the basis of their sexual content. In other words, challengers want to avoid appearing homophobic, so they go with a more socially acceptable reason, such as protecting children from sexual imagery. Dig a little deeper, though, and many of these challenges reveal themselves to be motivated by homophobia. For instance, after receiving complaints from parents, a Tacoma, Washington, superintendent removed *Geography Club* from high school and junior high libraries in late 2005 (Abe, 2004a, 2004b). Although this YA novel contains some mild same-sex sexual content, the superintendent said she yanked the book because of a scene in which two gay teens talk online and then agree to meet in person; she was worried that this might encourage teens to try risky online behavior. But local citizens and observers nationwide saw things differently. Librarians posting on a YALSA listserv pointed out that if the superintendent removed *Geography Club* because of its Internet angle, she should also ban the memoir *Katie.com*, about a straight girl who chats with strangers online and agrees to meet them afterward. After a firestorm of protest against her actions, the Tacoma superintendent restored the book to the high school library but kept it out of the junior high stacks. The irony is that Tacoma, Washington, is the hometown of *Geography Club* author Brent Hartinger.

HANDLING CHALLENGES APPROPRIATELY

The First Amendment guarantees the right to free speech to everyone in the United States. In the more than two hundred years since free speech was enshrined in our Bill of Rights, a consensus has formed that when a person is offended by another person's speaking his mind, the best remedy is not to censor the offensive speech, but to make room for more speech—in other words, to provide for balance. Today, the principle of balance guides public discourse in everything from journalism and governmental proceedings, to classrooms and libraries. As a librarian, your first and best defense against book challenges and other threats to open access will be to maintain as balanced and comprehensive a collection as possible. Thus, if someone objects to a queer-themed book, you can point to a book that balances it with an opposing viewpoint—giving everyone, not just queer-friendly people, equal representation in your library.

Where might you find books that feature alternative views of homosexuality? A great starting point is the *Homosexuality* volume, edited by Helen Cothran, in Greenhaven Press's "Current Controversies" series. It offers essays both "for" and "against" different aspects of homosexuality, such as what makes a person queer and the struggle for equal rights. The series also offers two similar volumes specifically focused on gay rights and gay marriage. David Hudson's *Gay Rights*, in Chelsea House's "Point/Counterpoint" series, offers similar issues presented in "pro" and "con" style. Another genre of books with alternative views about homosexuality are those that argue people can change their sexual orientation. As James P. Danky noted in an article on ultraconservatives and the queer community, "reparative therapy" is the one topic that unites both groups in dialog (Danky, 2006). To this end, a burgeoning genre of books written by so-called "ex-gay" Evangelical Christians aims to forge common ground and nurture tolerance between the two groups (Ford, 2004; Thompson, 2004). There are certainly other materials out there, but you can find them yourself. The viewpoints of ultraconservatives may be as under-represented in library collections as those of queer people, as Danky has argued, but these viewpoints warrant a separate book.

Aside from maintaining a balanced collection, your primary recourse in handling challenges is to consult your library's collection development plan, which will spell out the specific procedures unique to your library. Typically, a challenger must complete a form that asks which passages in a book he or she finds objectionable; the form also asks whether or not the challenger has actually read the book; and finally, the form requests the challenger's name and contact information. The form then circulates to a library's department heads, collection development team, and, in some cases, the trustees. Along the way, the challenger may be asked to speak with librarians, or resubmit the form with additional information, so the process can become fairly intensive. This lengthy process deters some challengers—indeed many people have not actually read the book they are challenging, while others are reluctant to give out their names—but it is meant to ensure that the objections of a person challenging the book are weighed against the book's merits and the rationale for why it was included in a collection.

Another reason why you should refer to your library's collection development plan is that this document will contain language stating why your library collects the materials that it does: language that guarantees open access as well as a diverse, balanced collection. When your library's directors review a challenge, they will refer to these passages for guidance. You should also refer to them when someone approaches you and objects to a book. Explain to the would-be challenger that your library includes queer-themed books because there are LGBTQ people in your community, and that your library seeks to be as representative as possible. Show the would-be challenger that you maintain a balanced collection, pointing out materials containing opposing viewpoints, and note that simply including materials in your collection does not mean that your library endorses their views. Hopefully this conversation will diffuse the immediate ire of a would-be challenger, convincing him or her not to file an official challenge. Sometimes, people just want to vent and have their voice heard.

Speaking on a panel about LGBTQ books at the ALA's June 2006 conference, Erin Downey Howerton, a school liaison for the Johnson County Library in Overland Park, Kansas, recommended trying to empathize with would-be challengers. "Try to find common ground by saying things like, 'Yeah, it can be tough to talk to kids about sexuality.' Sometimes just listening takes the temperature down." Howerton added that librarians can also try to focus on universal themes in a book, rather than dwelling on its LGBTQ content. For instance, she noted that the YA novel *Bermudez Triangle* portrays a triumvirate of three female friends, two of whom become romantically involved. While not everyone can relate to that exact scenario, everyone can relate to feeling left out. Sometimes focusing on common themes like this helps people remember that LGBTQ books are just like any other. And, again, engaging in dialog helps to diffuse tension.

But in cases when talking isn't enough and a challenger wants nothing less than the removal of a book, you should be prepared to fight for a book's presence in your library—and fight loudly. Noise is better than silence. In an October 2005 interview, Beverly Becker, associate director of the ALA's Office for Intellectual Freedom, observed: "It's more scary when books disappear and no one makes a fuss." She added that many librarians acquiesce to a challenger's wishes without initiating any official review process. There is no need to be like these librarians. If someone objects to the presence of an LGBTQ-themed book in your YA collection and you are unable to reason with that person, ask him or her to fill out a challenge form. Take the form to your department head and let the official process run its course. Be prepared to fight. You include LGBTQ books in your library's YA collection for a good reason: to represent queer and questioning teens in you community. Remind people of that reason and don't let censors off the hook. In the end, you stand a good chance of prevailing. Although the ALA doesn't track the outcome of book challenges, Becker said, "Our sense from talking to librarians is that most challenges are not successful, especially when they follow the policy in place."

FRIENDS AND FOES

Fighting challenges often seems daunting, in part because challenging books has become something of a cottage industry in the United States. Several national organizations, in fact, exist solely to assist people in finding and challenging books. The most prominent group, Parents Against Bad Books In Schools (PABBIS), maintains a Web site, www.pabbis.org, that lists more than 1,300 books that it finds objectionable; many of these contain queer content. The group posts excerpts from these titles so that parents may review them—and, of course, become incited enough to file challenges. PABBIS also advocates the creation of rating schemes and parent review boards to help keep "bad books" out of schools and the library. We urge you to stand up to PABBIS and other organized censorship campaigns. As YA author David Levithan said at the ALA's panel on LGBTQ books at its June 2006 conference, "Just because the other side is loud and can make your life a living hell doesn't mean you should back down."

It's also important to remember that even if you are challenged, you'll have plenty of allies ready and willing to come to your defense and recognize your efforts. Each year the University of Illinois's Graduate School of Library and Information Science awards the Robert B. Downs Intellectual Freedom Award to people who stand up to censors. In 2001, it recognized Deloris Wilson, a Louisiana high school librarian who successfully fought attempts to remove a queer book from her collection. The Pen American Center also recognizes librarians who fight for intellectual freedom with its annual Pen/Newman's Own Award. And it's only fitting that censors also get their due. The Thomas Jefferson Center for Protection of Free Expression doles out "Jefferson Muzzles" to people and organizations that disregard Jefferson's warning that freedom of speech "cannot be limited without being lost."

While not advocating self-censorship, we recognize that librarians in some parts of the country may not be able to push the envelope too far, too fast in acquiring and programming queer-themed YA materials. For this reason, Chapter 8 outlines four separate approaches that you might take to building an LGBTQ collection: a slow, medium, and fast track, as well as a school track, each of which is sensitive to your community's standards.

PROTECTING OPEN ACCESS

Open access to information is a fundamental principle of the library that encompasses the freedom of all people to use the library, and the freedom to be represented by the library's collection. The library's mission is to be as inclusive as possible, representing all viewpoints in a community. Including a book in its collection does not mean that a library endorses the book's message any more than the landlord of a convention center endorses the views of people who use the facility as a gathering space. It is not for librarians to pass judgment on the content of the materials they collect for their communities, or for librarians to allow the tastes of some people in the community to limit the intellectual freedom of others. Acquiescing to the objections of a minority and limiting access is tantamount to censorship. As Henry Reichman explained in *Censorship and Selection: Issues and Answers for Schools*, "Censorship is the removal, suppression, or restricted circulation of literary, artistic, or educational materials—of images, ideas, and information—on the grounds that these are morally or otherwise objectionable in light of standards applied by the censor. . . . In the final analysis, censorship is simply a matter of someone saying: 'No, you cannot read that magazine or book or see that film or videotape—because I don't like it'" (Reichman, 1993:2).

The librarian's job is to serve all people in the community—including people who want or need access to queer-themed materials. Thinking that there are no queer people in your community is no excuse. As Beverly Becker, associate director of the ALA's Office for Intellectual Freedom, said in an October 2005 interview,

> We hear it a lot from librarians: "We're in a small town, we're in a conservative state, we don't have any gay people so we don't want to include these materials," but this misses the point. The point of the library is not just to serve the majority, but to make sure that they have something for every individual person. So if you're in the kind of environment where gay people are invisible, that's where these materials are absolutely essential. People are not going to ask for these materials, so you should just make them available. The library is a source of information for everyone, regardless of their social status or their ability to pay. Removing a book because someone objects to content is a real barrier to some people. Not everyone can buy books from Amazon. The library is the only place for everyone to get information they need. It's really a unique institution and important if you're going to have any kind of democracy.

WHEN FUNDING BECOMES A WEAPON

In a democratic society, people choose their elected officials and, in return, elected officials vow to serve all of the people they represent. Some politicians, however, lose sight of this covenant, and when this happens, more often than not, the library becomes a battleground in their efforts to limit and revoke people's rights. It's not just open access and intellectual freedom that fall into jeopardy in these situations; the library itself is threatened with financial retribution unless it agrees to censor certain items. For instance, in 2004, an Alabama state legislator sought to ban books with LGBTQ content, as well as books written by queer authors, from libraries in order to "protect" children (Barack, 2005; Johnson, 2004a, 2004b). Institutions that failed to remove these books would see their state funding revoked. Fortunately, community groups pointed out that this measure would effectively empty all library shelves—even Shakespeare would get the boot because his plays mention gay men—and the legislation failed to pass. A similar bill failed in Louisiana, but comparable legislation passed in Ohio (Goldberg, 2006).

Tying censorship to funding is an increasingly popular tactic and it's not just limited to removing books. In 2005, citizens in Tampa Bay, Florida, objected to a display that a YA specialist at the WestGate branch had organized to recognize Pride Month (Alexander, 2005). The "display" in question was merely a small shelf of twenty LGBTQ titles plus an accompanying bibliography. After citizens objected to a similarly modest display at a nearby branch, Tampa-Hillsborough County commissioners passed an ordinance declaring that the county would refrain from "acknowledging, promoting, and participating in" Pride celebrations (Alexander, 2006:24). This decision meant that the library, which receives county funds, would have to remove its displays. The library's district administrator acquiesced, and the displays came down. Librarians nationwide objected that this set a bad precedent for those who seek to limit intellectual freedom. "Next week is someone going to say, 'I don't like foreigners, and I don't want displays'? It's the wedge that opens the door," Judith Krug, director of the ALA's Office for Intellectual Freedom told a Florida newspaper (Parker, 2005). But the administrator disagreed. The library still carries queer-themed books, he reasoned; the only difference is that it no longer promotes them—so intellectual freedom was preserved.

But it would appear that for this administrator, his choice to remove Pride displays also came down to money. The Tampa-Hillsborough County system relies on taxpayer dollars for capital projects, such as its future plan to build five new branches. To keep public funds flowing, the library must follow the dictates of the taxpayers' elected officials. The administrator's priorities were clear, as he told a local newspaper: "[The new branches] will have a long-term impact on children and adults in this community. I have to keep my focus a little higher up than any display or controversy going on right now" (Parker, 2005). Many Tampa residents agreed with his priorities. One man told the local newspaper that while he defends the right for librarians to include whatever books they want in their collections, "It's not [librarians'] job to promote books" (Parker, 2005).

This man's comments reflect a deep misunderstanding of the librarian's job and what it means to promote books. Promotion includes both programming and readers' advisory, and, as such, it is central to the librarian's mission—in fact, the ability to promote books distinguishes the librarian as a skilled professional. The librarian's job is threefold: to keep abreast of new titles and materials available for the library; to study the needs of a community and make judgment calls about which materials the community wants and which materials will satisfy these needs; and to spread the word about materials in the library through readers' advisory and programming. Without promotions, how can patrons feel confident that they're finding the right books? How can people gauge whether or not they might like a book? How will people know which books are in the library? Why, in short, would people even have a reason to visit the library? Without promotions the library would be little more than a glorified book depository, and its staff would only require training in how to shelve books. Whether or not taxpayers realize it, in most cases they're paying for the librarian's expertise in promoting books.

As the Tampa example illustrates, the threat of diminished resources is a danger both to intellectual freedom and to libraries themselves. Indeed, the ALA was so concerned about events in Florida that in June 2005 it passed a special resolution addressing LGBTQ materials. It encouraged ALA chapters to "take active stands against all legislative or other government attempts to proscribe materials related to sex, gender identity, or sexual orientation," and it reminded all libraries to "acquire and make available materials representative of all the people in our society" (ALA, 2005b). Beverley Becker, talking again in an interview, explained that even though prior resolutions had addressed the inclusions of sexual diversity in library collections, the ALA believed that something more forceful was necessary. "There was a strong feeling that GLBT materials are really being targeted right now and the ALA wanted—and needed—to take a position. . . . People felt we needed to say something specific because we wanted librarians to feel they have support behind them when they decide to put these materials in their collection."

PHYSICAL AND CYBER BARRIERS TO ACCESS

Book challenges attempt to limit the scope of a library's collection, but they're not the only threat to open access. People frequently attempt to limit access by creating physical or psychological barriers that prevent patrons from easily finding LGBTQ materials—not as absolute as banning books, but every bit as effective. For instance, many libraries nationwide have acquiesced to censors' wishes and placed children's picture books, such as *And Tango Makes Three* and *King & King*, both about queer families, in adult stacks to prevent children from accessing them (Associated Press, 2004). Taking this strategy to an extreme, the Ohio state legislature in early 2006 passed a bill that seeks to revoke funding from libraries that fail to shelve children's and YA queer-themed books in a separate, adults-only area. The bill also seeks to create a list of books that should be kept out of children's hands—a blacklist, if you will—because these books contain LGBTQ or sexual content (Goldberg, 2006).

Periodicals and books are not the only information sources at the library, of course, so it's no surprise that censors also seek to limit access to LGBTQ content on the Internet. In 2000, Congress passed the Children's Internet Protection Act (CIPA), which prevents schools and libraries from receiving federal funding to purchase computers unless they install Internet filters that block access to pornographic material, and, as of the writing of this book, similar new legislation, called the "Deleting Online Predators Act," is making its way through Congress. The problem with Internet filters, however, is that they are often so broad that they also block nonpornographic Web sites that discuss LGBTQ issues. In fact, several studies have found that innocuous Web pages containing queer content are usually mischaracterized as pornography (Cianciotto and Cahill, 2003). The result, of course, is that gay and lesbian sites are disproportionately blocked compared to all others (Kaiser Family Foundation, 2002).

CIPA has survived a challenge in the Supreme Court, because the law only applies to libraries that receive federal funding, but most observers maintain that it is discriminatory due to the flaws in Internet filtering software (Miltner, 2005). The problem, of course, is that many libraries cannot afford to pass up federal money and thus must implement filters. This situation is especially unfortunate for teens who rely on their library as their online gateway. Much as the library allows impoverished populations to access books they cannot afford, it also provides free Internet access to them. And for LGBTQ teens seeking to access the Internet privately, the library is often their only option. Indeed, the Supreme Court case that challenged CIPA was initiated by a lesbian teenager who was unable to access the Internet from home to find information about LGBTQ concerns (Forbes, Gregoire, Tejada, and Rogers, 2003).

While it is beyond the scope of this book to examine the ever-expanding role of the Internet in libraries, it would be remiss to fail to mention it. The Internet gives people access to a world of information that was once only available at the library. Fortunately, the library still has a place in this brave new digital world—for starters, as an access point to the Internet. Indeed, a recent study commissioned by the ALA found that two-thirds of Americans say that providing computers and online access are the library's top services (ALA, 2006). Libraries also have an important role to play in our digital age because they are uniquely positioned to help people use the Internet more effectively; librarians are trained professionals in searching for information, a skill that many Web users need. For both these reasons, many observers predict that while the library will always contain books, in the not too distant future it will contain more computers than anything else—a digital commons (Murdock, 2006). So, just as we cannot limit access to books, we cannot limit access to the Internet.

VANDALISM OF LGBTQ MATERIALS IN THE LIBRARY

Sometimes censors don't want to bother with initiating a book challenge, placing books in a restricted area, or formulating Internet access policies. For these people, the most efficient strategy of limiting access to books is to disable the electronic "tattle tape" strips and steal books, or legitimately borrow books and then fail to return them. If you notice that queer-themed materials are disappearing from your collection at a higher rate than others, perhaps a *sotto voce* censorship campaign like this is at work. If you notice that queer-themed materials and displays are being maimed and defaced with anti-gay slurs, you'll have an even better idea that homophobia is at work—but not always. In June 2006, someone set fire to nearly eighty queer-themed and African American books in the Chicago Public Library's Merlo branch. While many observers in the city's queer community believed that the incident was a hate crime, a homeless woman later admitted that she set the fire to protest the library's allegedly unfair treatment of homeless people—that the damaged books were queer and African American, she claimed, was purely coincidental (Noel, 2006a, 2006b).

If queer-themed materials in your library are stolen or vandalized, regardless of the motivation, it's critical that you replace these items as quickly as possible. When people see that your library stands behind its collection and replaces LGBTQ items, would-be censors will realize that their efforts are fruitless. If vandalism persists or escalates, you should speak with your library directors and, at their discretion, contact the ALA's Office for Intellectual Freedom and groups such as the American Civil Liberties Union. Speak up and make your voice heard as a defender of open access. And, forgive the cliché, you should also attempt to make lemonade out of lemons. In 2001, when more than 600 materials were vandalized at the James C. Hormel Gay and Lesbian Center at the San Francisco Public Library, the library sent these damaged items to artists nationwide who could turn them into works of art. The library then sold the artworks and used the proceeds to replace materials in its collection (Hammond, 2006).

6 IDENTIFYING AND ACQUIRING COLLECTION COMPONENTS

INTRODUCTION

The year 2003 marked a turning point for queer people living in the United States. On the civil rights front came two stunning legal victories. The U.S. Supreme Court, ruling in Lawrence *v.* Texas, struck down sodomy laws nationwide. Then, the Massachusetts Supreme Court ruled that denying gay and lesbian couples the right to marriage was a violation of that state's constitution, paving the way for couples there to marry the following year. On the airwaves, meanwhile, the "Fab Five" of cable television's *Queer Eye for the Straight Guy* joined an already crowded slate of other queer-friendly programs, including *Will & Grace*, *Queer as Folk*, and *The L Word*. And, of great interest to YA librarians, 2003 saw the publication of an avalanche of LGBTQ teen lit with the release of novels by Brent Hartinger, Julie Anne Peters, Alex Sanchez, and, most notably, David Levithan, whose novel *Boy Meets Boy* was hailed as a "revolution" in YA literature because of its problem-free portrayal of queer teen life (Cart, 2003). So revolutionary was this book's vision, in fact, that many people described the world it portrays as a "gaytopia" (Lewis, 2003).

Levithan's gaytopia was a long time coming. Even though the history of queer characters in YA lit is short, it is decidedly less than sweet. This chapter will begin with an examination of the continuing importance of novels—even in this multimedia age—in the life of teenagers, and will provide a tour of the history of queer YA fiction. The remaining gaps in the canon, such as the dearth of bisexual and trans characters, will be discussed, along with a few predictions about where things are heading now. Eleven key areas of nonfiction and non-print items, such as films and Web sites, also will be explored, followed by advice on how to keep your collection current, including tips on how to find new queer-themed YA materials, as well as guidelines for evaluating whether or not they'll work within your collection and your community. To that end, this chapter includes a discussion on how to evaluate adult materials that may be suitable for teens: how to determine how much sexual content is too much for younger audiences. The chapter closes with a discussion of the importance of recognizing crossover audiences for queer-themed teen materials because, as noted before, LGBTQ-themed YA items are not just for queer teens, they're for everyone.

APPRECIATING THE EVOLUTION OF LGBTQ CHARACTERS IN YA FICTION

Traveling, even just to another town, gives us perspective on our lives; it provides a negative mirror, a way of defining oneself by seeing what one is not. Reading a good novel produces exactly the same effect. Novels take us on mental journeys. The best ones give us insight into the human heart, and this power comes from an author's ability to get inside a character's head, enabling readers to do the same (Cart, 1996). As noted in Chapter 1, teens want to get inside the heads of characters. They read to be entertained, of course, but they mainly read to know themselves: to find role models that suggest how they might handle similar situations in their own lives. The need to find oneself in a book is especially acute for LGBTQ teens. Queer and questioning teens crave true stories as well as fictional accounts of kids like themselves—proof that they are not alone and a way to begin envisioning their own place in the world (Hamer, 2003; Linville, 2004).

Historically, the only places in YA fiction where teens found LGBTQ characters were so-called "problem novels," or "issue books." A problem novel centers around a single issue that a teenaged protagonist must solve: everything from substance abuse and unwanted pregnancy to eating disorders and suicide. While these issues are not unique, and indeed are explored in other types of books, in a problem novel the issue takes precedence over character development and plot (Cart, 1996). Although authors usually don't set out to write problem novels, as scholar Michael Cart has observed, many YA books of the 1970s fit the description because adults at the time held the view that teenagers were under siege and needed guidance to make it through adolescence safely. Homosexuality, which had only just begun entering the national media spotlight, appeared in YA books for the first time, presented as another problem that needed to be addressed. To this end, early books with LGBTQ themes addressed the difficulties of coming out (Cart and Jenkins, 2006).

For the most part, being queer is no longer relegated to problem novels, but many authors continue to write about the coming out process. This is understandable, in one sense, given that YA books generally capture the adolescent experience; coming out takes place during these years, so the fit seems natural. But we believe that the best LGBTQ-themed teen novels, whether they're about coming out or something else entirely, provide insight into the minds of queer teenagers. The best queer novels, just like other good novels, enable teens from all walks of life to experience emotions vicariously and gain confidence in themselves to work through their own emotional concerns. Rich with character development and plot, these books show LGBTQ teens that they are not alone, and, just as important, they help queer and straight teens alike to reinforce their own ideas of who they are and what they want to become in our society.

As Michael Cart and Christine A. Jenkins observed in *The Heart Has Its Reasons: Young Adult Literature with Gay/Lesbian/Queer Content, 1969–2004*, their study of queer teen books, the arrival of LGBTQ characters in YA lit followed the same three-step path to prominence forged by people of color and other previously unseen characters: visibility; assimilation; and consciousness/community (Cart and Jenkins, 2006). The first phase is visibility: being present and identified in a book, which for queer characters either means coming out or being involuntarily outed. These types of books mainly appeared in the 1970s and 1980s, but even today a number of queer novels are stories about visibility. The second phase of evolution is assimilation, a common theme in the 1990s. In these books, characters appear and happen to be queer, but being queer is not the book's central plotline: Assimilated queer characters, in fact, often play cameo roles. We see characters who are both in and out of the closet, crushing, falling in and out of love, and interacting with their friends and families. The final phase of evolution, which in many ways is still in its infancy, is queer consciousness and community: Books that show LGBTQ teens interacting with many other teens and adults, often ones like themselves. Here we see queer teen characters out of the closet in their homes and schools, attending local LGBTQ community centers, forming gay-straight alliances at school, or, as in Ellen Wittlinger's *Hard Love*, visiting queer-friendly meccas such as Provincetown, Massachusetts.

At the same time as queer characters have come out, assimilated, and found a community of people like themselves, they've also stepped into the spotlight. Early books tended to feature secondary queer characters rather than stories told from the point of view of a first-person narrator (Cart and Jenkins, 2006). While these books were invaluable in helping straight allies find a place for themselves in the world, queer teens need stories told from their own perspective. Thankfully, more books today use the first-person voice—a reflection of the increased visibility of queer authors and publishers' willingness to handle these perspectives, not to mention the overall increased visibility of queer people in society. Be that as it may, you need to be aware of an LGBTQ character's point of view and to offer a collection rich with both first-person queer narrators as well as LGBTQ characters who play secondary roles.

> **Twenty-Five Years of YA Novelties**
>
> 1969—*I'll Get There, It Better Be Worth the Trip*, by John Donovan, the first novel to feature an LGBTQ character, a gay teen
> 1976—*Ruby*, by Rosa Guy, the first novel to feature a lesbian teen and the first about a queer person of color
> 1994—*"Hello," I Lied*, by M. E. Kerr, the first novel to feature a bisexual teen
> 2004—*Luna: A Novel*, by Julie Anne Peters, the first novel to explore a trans character in depth

FIRST STIRRINGS—GAY CHARACTERS COME OUT

Young adult literature, as a recognized genre, had been around for more than three decades before the first acknowledged queer character graced its pages in 1969—coincidentally, the same year as the Stonewall uprising in New York City's Greenwich Village. *I'll Get There, It Better Be Worth the Trip*, by John Donovan, tells the story of a thirteen-year-old boy named Davy Ross who falls for his new friend, Douglas Altschuler. The boys fool around once or twice until Davy's overbearing, histrionic mother eventually discovers them. She takes his beloved dachshund, Fred, out for a walk while the boy and his father discuss what happened. Davy glances out the window and happens to watch just as Fred slips his leash and is struck dead by a car. Davy interprets this tragedy as the spiritual consequence of his same-sex explorations and is scared straight. Although to modern eyes Davy's reasoning seems illogical, teen readers of the time identified with his plight—perhaps out of sheer hunger for a character even remotely like themselves (Cart and Jenkins, 2006).

I'll Get There's denouement reflected society's then prevailing attitude that sexual orientation was open to change and, indeed, that homosexuality itself was a disorder that could be corrected. Unfortunately, these perceptions—which we now know to be false—defined the pattern for most early queer YA novels. Many of these books followed *I'll Get There*'s themes to the letter: They featured wealthy white boys discovering or questioning their homosexuality in a lonely and hostile world devoid of positive role models. Fully three-quarters of queer-themed YA books published during the 1970s and 1980s featured only gay boys (Cart and Jenkins, 2006). And, like *I'll Get There*, most early novels featured a character's death—usually in an automobile accident. As Michael Cart has wryly observed, "Early gay literature featured the worst drivers this side of my grandmother!" (Cart, 1996:225).

Another common scene that figured prominently in early queer novels was the drama club, but not even this stereotypically gay refuge was safe. In Sandra Scoppettone's 1974 *Trying Hard to Hear You*, a gang of homophobic summer stock actors attempt to tar and feather Jeff, a fellow actor, whom they've just discovered making out with Phil—a boy who, tellingly, listens to Judy Garland records. Jeff escapes this fate, thanks to a contrived scene involving a gang of African Americans, who save the day by using the most stereotypical jive-talking slang imaginable. But Phil ends their relationship and attempts to set himself straight by bedding the first girl he finds. Phil's plans are wrecked, literally, when he drinks too much and dies in a car wreck.

Although Scoppettone's book would seem to suggest that bad things await queer people who act on their impulses, the author later defended *Trying Hard to Hear You* by explaining that Phil died because he was trying to be something he was not: straight (Cart and Jenkins, 2006). But this message was probably lost on many readers. Intentional or not, like most early queer teen novels it sent the tacit signal that being attracted to someone of the same gender was an awkward phase of adolescence that "normal" teens should outgrow. Up to a point, this is true—as noted in Chapter 1, most ostensibly straight teens have same-sex crushes as a normal part of growing up—but these books did readers a disservice by implying that gay and lesbian people "choose" to pursue same-sex desires as an ongoing lifestyle. It wasn't until 1982 that the literature would address the reality that people have no choice in who they are, but they can choose to be honest about it.

YA LIT TAKES A NEW DIRECTION

In many ways, honesty is the underlying theme of Nancy Garden's 1982 novel *Annie on My Mind*, which realistically explores the complexities of a burgeoning relationship between two high school girls. The characters, Liza and Annie, must not only admit their feelings to themselves and to others, they must also deal with Liza's violating the trust of a couple who ask her to watch their house while they're out of town. *Annie* was the first LGBTQ-themed YA book to feature fully realized teen characters who not only come out but are able to experience the first positively portrayed same-sex romance. Indeed, although Liza and Annie have their ups and downs, the book ends on an exuberant note.

The next notable YA novel to portray happy queer people was Francesca Lia Block's *Weetzie Bat*. Published in 1989, it was to become the first book in the *Dangerous Angels* series. Block's almost fantastical vision of Los Angeles is chock full of magic lanterns, pink convertibles, mohawked punks, and queer-friendly protagonists who prefigure a time when queer people are embraced without hesitation. For instance, when the title character, Weetzie Bat, has dinner with her ex-boyfriend, Dirk, and he comes out to her, Weetzie's reaction is simply: "It doesn't matter one bit, honey-honey" (Block, 1991:9). The pair proceed to find their true soul mates, and the foursome lives happily ever after. Block's novel is definitely a fairytale, but it is hardly far-fetched. Her world is one in which being queer is acknowledged but not dwelled upon as a problem.

The *Weetzie Bat* vision of an assimilated queer-straight world blossomed in YA lit of the 1990s, but not without some interesting side effects. During that decade, more books featured LGBTQ characters than in both previous decades combined. Numerous gay uncles, gay teachers, and lesbian mothers appeared as secondary characters in novels that were mostly sympathetic and unfussy in their portrayal of being queer. The increased visibility of these characters—both in print and in popular media of the time—was an important step in helping LGBTQ teens see themselves in the world, and in helping straight teens do the same. The irony, though, was that the vast majority of queer characters were primarily bit players, not the protagonists (Cart and Jenkins, 2006).

One day soon, YA books will routinely feature happy, well-adjusted protagonists who just happen to be queer: books in which the plotline is something other than coming out, in which characters are relieved of the stigma of homophobia, and in which they can simply be themselves. David

Levithan's *Boy Meets Boy*, published in 2003, was exactly this kind of book. In case the title leaves any doubt about content, the book's cover—featuring pastel-colored candy hearts on a baby blue background—assures readers that *Boy Meets Boy* is, in fact, a gay love story. The book contains drama, to be sure. Paul, the protagonist, meets Noah and falls in love, then loses Noah and must win him back. Being gay and coming out, though, is not the issue. Paul came out in kindergarten.

Observers have described Paul's world as "post-gay" or "gaytopia" (Lewis, 2003; Murdock, 2004b). It's easy to see why, given that the book features characters such as Infinite Darlene, a drag queen who happens to be the high school's star quarterback. Levithan admits that he wrote his novel in the same magical style favored by Francesca Lia Block. He wanted to write a book in which being gay was not a problem—a reaction to what he saw as the ongoing recurrence of gay-themed problem novels. Levithan instead set out to write the long overdue "dippy, happy gay love story" (Murdock, 2004b:15). But rather than describe the world in *Boy Meets Boy* as a utopia, which implies an impossibility, he prefers to think of it as one possible version of our own world. Thus, when readers ask Levithan where Paul's town is located, he replies: "It exists ten minutes away" (Murdock, 2004b:15). In reading Levithan's uplifting novel, queer teens can finally envision a positive future for themselves, a world in which they will not be alienated because of their sexual orientation, and a world fully populated by other queer people.

Levithan's world may be farther away than just ten minutes, but happily, other authors share his vantage point. Alex Sanchez, for instance, also writes about well-adjusted teens in his *Rainbow Boys* trilogy, which follows three gay high school boys as they mature into young men. Sanchez's world is more like our own, and the stress of coming out is a big theme in the Rainbow books, but the trilogy is mainly a humorous, soap-opera-like romp through high school corridors, starring three very different gay personalities: a jock, a brain, and a flaming Nelson. An even more diverse cast of queer characters appears in Brent Hartinger's *Geography Club*, published in 2003, which features a gay white boy, his closeted boyfriend, a bisexual Chinese American girl, her girlfriend, and a female African American straight ally. These two books signal the arrival of community and consciousness, the third stage in the integration of LGBTQ characters into YA lit.

REMAINING GAPS IN THE CANON

Although books of the new millennium are the most diverse yet, there is still room—lots of room—for additional LGBTQ voices and perspectives. For instance, although there are now a generous handful of books about queer people of color, such as the lesbian books *The House You Pass on the Way* and *Orphea Proud*, only one title, *True Believer*, features a gay black boy—and he's just a secondary character, not the protagonist. Talk about being on the down low! (For those of you who don't remember from Chapter 1, the down low, or DL, is African American slang for self-identified straight men who secretly have sex with other men.) Alex Sanchez, meanwhile, is finally putting the stories of queer Hispanics onto the page with his 2006 novel *Getting It*, about a gay Latino who helps a straight boy improve his image; and Sanchez's 2005 tween novel *So Hard to Say* portrays a Latina straight ally.

In addition to portrayals of people of color, another oddly persistent publishing gap remains for lesbian YA novels. While the proportion of gay to lesbian titles is slowly balancing out from its lopsided three-to-one ratio, it remains biased toward gay books (Cart and Jenkins, 2006). Helping to correct this bias, Julie Anne Peters has fast become a popular author in lesbian YA fiction since the 2003 publication of her first queer-themed book, *Keeping You a Secret*. Peters has since written two more novels that prominently feature lesbians: *Far From Xanadu* and *Between Mom and Jo*. That said, while Peters' books are devoured by teens nationwide, they tend to focus on the struggle of coming out. Someone has yet to write the equivalent of a dippy, happy lesbian love story—a "Girl Meets Girl."

Even more glaring queer gaps remain. Not until 1997 did the first bisexual character appear in a YA book, in M. E. Kerr's *"Hello," I Lied*. Sara Ryan's *Empress of the World*, published in 2001, became the second major portrayal of bisexuality in teen literature. But still other queer identities are only just coming out of the literary closet. Not until 2004 did a novel prominently feature a trans character, the eponymous Luna of Julie Anne Peters' *Luna: A Novel*. The story focuses on Regan, a teenaged girl who helps her brother, Liam, transition into his true self, a girl named Luna. As of this writing, *Luna* remains the only novel-length treatment of transgender issues—one reason why it is especially popular with teens nationwide—although author Ellen Wittlinger is expected to publish a trans novel in 2007. Along with bisexuality, trans identities remain an important avenue that YA lit has yet to explore. From a collection development perspective, therefore, you should be alert for any new titles.

In addition to featuring increased diversity, the future of queer YA lit will hopefully look something like *The Bermudez Triangle* and *Pretty Things*, books that humorously portray the mutability of contemporary teen sexual identities. In these novels, characters don't so much question their sexuality as seamlessly slide back and forth between identities in the larger pursuit of love. The future of queer-themed lit may also look like Brian Sloan's 2005 book *A Really Nice Prom Mess*. This novel is a coming out story, but the "problems" it depicts lead to utter hilarity. Cameron, the protagonist of *Prom Mess*, tries to stay in the closet but is outed in a series of madcap events that involve a gay mobster and a deaf stripper. There's not a shred of homophobia in the book, except for the internalized homophobia harbored by Cameron's closeted boyfriend, which Sloan converts into humor. *Prom Mess* appeals to a broad range of ages and sexual identities—one reason why YALSA named it a Quick Pick in 2006. Even straight boys borrow the book, attracted initially by its cover art, and stay hooked because of its rollicking plot. Surely this is future of the queer novel: a book that everyone wants to read.

INCORPORATING KEY AREAS OF NONFICTION AND NON-PRINT ITEMS

Fiction is only one of many different kinds of LGBTQ materials: everything from nonfiction and poetry, to non-print items such as television shows and music. Nonfiction titles for teen audiences, particularly those that focus on queer issues and people, are few and far between. However, queer themes abound in graphic novels, and there are a ton of non-print items to consider. Indeed, teenagers are always interested in popular culture; popular culture itself is produced mainly for their consumption. Offering films, TV shows on DVD, music CDs, books on CD, and online zines is a great way of helping teens feel connected to your library.

NONFICTION

Queer-themed nonfiction is relatively easy to locate in library catalogs thanks to the specificity of nonfiction cataloging compared to fiction cataloging. Ironically, however, there are only a small number of LGBTQ nonfiction titles available for young adults. Most YA nonfiction, queer and straight, takes the form of expensive hardcover series by publishers such as Chelsea House and Gale. These books are intended to fill gaps in school curricula. Written in stale, textbook-like tones, such titles are less than scintillating, which is too bad, because, as already noted several times, queer teens crave factual information about real people like themselves.

In addition to series, each year publishers release a small handful of one-off nonfiction titles written expressly for teens, including the fabulous field guide *GLBTQ: The Survival Guide for Queer and Questioning Teens*; the well-balanced anthology *The Full Spectrum: A New Generation of Writing about Lesbian, Gay Bisexual, Transgender, Questioning and Other Identities*; and the essential reference book *The Advocate College Guide for LGBT Students*. Unfortunately, as excellent as some of these books are, many go out of print within just a few years. Likewise, there are always a few special-format nonfiction titles published each year that contain light amounts of text and plenty of pictures: books such as *Kings & Queens*, *Queers at the Prom* and *When I Knew*. Everyone enjoys leafing through these books for fun, because they contain so many pictures and don't need to be read from cover to cover; they're especially ideal for reluctant readers.

BIOGRAPHIES AND MEMOIRS

Like general YA nonfiction, most biographies written for teens are expensive hardcover series titles intended for high schools. Chelsea House, for instance, released a new "Gay and Lesbian Writers" biography series in 2005, picking up where its now out-of-print series "Lives of Notable Gay Men and Lesbians" left off. The first series profiled Oscar Wilde, Sappho, and Martina Navratilova, among others. The new series includes books on Adrienne Rich and Walt Whitman.

When it comes to biographies that are not part of a series, even fewer titles exist; many excellent books, such as Adam Mastoon's *The Shared Heart*, are now out of print. Moreover, many famous queer people are known for other things aside from being queer, so biographies about them often omit any mention of homosexuality. In a way, this is the long-hoped-for ideal of queer assimilation—that we recognize people for their accomplishments, not their sexual identity—but it does a disservice to LGBTQ youth seeking queer role models. Only one biography that's a bona fide YA title, *Andy Warhol Prince of Pop*, discusses its subject's queer sexual orientation at length. Given the lack of YA biographies about queer people, should you recommend that your teen patrons head for the adult stacks, or provide a list of adult materials you've already found and can recommend? Well, before you do, consider the added irony that many adult biographies of famous queer people are now out of print. If your library was lucky enough to buy these titles when they first came out, and if no one has since weeded them, you can consider recommending them.

Recommending adult books has its drawbacks, which will be examined in detail later in this chapter, but memoirs are a special case. Any number of famous queer people currently have memoirs on the market—and a lot of them are humorous, which definitely boosts their teen appeal. For instance, there's Ellen DeGeneres's memoir, *The Funny Thing Is*; comedian Margaret Cho's *I'm the One That I Want*; and David Sedaris's books, such as *Naked*. These are sophisticated titles written for adults, but they might appeal to some high-school-age readers. Indeed, they can fill an important gap in that they are written by current public figures and potential role models.

Clearly, more famous queer people should step up to the plate and write their memoirs—or someone should step up and do it for them—particularly if it can be done in a teen-friendly length of 300 words or less. There is a small handful of queer memoirs that either have been published expressly for teens or have genuine teen appeal: Billy Merrell's *Talking In the Dark*; Kirk Read's *How I Learned to Snap*; and Kevin Jennings' *Mama's Boy, Preacher's Son*. All three are reviewed in Chapter 9. While these authors are not necessarily celebrities—perhaps with the exception of Jennings, who is the founder of the Gay, Lesbian and Straight Education Network—they have compelling, valuable stories to tell, and their books would be a major asset for your collection.

By the way, if you're wondering how to sleuth out a famous person's sexual identity, we recommend *LGBT Encyclopedia of Lesbian, Gay, Bisexual and Transgender History in America* and *GLBTQ: The Survival Guide for Queer and Questioning Teens*. You could also try the online queer encyclopedia at www.glbtq.com. All three sources contain lists of notable out people as well as historical figures widely believed to have been queer. After perusing the lists, cross-reference your library's catalog or go online to find biographies of these people.

POETRY

Whether it's reading their favorite poets, or writing their own works, most teens love poetry—straight and LGBTQ teens alike. That said, there are only a handful of queer poetry books published for teenagers. Recent offerings include Billy Merrell's memoir *Talking in the Dark*, which is written as a series of poems, and *The Full Spectrum: A New Generation of Writing about Gay, Lesbian, Bisexual, Transgender, Questioning, and Other Identities*, an anthology edited by David Levithan and Billy Merrell. *The Full Spectrum*, which is no doubt destined to become a teen lit landmark, is an all-out collection containing real coming out stories mixed with poetry by queer teen and twenty-something authors. Another YA anthology focuses exclusively on poetry: *Bend, Don't Shatter: Poets on the Beginning of Desire*. Its poems explore feelings of love, attraction, intimacy, obsession, and what it's like to be queer. While teens may not recognize the authors, they'll certainly understand the emotions and feelings conveyed by their words. Anthologies such as these will likely inspire other young queer writers to publish their work.

As with biographies and memoirs, there are any number of adult queer poets whose work you might also want to include in your YA collection. Whether or not you include these poets depends on your library and your community's tolerance level for sexual imagery and strong language. Allen Ginsberg's work, for instance, contains many graphic images, yet his poem "Howl" is virtually a teen manifesto. Walt Whitman, Ginsberg's muse, also includes sexual imagery in his poems, but since these images are less obvious, his work is taught in many high school English classes nationwide. Whitman, "the great grey poet," is best known for works such as "O Captain, My Captain!" written after the assassination of President Abraham Lincoln, but this poem is often the least favorite of Whitmaniacs—not to mention teens who are assigned to read it in school. Perhaps LGBTQ kids would enjoy Whitman more if they were looking for veiled references to homosexuality. Whitman, who lived from 1819 to 1892, never self-identified as gay or bisexual—indeed, the word "homosexual" did not come into use until the 1890s—but scholars have shown that many of Whitman's greatest poems refer to his desire for other men (Reynolds, 2005).

A list of lesbian, gay, and bisexual poets, in addition to Whitman, is provided in the sidebar. You will note that some names are familiar but not necessarily within a queer context—for example, William Shakespeare. But the great bard wrote several sonnets that express tender and erotic feelings for men. The list contains mostly older writers whose work is now considered classic, so it should be supplemented with more contemporary voices for a well-rounded collection.

GRAPHIC NOVELS

Graphic novels, a genre barely thirty years old, are an increasingly important part of any YA collection because they greatly appeal to teen sensibilities. Kids today are surrounded by television, reality game shows, highly sophisticated video gaming systems, and digitally engineered pop music. Graphic novels—with their colorful art, jump panels, stylized vocabulary, and studies of interpersonal relationships—are the perfect embodiment of teens' multimedia lifestyle. Graphic novels also have tremendous potential to draw reluctant readers into the library, opening their sensibilities to even further ventures in reading. Indeed, in his nonfiction cartoon book *Understanding Comics: The Invisible Art*, artist Scott McCloud explains that the lack of photorealism in graphic novels forces readers to see themselves inside the world of the cartoon—the ultimate mental journey (McCloud, 1993). It's no wonder that many public libraries now offer extensive graphic novels collections, and schools are also building collections that fit their curricular needs.

Comic book vendors such as Marvel, Viz, and DC Comics all offer queer-themed titles available for purchase by libraries. None of these publishers feature an LGBTQ search key to locate such materials, however, so the best way of finding queer graphic novels is to post a query on the YALSA-BKS LISTSERV, which is read by many avowed graphic novel aficionados. There's another graphic novel listserv available, too, at http://lists.topica.com/lists/GNLIB-L/. You can also find these books by browsing the graphic novel sections of national bookstore chains and local independents. Graphic novels come in a variety of formats, and, long before DC Comics outed Bat Woman as a lesbian, queer characters have been featured prominently in all of them. What follows are brief descriptions of the primary categories of graphic novels, as well as queer examples within each category:

> ▼ *Superhero stories* involve fictional characters who possess superhuman powers, caught up in stories rich with complex plots and characters. Some well-known queer superheroes are the Green Lantern, Shade the Changing Man, and Enigma. What queer kid can't relate to having a secret identity—and what queer kid doesn't want to feel like a superhero?

Gay and Lesbian Poets

- ▼ W. H. Auden
- ▼ Elizabeth Bishop
- ▼ William S. Burroughs
- ▼ Lord Byron
- ▼ Catullus
- ▼ Allen Ginsberg
- ▼ Jack Kerouac
- ▼ Langston Hughes
- ▼ Audrey Lorde
- ▼ James Merrill
- ▼ Edna St. Vincent Millay
- ▼ Paul Monnette
- ▼ Adrienne Rich
- ▼ Muriel Rukeyser
- ▼ Sappho
- ▼ Anne Sexton
- ▼ William Shakespeare
- ▼ Gertrude Stein
- ▼ May Swenson
- ▼ Alice Walker
- ▼ Walt Whitman
- ▼ Oscar Wilde

▼ *Human interest stories* are the cartoon version of fiction. In the world of graphic novels, LGBTQ people live lives just like their straight counterparts: in other words, normal ones. Queer titles and series include *Stuck Rubber Baby*, *Hopeless Savages*, *Dykes to Watch Out For*, and the works of Ariel Schrag, a young artist who creates memoir-like books about a lesbian high schooler.

▼ *Nonfiction* graphic novels are narrative comics about real subjects, along the lines of Art Spiegelman's *Maus: A Survivor's Tale* and Larry Gorton's *Cartoon History of the United States*. Check out Judd Winick's classic queer biography *Pedro and Me*.

▼ *Adaptations and spinoffs* are stories of well-known characters, such as Captain Nemo or Zeus, told in cartoon format.

▼ *Satire* calls into question political systems and social mores, such as the work of Robert Crumb.

▼ *Manga* is an immensely popular form that arose in Japan and now accounts for most of the graphic novel market worldwide. Manga typically falls into two categories, *shonen* and *shojo*, both of which feature queer subgenres. *Shonen* usually revolves around a male character and features a fast-paced plot that is mostly driven by action sequences mixed with extreme physical humor. The *shonen-ai* and *yaoi* subgenres feature boys falling in love with boys and are especially popular with female readers (Cha, 2005; Ferber, 2005). One example of *shonen-ai* is the *Eerie Queerie* series. And, late in 2005, TokyoPop, the main distributor of manga in the United States, launched the BLU imprint specifically for *shonen-ai* titles. *Shojo* plots, in contrast, are slower paced and usually center on the relationships and love triangles of a central female character. The girl often becomes infatuated with good-looking androgynous males, called *bishonen*, or "other girls." In *yuri* books, girls fall in love with girls. Some manga titles, such as *Gundam Wing*, combine genres. *Peach Girl*, for instance, features both gay and lesbian characters, and *Les Bijoux* depicts trans teens.

PERIODICALS

There is only one periodical that's dedicated solely to covering all facets of LGBTQ teen life. Titled *YGA*, an acronym for Young Gay America and an anagram for the word gay, this Canadian magazine offers real-life stories of queer teens; interviews with queer celebrities and celebrities of interest to queers; reviews of media such as books, music, and movies; and close-up examinations of issues like proms, combating homophobia, and how to meet other queer people. As of early 2006, however, *YGA* was taking a temporary hiatus to revamp its look and attain a more stable financial footing. It plans to come back louder and prouder than before, reaching a wider audience.

Another periodical geared toward queer teens is also on shaky financial ground: *XY*, a bimonthly magazine devoted to the life of the gay teen boy. Although its focus is gay boys, *XY* is filled with media reviews and stories that are of interest to all youth. It is difficult to recommend *XY*, though, because it regularly runs photo spreads of young men who seem to lose a major article of clothing with the turn of every page; by the end, they're all but naked, with only a strategically placed object or languidly draped limb concealing key parts of their anatomy. We're sure that gay boys would be more than ecstatic to get their hands on this periodical in your library, and perhaps if you're in an extremely liberal community you can acquire it. But most librarians should probably think twice about this publication since *XY* pushes exactly the hot-button issue—teens and sex—that inflames social conservatives faster than you can say the word "censorship."

After these YA-oriented periodicals, we are left with some adult stand-bys: *The Advocate* and *Out*, two mainstream queer magazines that are carried by most retailers including Barnes & Noble and Borders. Akin to *Time* and *Newsweek*, *The Advocate* is a biweekly newsmagazine for the queer community. Of interest to teens, *The Advocate* features a regular department called "Generation Q," which profiles LGBTQ teens and twenty-somethings. *The Advocate* also offers interviews with queer newsmakers and reviews of books, films, music, and television, making it an excellent addition to a well-rounded YA collection. *Out* is the more entertainment-focused of the two periodicals. This monthly magazine is chock full of interviews with queer celebrities, as well as features about film, music, and fashion. It also offers articles on "lifestyle" topics, such as facial products, as well as a regular fashion spread that can get a little risqué, but no more so than those in mainstream heterosexual magazines. In the past, *Out* claimed that it was targeted at all queer audiences, but the magazine clearly favored gay men. This might change under the auspices of its new editor, who was relaunching *Out* in late 2006.

There are two other U.S.-based queer periodicals, *Genre* and *Instinct*, but both are geared at twenty-somethings and thirty-plus gay men, so they are not appropriate for queer teens. Be sure to see what local periodicals are available in your own community. Many large and medium-sized cities boast their own queer newspaper and circulars. For instance, *In Newsweekly* covers most of New England, while the company Windows Media publishes a series of newspapers around the nation, including the queer-themed *New York Blade*, *Washington Blade*, and *Southern Voice*.

These periodicals are generally distributed for free and are suitable for all ages. And don't forget to be on the lookout for queer zines. Your best shot at finding these will be to visit local coffee houses, or ask around at your local queer community center.

ONLINE OFFERINGS

The Web sites of eleven national queer groups were profiled in Chapter 4, all of which can be highly recommended to LGBTQ teens seeking online resources. However, there are several other queer offerings on the Internet. For starters, there are online zines. While most people think of zines as homemade print periodicals, a few Web sites re-create the zine concept online. Among them, *Oasis*, at www.oasismag.com, is a teen-only, adult-moderated site that provides opportunities for kids to sound off about events in their lives and national news, share their creative writing, and chat with each other. Unlike similar sites that have come and gone, *Oasis* has been going strong since 1995. Akin to online zines, blogs provide an opportunity for teens to share their thoughts and opinions—including those of queer and questioning teens—but these will-o'-the-wisp affairs are more difficult to find and often not well maintained. One reliable site is called *Good as You*, www.goodasyou.org, in which a twenty-something gay man serves up a humorous take on daily news as it relates to queer people. The blog's motto: "Using humor and irreverence rather than anger and protests, *Good as You* represents a new generation of GLSBT activism." It's not clear what the letter S stands for in that motto, but *Good as You* boasts guaranteed appeal to readers of all ages and sexual identities.

Fanfiction Web sites often imagine queer twists on popular straight favorites—such as gay encounters between Harry Potter and Draco Malfoy—as well as an opportunity to deepen existing queer storylines, such as the romance between Willow and Tara on the television show *Buffy the Vampire Slayer*. Queer fanfiction is known as "slash." While it is difficult for libraries to "collect" these kinds of ephemera, Paulette Rothbauer and other researchers have documented the importance of fanfiction in the reading diet of young queer people (Rotherbauer, 2004). To that end, you should consider perusing some of the more popular fanfiction sites, such as www.fanfiction.net, and making a list of the better queer-themed offerings. You could add this list to your library's home page, or generate a poster for the YA room.

Finally, any discussion of online queer resources wouldn't be complete without mentioning author Web sites. Although some of these sites are primarily marketing vehicles designed to benefit the publisher, others offer a wealth of helpful resources specifically for LGBTQ teens: everything from bibliographies and links to national queer resources, to author blogs and opportunities to contact the author directly, which many readers want to do.

Among the many excellent sites are those maintained by Brent Hartinger, David Levithan, Julie Anne Peters, Sara Ryan, and Alex Sanchez. To find them, simply add the www. prefix to the start of the author's name and then tack the .com suffix onto the end of it.

RADIO AND AUDIO ON THE WEB

If your library has satellite radio, and probably only a few do, the service Sirius Satellite Radio offers a channel called OutQ that is entirely devoted to queer programming. Online, meanwhile, there are a plethora of radio-like audio offerings. Podcasts, for instance, are essentially radio programs that are made available for listening online or for download to an MP3 player, such as Apple's iPod. Listeners can subscribe to podcasts for automatic download, but subscription is almost always free. Moreover, podcasts don't have to be professional-quality radio. Anyone can produce a podcast and post it on the Internet for others to download without a subscription service. Since the first podcasts appeared in late 2003, this technology has boomed. There may soon be a host of queer-themed podcasts out there for teens—perhaps even some created as a result of our "Create Your Own Coming Out Podcast" program offered in Chapter 12. In the meantime, check the Web site http://qpodder.org, which offers links to more than 150 queer-themed podcasts, mainly for adult audiences.

AUDIO BOOKS AND E-BOOKS

Several queer YA fiction titles are available as books on CD, including *Boy Meets Boy*, *My Heartbeat*, *Deliver Us from Evie*, and *Hard Love*. To find these items, look on amazon.com; check with book distributors such as Baker & Taylor; or contact vendors directly for their catalogs. As of this writing, there were no queer YA titles available in e-book format, but it's only a matter of time before this format also takes off.

MUSIC

Building a popular music collection for LGBTQ teens is something of a misnomer. Indeed, to the extent that you already survey all patrons in your YA room to see what music they want, you're already satisfying the needs of queer and questioning teens. LGBTQ teens, in other words, are no more or less likely to listen to a given type of music than straight teens. That said, if you want to build a collection of popular music produced by queer artists, or artists who are hits with the national queer community, a few suggestions can be offered. Queer teens need role models—so why not provide them with music written or performed by openly out artists.

In terms of queer favorites—i.e., artists that appeal to queer listeners regardless of the performer's sexual identity—a basic list might include Madonna, Celine Dion, Britney Spears, The Magnetic Fields, and Belle and Sebastian. You could also include the soundtracks to *Queer as Folk* or *The L Word*. As for openly queer artists, you might collect music by David Bowie, Ani DiFranco, Melissa Etheridge, Jason and deMarco, the Indigo Girls, Janis Joplin, Elton John, K. D. Lang, the Scissor Sisters, Meshell Ndegéocello, the Pixies, Sigur Ros, the Smiths, and Rufus Wainwright. If you're looking to build a more obviously queer collection, and if your budget allows, check out in-your-face bands such as The Homosexuals, Pansy Division, and The Queers. To keep your collection current, aside from asking patrons what they like, periodicals are your best source for information about cutting-edge music. *The Advocate* and *Out*—especially *The Advocate*—do good jobs of covering obscure artists. Another queer periodical, *Instinct*, boasts a vast section of CD reviews and artist profiles, but the magazine itself is better suited to adult readers.

FILMS

There are any number of wonderful, touching, and valuable features films that portray the lives of queer teens. However, these films are often rated R due to strong language and partial nudity. It's unfortunate that these films carry the R rating, which makes it seem like being queer itself is taboo, because the rating is often enough to keep these films out of many YA collections. That said, the Young Adult Library Services Association includes R-rated movies, such as the 2005 hit *Brokeback Mountain*, in its list of recommendations for libraries seeking to build queer-themed YA collections, so you should definitely consider adding them to your own collection (YALSA, 2006).

A list of queer coming-of-age films that feature minimal nudity or offensive language appears in Chapter 10. There are also detailed reviews for several of these films in Chapter 9. One of the all-time best LGBTQ films for teens remains the 1995 movie *Beautiful Thing*, about two boys in a working-class London suburb who fall in love. For a lesbian romance, meanwhile, there's *The Incredibly True Adventure of Two Girls in Love*, but be aware that it features a strong sex scene. For a portrayal of transgendered characters on screen, *Hedwig and the Angry Inch* can't be beat—this popular rock musical will have all teen audiences tapping their toes. Finally, one essential work of queer cinema that may be of interest to teens is *The Celluloid Closet*, a documentary that examines the history of queer people in movies. *The Celluloid Closet* carries an R rating—due to language and partial nudity—but this lavender look at Hollywood's queer subtext is an affirming work for queer people of any age.

TELEVISION

In the years since 1997, when Ellen DeGeneres came out as a lesbian on her sitcom *Ellen*, the number of out queer people in regular roles on network and cable television programs has exploded. Queer teens can now watch any number of out role models on the airwaves: everyone from Ellen, who now hosts a daytime talk show, to the "Fab Five" style gurus on Bravo's *Queer Eye for the Straight Guy*. Queer people also populate so-called "reality" television programs, such as MTV's *RealWorld* and CBS's *Survivor*. The increased visibility of queer people behaving normally—well, as normally as the contrived settings of "reality" television allows—helps even the most geographically and socially isolated LGBTQ teens see that they are not alone in the world. Plus, the range of characters depicted has diversified. Queer people on television have moved beyond the odd cameo role or stereotypical bull dykes, flaming queens, and simpering fairies, such as the closeted Monroe on the 1980s sitcom *Too Close for Comfort*. Remember him?

Given the wide range of queer people that populate the airwaves today, you don't need to acquire every single program available on DVD for your YA collection. This is impractical, both for budgetary reasons and because many shows are intended for adult audiences. For instance, queer teens enjoy the cable-only favorites *Queer as Folk* and *The L Word*, but the strong sexual content in these shows may relegate them to your library's adult department. While you should feel free to help interested teens find these shows, you might also point them toward *Will & Grace*, a primetime sitcom on NBC, whose lighthearted content makes it an easy match for a YA collection. There are several teen-oriented television programs that you can acquire; a list of them appears in Chapter 10, and Chapter 9 offers reviews of *Buffy the Vampire Slayer* and *My So-Called Life*. These two shows are ostensibly straight, but feature prominent LGBTQ characters. It's only a matter of time before a queer character steps into the lead role of a teen-themed show.

One final word about television. If your YA room has a TV set that's always on, there are two queer cable networks that you might tune in: Here and Logo. These channels offer a mix of syndicated programs and reruns, as well as talk shows and other original programming. If you do tune in, however, be alert for content that is intended for adult audiences.

FINDING NEW MATERIALS

The remainder of this chapter contains tips and resources to help you keep your LGBTQ collection current and relevant. New queer YA books once appeared at a rate of only two or three a year; now publishers release a dozen annually. Finding the best of future titles should be a snap—in fact, it will be little different from how you'd approach finding most other new YA books. For starters, check out *Booklist, Kirkus Reviews, KLIATT, Publishers Weekly, School Library Journal, Voice of Youth Advocates*, and other periodicals that review books for teenagers. Their reviews usually supply a snapshot of a book's plot and literary quality, as well as comment on its overall contribution to the world of YA lit. Moreover, most reviews will likely mention whether or not a book contains LGBTQ characters. *VOYA* is unique in that it actually prints reviews by real teenagers alongside reviews by librarians, enabling you to measure a book's literary quality simultaneously against its actual teen appeal. Here are some other places where you might look for new titles:

▼ Read YALSA listservs for word of mouth among librarians.

▼ Check out YALSA/ALA lists including Printz medal winners, Popular Paperbacks, Best Books for Young Adults, the Alex Awards, and Quick Picks for Reluctant Readers. Each year these citations usually flag a handful of queer titles.

▼ Search for books that have been cited by the Stonewall Book Awards, which recognizes books with LGBTQ themes.

▼ Peruse The New York Public Library's *Books for the Teen Age*, an annual list of recommended recent YA books that contains a special section titled "LGBTQ: Being Gay." Every title in *Books for the Teen Age* is read and reviewed by a young adult librarian from The New York Public Library. An online version is available at http://teenlink.nypl.org/index.html.

▼ Read book reviews in queer periodicals such as *The Advocate* and *Out*.

▼ Search the catalogs of queer publishing houses, including Advocate Books, Alyson, Kensington, Naiad, and Soft Skull.

▼ Surf over to amazon.com for queer YA titles you're already aware of, then check out the "You may also like" recommendations from amazon.com's database, or entries in the "Listmania!" section, which are compiled by other customers with shared interests.

▼ Use a search tool such as NoveList, a subscription database that contains fiction records that are searchable by subject headings and are hyperlinked to similar materials. Keywords to search include: lesbian, gay, bisexual, transgendered, coming out, homosexuality, and teen sexuality.

▼ Visit chain stores, such as Barnes & Noble and Borders, as well as independent bookshops for inspiration. Queer specialty bookstores, if your town has them, will offer you the best suggestions. Plus, you'll get the chance to browse before you buy.

TALK TO TEENS

Aside from reading booklists and reviews, your best resource for finding new materials will always be your patrons—LGBTQ teens, their parents, and straight allies—and the best way to find out what your patrons want is simply to ask them. As discussed in Chapter 5, queer teens may or may not make their presence known in your library. But if you do have visible queer teens, talk to them. Some questions you might ask include:

▼ What are you reading now?

▼ What do you want to read?

▼ What are your friends reading?

▼ Would you like to read fictional stories about LGBTQ teens?

▼ Would you like to read coming out stories about real teenagers?

▼ Do you want to read books about famous queer people or queer history?

▼ Do you want information about health concerns such as safe sex?

If you can't ask openly queer teens, you should still survey—simply add a few LGBTQ-related questions to your regular reader questionnaire. Your patrons' answers will be gold. They'll reflect the needs of your community, which is exactly what your library's collection development plan states you should be matching.

EVALUATING NEW YA MATERIALS

Once you've found potential materials, the best way to judge if they are suitable for your collection is, of course, to read them and then apply your institution's collection development guidelines. Reading a book yourself is invaluable in determining its merits. Not only will you be able to make a professional judgment about the book's quality, you'll also find it easier to recommend the book to teens. And no one knows your patrons better than you do. Only you can make the final decision about a book, so it's best to be as informed as possible.

When you read a novel that you're considering for inclusion in your YA collection, some basic rules of thumb or questions to ask yourself include:

▼ Does the plot grab your attention immediately?

▼ Do the characters ease you into the book?

▼ How does the book grab your attention? Does it shock you, titillate you, or is it a familiar tale?

▼ How does the plot unfold: evenly with rising action, a climax, and then a resolution; or, does it come and go in spurts?

▼ Is the writing style dialog-driven? Does it plod along? Or, is it lyrical and descriptive?

▼ Are themes embedded in the novel's plot, or do the characters openly discuss them?

▼ Is the book's writing style new and engaging, or the same tired style that teens expect and loathe?

▼ What is the book's atmosphere?

▼ How does the book end: Does the author draw everything together, or not?

▼ What is the book's point of view?

▼ Does it have unique characters or a unique voice?

▼ Is there a character never seen in YA lit before, or a topic never before covered?

▼ What is the book really about?

▼ What can the book contribute to your collection?

THINKING ABOUT LGBTQ CONTENT

In addition to these general rules of thumb, evaluating queer materials involves a few extra steps. First, try to place a title within the larger context of queer-themed YA material: Is it a story about visibility, assimilation, or consciousness and community? (These categories, which were outlined by Michael Cart and Christine Jenkins, were explained earlier in this chapter.) Is it something altogether new and different? Next, ask yourself the following questions:

IDENTIFYING AND ACQUIRING COLLECTION COMPONENTS

▼ Does the book fill a particular gap in the YA queer canon: For instance, is it about a gay African American teen? A trans teen?

▼ Does the book present a fresh voice, as yet unheard?

▼ How sympathetic is the book's view of homosexuality?

▼ Is the LGBTQ character a protagonist or a secondary character?

▼ Does this queer character find and consummate romance?

▼ Does the book make sense as a whole?

▼ Does the book portray a believable teenager?

If the book is about visibility, i.e., a coming out story, ask yourself the following questions:

▼ How does the queer character's process of coming out compare to other treatments you've read in the past?

▼ Is the book didactic or nondidactic?

▼ Are the characters multidimensional? Is there more to them than being queer, or being homophobic?

▼ How does the book end? (Not with a fiery car crash!)

▼ Does the book's conclusion show any reconciliation?

▼ Is the character able to interact with other queer characters or straight characters in a believable way?

▼ Does the book make you want to read more coming out stories?

▼ Does it make you want to read more books about queer people?

▼ Is the book satisfying as a novel and does it give you perspective on life or the human condition?

If the book is about gay assimilation or queer consciousness/community, ask yourself:

▼ Is being queer the focus of the book?

▼ Is homosexuality a subplot of an altogether larger plot? If so, how well do those two topics come together and how big a role does sexual identity play in the book?

▼ How is the queer character treated by friends and family?

▼ How do other characters in the book treat homosexuality?

▼ How does the queer character interact with other queer people, and do these interactions seem realistic?

▼ How isolated from, or connected to, the broader queer consciousness are the queer characters?

▼ Is there a queer community depicted and how big is it?

▼ Is the character active in the queer community by forming a gay-straight alliance, going to community centers, hanging out at coffee shops, etc.?

Finally, and this is the most important step, think about the book in relation to your patrons:

▼ Do kids like the book, based on YALSA listserv chatter or *VOYA* teen reviews?

▼ Are teens in your library asking you for the book?

▼ Will adding this title contribute anything new to your collection, or is your money better spent on something else?

SELECTING ADULT MATERIALS SUITABLE FOR TEENS

A general rule of thumb for building any YA collection is that teenagers like to see themselves reflected in the things that they read as well as the movies and television shows they watch. This rationale often opens the door to adult materials that feature teen characters and teen voices. For instance, several novels originally written for adults have since become YA classics, including *Catcher in the Rye* and *A Separate Peace*. These novels are coming-of-age stories with which teens readily identify. Some of these adult classics, we should add, contain queer themes. For instance, there's an unmistakable gay subtext running through *A Separate Peace*; the author, John Knowles, later admitted as much (Cart and Jenkins, 2006). While this book is routinely assigned in high school English classes, teens also read it for pleasure. The same cannot be said of other queer-themed adult novels written during the same era, such as Gore Vidal's *The City and the Pillar* and James Baldwin's *Giovanni's Room*. Kids are aware of these books and will read them when assigned, but they're hardly Quick Picks. An easier sell are newer coming-of-age adult novels such as *Leave Myself Behind* and *The World of Normal Boys*.

The paucity of queer fiction, nonfiction, and non-print items for teen audiences virtually guarantees you'll need a few adult materials to round out your collection. Fortunately, several resources exist to help you find the best and most appropriate of these materials. For instance, *School Library Journal* and *VOYA* publish lists of adult titles for teens. Moreover, each year the American Library Association announces its Alex Awards, which are given to ten adult books that YA librarians nationwide have deemed suitable for younger audiences. Past awardees with queer-themed content include *Donorboy*, *The Year of Ice*, and *Leave Myself Behind*. In evaluating these titles, librarians examine whether or not the book contains teenaged characters or coming-of-age themes, and whether or not teenagers are asking for the book.

In evaluating adult materials for your own YA collection, begin by referring to your library's collection development plan for any guidance that it contains. Next, and this is a crucial step, read the book yourself: There's no better way to judge its suitability for your library. When reading an adult book, ask yourself the following questions:

▼ How well do you know your teen audience?
▼ How well do you know your community, and will it object to certain content for teens?
▼ Are teens asking for the book (or the movie, etc.)?

Only you know the answers to these questions as they relate to your library's patrons and its community. And remember, you shouldn't base your purchases simply on an author's previous track record. For instance, Bart Yates's first novel, the Alex Award–winning *Leave Myself Behind*, was really a YA novel in disguise; but his latest book, *The Brothers Bishop*, lacks any teen appeal. Many adult books simply don't interest teens because their themes and ideas fly over younger people's heads.

ADULT NONFICTION

As we noted earlier this chapter, the lack of queer-themed nonfiction specifically written for YA audiences means that you might be tempted to fill this gap with adult titles. Although this can be expensive, and there will be a chance of creating overlap with your library's adult collections, we recommend doing so because it's important that teens have the option of finding adult nonfiction within the YA room itself. If you're fortunate enough to have a separate budget to purchase adult materials that appeal to teenagers, refer to Chapter 10 for a list of suggested queer biographies and memoirs that fill these gaps in YA publishing. If you don't have a budget for adult materials, you could simply generate a list of titles available in your library's adult stacks. Or, if you're a school media center specialist, you could list materials that are available at your nearby public library and then post it near the nonfiction stacks in your YA room.

LET'S TALK ABOUT SEX

Despite the teen appeal inherent in many adult books, certain adult titles are classified that way because they contain content that some people have deemed inappropriate for readers under the age of eighteen. This content varies, but generally includes strong language, explicit drug and alcohol use, extreme violence, and sex. But, let's face it. Although teenagers live in a world that's saturated with curse words and extreme violence in everything from movies to video games—many of which are marketed specifically to teenaged boys—some adults would sooner expose children to this violent material than to sex.

The United States has a love/hate relationship with sex. Founded by puritans, it remains far more prudish about sex than most other Western nations. Yet hypocrisy abounds. Sex, mainly aimed at heterosexual consumers, is everywhere: in music, on television, in movies, on the Internet, on roadside billboards, and in books. There is literally no escaping sexual imagery, and yet many adults attempt to shield teenagers from it. They have a hard time, obviously, but schools and public libraries are one place where they can attempt to exert control. These institutions exist to serve their communities and, within reason, must follow a community's standards of decency. A few states, in fact, have passed parental consent laws mandating that teachers seek parents' permission before discussing sexual material in class (Cianciotto and Cahill, 2003). That said, it's critical that teens be able to find sensitive, realistic portrayals of sex in both fiction and nonfiction—and where better to find this material than in the library? Whether or not society should condone teenage sexual activity is not for librarians to decide. Instead, librarians should provide accurate, realistic information that can help teenagers make safe, well-reasoned choices.

The reason why libraries should ensure the availability of fiction and nonfiction materials containing sex is the unfortunate reality that while teenagers are surrounded by sexual imagery in popular culture, very little of what they see is accurate or helpful. All teens, straight and queer alike, are curious about what sex actually is, what it means or should mean, and how it relates to love. It's important that teens receive accurate information about sex because, whether or not adults like it, teens are sexually active. Nearly half of all high school students claim that they have had sex, and 7.4 percent of them report that their first sexual encounter occurred before the age of thirteen (Escobar-Chaves, Tortolero, Markham, Low, Eitel, and Thickstun, 2005). For the teens who are not having sex, it's still important that they learn about it because all teenagers undergo puberty: the physical maturation of the body and its sexual organs. Teens want to know what's happening to their bodies, and high school health class often doesn't cut it. Teens also want to read fiction and nonfiction books that explore the mechanics of sex and, more important, the feelings that accompany it.

Since coming of age and puberty occur during the teen years, these subjects make excellent fodder for YA novels—as does sex. Sexual scenes are a staple of YA lit and have become increasingly frank since Judy Blume's *Forever*, a milestone in teen sex talk, was published in 1975. Given the amount of sex in YA novels today, it's only fair that YA librarians should not discriminate against adult novels that contain a similar amount of sexual imagery. But how much sex is too much? In evaluating adult books for teens, some libraries, such The New York Public Library, use a standard that sex scenes should be portrayed as natural, safe, and within the realm of belief of a story, and that they should not be gratuitously explicit. Your library might have a similar standard; if it doesn't, you can encourage your library to formulate one.

Do some communities apply a double standard to queer sex? Not necessarily. Some communities object to any depictions of sex, regardless of its orientation. Others, however, unfairly and inaccurately lump all LGBTQ material—whether or not it contains sexual scenes—in the same category as outright pornography. You know your community best and where it falls on this spectrum. Films are somewhat different than books because, as a visual medium, they leave less to the imagination. Many films receive an R rating for only the briefest suggestion of nudity. For instance, in the 1995 British coming-of-age film *Beautiful Thing*, a male actor's bare buttocks appear for less than a second of screen time, but the film is otherwise fairly tame. Some same-sex kissing occurs in the film, too, but these scenes are hardly gratuitous and indeed are far less graphic than most heterosexual content found in PG-13 movies. Some observers feel that latent homophobia in Hollywood forces the R rating onto many queer films that would otherwise deserve a less stringent restriction. Film critic Roger Ebert said as much in his review of the coming-of-age lesbian romance *The Incredibly True Adventure of Two Girls in Love* (Ebert, 1995).

Suffice to say, whether evaluating books or films, don't let censors get away with discriminating against homosexual sex while turning a blind eye to heterosexual sex. Apply the same standard to everything. To that end, the only measuring stick that you or your community should use to evaluate the suitability of materials with sexual content for younger audiences is the degree of sex and how explicit it is. And, again, the best thing you can do is to read the book or watch the film yourself: not just to gauge the level of sexual content, but to determine its overall teen appeal.

RECOGNIZING AND SATISFYING THE NEEDS OF CROSSOVER AUDIENCES

After discussion of adult materials suitable for teens, it's time for the flipside: adults and other crossover audiences who read queer-themed teen materials. A good YA novel is simply good literature and can appeal to readers of all ages and sexual identities. One sign that YA lit has truly come of age is the fact that publishers now battle it out internally over which division, YA or adult, will publish certain books. David Gale, editorial director of Simon & Schuster Books for Young Readers, told us in a July 2004 interview that this was the case with Brian Sloan's *A Really Nice Prom Mess*, which was eventually published as a YA novel.

Often queer adults are drawn to queer YA books for a simple and poignant reason: These kinds of books didn't exist when they themselves were growing up. David Rosen, former editor-in-chief of the book club InSightOut Books, explained that by reading YA titles, queer adults are able to reclaim part of their own adolescence. "Many of these books involve romance. We're finding the adult market really wants these stories and cannot get enough of them. It's very empowering to turn what were very difficult years into romantic ones" (Murdock, 2004c). For instance, the books in Alex Sanchez's *Rainbow Boys* trilogy are among the most popular queer YA titles read by adults. In a July 2004 interview, Sanchez said he is very aware of this crossover audience and acutely understands the books' appeal. "*Rainbow Boys* is the book I wish I'd had when I was in high school—you know, a book that would have told me it's okay to be who you are, just that validation of knowing there was at least one other person out there in the world like me."

It's not just adults who read queer YA books. Straight allies and siblings of queer teens also read them. As noted in Chapter 1, today's generation is the most tolerant yet of the queers in its midst, and nearly 80 percent of high school and middle school students know someone who is queer (GLSEN, 2005). These teens want to read about other kids in similar situations. And even those few teens who don't know any queer people also want to read these books. Teenagers, after all, are like cats—innately curious about the world around them.

One of the most significant crossover teen audiences for queer novels is straight girls. They read everything—from the obvious suspects, such as the *Rainbow Boys* trilogy, to the more obscure lesbian novel *Orphea Proud*. They also devour *shonen-ai* and *yaoi*, two manga subgenres that feature romances between boys. Straight girls are attracted to books about gay boys out of more than just curiosity. The presentation of these books has a lot to do with the appeal. The book jackets of Alex Sanchez's *Rainbow Boys* trilogy, for instance, feature three attractive boys who could have just stepped out of an Abercrombie & Fitch catalog, which significantly boosts their appeal. Sanchez explained, "Teenage girls come across the book and they see these cute guys and they pick it up and they start reading the dust jacket and they're like, 'Oh, my gosh! They're gay!' Then they're more intrigued and then they start reading it" (Murdock, 2004b, 2004c). And once they start the book, he added, they discover it's a love story—which keeps them hooked.

Even straight boys will read queer books, and they too are initially attracted by things such as the cover art; they keep reading because of the good writing. Brian Sloan's hilarious novel *A Really Nice Prom Mess* is a hit with straight boys because the book's cover photo leads them to believe it's about a racy heterosexual evening at the prom. But by the time they discover the book's gay storyline, they're already hooked into its fast-paced plot and humor—one reason why this book was named a YALSA Quick Pick in 2006. Straight boys also enjoy *Geography Club*, about a group of queer teens who form a secret gay-straight alliance in their high school. As author Brent Hartinger explained during a seminar at the ALA's June 2006 conference, everyone can relate to keeping a secret—it's a universal theme.

The point of this discussion is to remind you that queer-themed YA materials are not just for queer teens, they're for everyone. Many feel that the more that straight kids read about queer people, the more they'll come to understand them. Teens read to understand themselves, but, just as important, they read to empathize with others. One self-identified straight teenage girl told us in a July 2004 interview at The New York Public Library: "I read gay novels with teenagers in them to see how teenagers feel about being gay." She paused and then added that when she began school again in the fall, "Maybe I'll try to make more gay friends just to see how they really feel." The more teens who do this, the better, bringing us closer to the day when ignorance and homophobia are finished.

7 INTEGRATING LGBTQ THEMES INTO EVERYDAY PROGRAMS AND SERVICES

INTRODUCTION

This chapter begins to synthesize all the concepts outlined up to this point, starting with a look at programming. Offering queer materials in your library is a critical first step in creating a queer-friendly environment—but it is only the first step. To get kids actually walking through the doors of your library and reading these books, watching these films, and going online, you need to complement your collection with programming. This chapter begins with advice on how to offer effective programming for all teens; there are also specific pointers for designing LGBTQ-themed programs. One basic rule of thumb is that any type of display or program can be given a queer twist—or, if necessary, the queer twist can be straightened out. It's all about the degree to which you integrate queer themes into your regular programming. Booktalking is similar: Use your discretion in deciding whether or not to reveal a book's LGBTQ content. Indeed, this chapter also offers suggestions for overcoming anxiety about queer books, as well as basic booktalking tips. Finally, the chapter closes with a self-evaluation exercise—a series of questions paired with solutions—designed to help you rate your current library service and target ways to improve it.

CUSTOMIZING SUCCESSFUL LGBTQ-THEMED PROGRAMS

Throughout this book, the YA librarian's role is presented as expansive. As a YA librarian, you should focus not only on providing quality materials for kids, but on providing excellent service—and helping teens realize their potential. Programming is a crucial part of service to teens. When it's done well, it helps forge a bond between you and your patrons: dismantling, one interaction at a time, the traditional stereotype of a librarian who scowls and "shushes" kids in the library. The more time you take to interact with your patrons and have conversations with them, the more they'll trust you and respect your opinion when it comes time to recommend materials. Programming is also critically important because it can empower teens, increase their sense of well-being, and help them gain developmental assets. If teens begin to associate these positive experiences with your library, they'll surely return.

Programs can integrate all forms of artistic expression, physical expression, and media types. Designing a good program is partly up to your creativity, partly up to the time and budget that your library allots to you. According to Patrick Jones, most good programs share the following characteristics:

▼ Programs give teens the opportunity to interact and form relationships with other teens and with adults.

▼ Programs offer teens chances to develop life skills, opportunities to contribute to their communities, and chances to enhance their own self-confidence.

▼ Programs can be tailored to match different skill levels among participants, offering everyone a chance to showcase individuals talents and contribute to a final product.

▼ Programs match the interests of teens in the community and offer an opportunity to broaden teens' horizons.

▼ Programming increases youth participation in the library and, when possible, includes outreach and partnerships with schools, community agencies, and families. (Jones, 1998)

Programming can be as simple or as complicated as you make it, but generally speaking, the longer a program is, the more opportunities for participation and creation it can provide for teens. Longer programs also ensure that teens will return to your library on a regular basis. A regular audience, in turn, will help you persuade administrators that you need a bigger programming budget. To this end, be sure to keep copies of a program's finished product: one for your archives, and one to share with co-workers and administrators.

DESIGNING PROGRAMS THAT ARE RIGHT FOR YOUR COMMUNITY

One of the goals of all programming is to provide teens with a safe, relaxed environment. Thus, the first tip is to make sure that hate speech and homophobia are not tolerated during any programs, regardless of whether or not they're queer-themed. Beyond that, programming LGBTQ materials in your library shouldn't be any more or less exotic than highlighting

Summer Reading, Black History Month, Women's History Month, or holidays such as Valentine's Day and Halloween. It can be as straightforward as displaying queer-themed titles against a pink bulletin board during Pride Month, or as complicated as hosting your own "Anti-Prom." That said, programming LGBTQ materials may be difficult for some of you due to your community's prevailing attitudes. Recognizing this, Chapter 8 outlines four distinct plans for how quickly you might implement queer programs based on how conservative your community is.

One final thing to stress is that just because the suggested programs are queer doesn't mean that participants have to be. Like everything else in the library, these programs should be open to everyone. To that end, the secret to designing a successful LGBTQ program is that it's possible to add a queer slant to virtually anything. Take a moment to recall your past programming hits. Did that "Meet the Author" program go over really well with kids last summer? Well, turn it into "Meet the Author of a Queer Book"—you've got queer programming! This rule of thumb works equally well in reverse. Want to douse the flames on a loud and proud program such as "Queer Eye for the Straight Guy . . . or Librarian"? Well, just call it "Extreme Makeover: Library Edition." It doesn't get any straighter than that. Whatever you end up doing, be creative and have fun. If you're not having fun, neither will the kids.

To complement the concepts outlined here, Chapter 12 offers eighteen suggested programs, each with step-by-step instructions on how to execute them. These programs run the gamut from cost-free to costly, from quietly queer to loud-and-proud, and from predictable to outrageous; they are listed in order of how "out" they are. Some programs are outcome-oriented, in which groups of teens create individual works and then collaborate to bring their pieces together into a cohesive whole. Others simply offer suggestions for making LGBTQ collections more accessible. The programs also include a range of technologies and forms of creative expression in the visual arts, writing, performance, and popular culture. You can follow the instructions step-by-step, or modify them to suit your library's unique circumstances. For that matter, you can use the programs without including any queer content at all—but best to add a queer twist at least once!

PRESENTING ENGAGING LGBTQ BOOKTALKS

Reports of booktalking's demise are much exaggerated. Though some librarians no longer have the time or inclination to do it, booktalking remains a vital way of bridging the gap between collections and readers. It is one of the librarian's signature skills: an integral part of programming and promoting, something that distinguishes the librarian from a page or circulation clerk. That said, many librarians find it difficult to stand up in front of thirty unruly teens and talk about a book. Talking about a queer-themed book might cause an embolism. If you're one of those librarians, the advice in the following pages can help. There are general tips to help knock any booktalk out of the park; some specific concerns that librarians have about booktalking LGBTQ materials; and, finally, solutions to overcome these concerns. (And, by the way, Chapter 11 offers six sample booktalks that show you how it's done.)

If you can banish your fears about booktalking LGBTQ titles, your reward will be a powerful one. Queer and questioning teens will learn that libraries carry materials of interest to all people and that the library is a safe place for all youth. They might even borrow the title you present. One anecdote illustrates this perfectly. Harriet Selverstone, an adjunct professor at the Pratt Institute's Graduate School of Information and Library Science, was for twenty-nine years the media specialist in a Norwalk, Connecticut, high school. Each year she'd make a Banned Books Week presentation in which she always booktalked a queer title. After one such presentation, a teen visited her office and came out to her. He said that he was being ridiculed by students as well as teachers. In a September 2003 interview, Selversteone recalled: "He was hurting so terribly. I mentioned the materials we had and that if he had any difficulty I could get him additional material." The teen visited Selverstone again a few months later. He said that he'd come out to his parents and they had taken the news well; they'd even driven him to a local LGBTQ community center. The next year the teen switched schools to one that had a gay-straight alliance. "He felt accepted," Selverstone happily concluded. And it all started with a booktalk.

BASIC BOOKTALKING TIPS

There are myriad opinions on how to booktalk, and individual library systems often have their own preferred method (Jones, 1998). Booktalking style also varies from librarian to librarian. You should test a variety of styles to determine which ones feel most natural for you. In this chapter, the booktalking recommendations are based on The New York Public Library's style. No matter what style you use, the most important rule of thumb when it comes to booktalking is to pick books that you've actually read, enjoyed, and can wholeheartedly recommend. In addition to choosing books you like, be sure to use books that have a definite hook (Jones, 1998; Langemack, 2003). Titles that are funny, tragic, suspenseful, gruesome, or fast-paced make for excellent booktalks; books with exciting pictures or poems also make great booktalks and add variety. By contrast, don't pick titles that you haven't read or did not like. If you didn't like the book, chances are kids won't like it either. Teens have an innate sensor that will immediately detect any insincerity in your presentation.

In deciding on the focus of your booktalk, pick an exciting scene near the beginning of the action that you feel represents the entire work. Using a few key words and phrases that illustrate the author's voice can help convey the book's tone and atmosphere, but instead of trying to memorize a scene exactly as the author describes it, write down as much as you remember in your own words. Most booktalking disasters are failed attempts at memorization: You forget what happens and your booktalk grinds to an unexpected halt. Your nerves are going to be tense as it is, without the extra stress of trying to remember something verbatim, so spare yourself this challenge. Plus, using your own words to describe the flow of events in a way that makes sense to you will mean that your presentation will sound more natural and convincing. And this is the key to a good booktalk. In fact, it's your only real task as a booktalker: You want to mesmerize your audience with a great story that will make them go racing for the book as soon as you're done.

Begin by announcing the title of the book and the author's name. Then, open your booktalk with an awesome quote that will immediately seize your audience's attention; end it with a line that will make your listeners drool with anticipation for more. Avoid inserting personal opinions into your booktalk. Instead, focus on relating the plot, like a film preview. You should also avoid saying something like, "If you want to find out what happens, then read. . . ." This is patronizing and usually results in nothing but groans from your audience. If possible, try to incorporate the book's title into your closing sentence. This will strengthen the audience's connection between the content of the book you just presented and the book's title. End by repeating the name of the book and the author. Your booktalk can be as long or as short as necessary, according to the information you are relating and your personal style. Many librarians present a ten- to twenty-second blurb about a book and can cover a dozen or so titles at a time. But in some library systems, such The New York Public Library, booktalks run between two and four minutes and librarians present an average of only three or five per class period, in addition to discussing general library information.

Booktalking "Dos"

Do inflect your voice while doing the booktalk.

Do always have a few extra books just in case you have more time or the books you have aren't working with the audience.

Do read teen periodicals that give you an idea of what kids are into now and the people they like, and then use this information to help you pick titles to booktalk.

Do read a lot of new and old titles.

Do have titles from different reading levels to cater to a wide range of audiences.

(cont'd.)

Booktalking "Dos" *(Continued)*

Do use poetry, photo books, biographies, etc.

Do act excited about the books.

Do use new books: Teens want whatever is new and exciting.

Do read from books if the passage is particularly good or illustrates the plot and/or characters really well.

Do learn your booktalk: Know how it flows from beginning, to middle, to end.

Do tape a copy of your booktalk—or important facts such as names, places, etc.—to the back of the book in case you need a quick reminder. (Martin and Ronyer, 2003)

Booktalking "Don'ts"

Don't be overly dramatic: It distracts from the task at hand, which is to convey information about the book.

Don't use a monotone voice or too many pauses.

Don't give too much away and show too much of the book.

Don't give a straight summary of the book.

Don't give your opinion of the book, except perhaps to say it is a favorite.

Don't say "this is a really good book because . . . ."

Don't read a long passage: There is a greater chance for the audience to get bored.

Don't use old books unless they have relevance or a great hook. (Martin and Rouyer, 2003)

OVERCOMING FEARS OF BOOKTALKING QUEER BOOKS

For some librarians, booktalking any book is nerve-wracking—and booktalking a title with potentially charged content, such as queer characters, is terrifying. Even experienced librarians are often reluctant to do so. Our advice is simply to present LGBTQ-themed titles in exactly the same professional manner that you use presenting other titles, using the same normal tone of voice. Remember: LGBTQ books are great books that everyone should read. Thus, embed LGBTQ characters and themes within an already exciting plot that's guaranteed to hook readers: stories about teenagers who have ups and downs, romances, conundrums, all the normal drama. Diana Tixier Herald, a librarian and Web master of http://genre fluent.com, shared this advice in an April 2005 e-mail:

> I always include LGBTQ titles when I'm booktalking in my workshops for librarians and teachers. I try to emphasize the humanity of the characters, not that Russell [a character in *Geography Club*] is GAY but that Russell is this wonderful, kind, feeling person, who is feeling like an outsider at school, that he despairs of ever finding romance

and that he is gay. Or, that *Luna* isn't about a transgendered kid. It is about Regan, who loves her brother Liam (who late at night becomes Luna) because he is her brother—but keeping his secret impacts her life. What I try to do in booktalking these titles is to not present them as problem or issue novels, but rather as good stories with empathetic characters.

The less you call attention to the queer content of a book, the more normal it will seem. And this is precisely the point. Queer books are just like any other books in your collection. It's important to reinforce this message. And remember, whatever else happens you should be fearless. You're already brave enough to stand in front of an audience of thirty-plus teenagers, so take it one step further and talk about a queer book! The stronger and more direct you appear, the more the kids will respect you—good advice for any type of booktalk.

Depending on the group of kids you have, or a teacher's comfort level with LGBTQ content, it might be simpler to ease your way into booktalking a queer title by placing it in the middle of your overall presentation so that you avoid distracting your audience with LGBTQ themes right at the start. Also, placing the queer title in the middle of a presentation makes it seem less incriminating: That is, it doesn't appear as though you're "promoting" an LGBTQ agenda, but that you're just sharing a pile of good books which represents the wide variety of materials, including LGBTQ titles, you have in your library. When visiting different grade levels, pay attention to the types of LGBTQ titles you bring—novels such as *Totally Joe* and *So Hard to Say* are perfect for younger teen audiences. Aside from that, it's up to you to decide what you think a class is ready to read, just as you would do when selecting any other title to booktalk. In the rest of this chapter, we'll look at a few common concerns that librarians may have about booktalking queer books, and how to overcome them.

Worries about a Disruptive Audience

If you are a public librarian visiting a school, you should not tolerate disruptions from a class—especially if they entail expending energy you need to conserve for meeting with other classes later that same day. In the classroom setting it is the teacher's responsibility, not yours, to discipline the class. That said, if the teacher fails to step in when you hear any snickers in the audience at the mention of an LGBTQ topic, your first reaction should be to ignore them. Experience shows that if you keep talking through the giggles, laughs, and the exclamations of "say what?," the perpetrators will usually catch on that the rest of the class is silently listening and so they will soon shut their mouths. But if the snickers continue and become too disruptive, don't be afraid to pause and tell the miscreants that you'll be glad to finish your presentation as soon as they're finished talking. If that doesn't quiet them down, other teens in the class will often begin to tell the disruptive parties to be quiet so they can hear. If the disruption continues or escalates, make your second warning. Tell the entire group that you can't talk above thirty kids and that if the class is disinterested in what you have to say, you will pack up and leave. That usually quiets everyone down immediately, but if it doesn't then you should be prepared to follow through on your promise. School librarians who cannot leave the classroom should use any "last resort" disciplinary tactics that are open to you. The point in leaving is not that you're surrendering to homophobia, but that you have more important things to do with your time than let kids waste it.

Worries that an Audience Will Turn on Itself

Are you worried that an audience member might pick on another kid in the class by shouting something like, "Hey, fag, this book should be perfect for queens like you!"? If so, first remember that you are presenting a title to the entire audience and that everyone is listening together: not just the LGBTQ teens who happen to be in the classroom. That kind of collective attention helps put a lid on a lot of this type of behavior, especially when an outsider is presenting information to a class. Usually a classroom full of teens, unless they are already in an agitated state when you arrive, will be respectful of outside presenters no matter what information they are discussing. Don't let your fears that a queer booktalk will foment homophobic comments prevent you from presenting these materials to classes. The positives always outweigh the negatives, especially when your booktalk can help closeted youth discover that there are materials in the library for them. Remember, any book you include in your presentation may be targeted for disrespectful comments, not just queer books, so you should be prepared to respond to all sorts of remarks.

If you are a public librarian visiting a school, you should not be in a classroom full of kids alone: In other words, there should always be a teacher or school official present. Public librarians often are not trained in classroom management, and our role when visiting schools is not to discipline disruptive students. Rather, our job is simply to present library information and booktalks to a class. If students become disruptive, the teacher should bring them back to order. If the teacher doesn't react, you should make clear that you'll be prepared to leave. If you are a school librarian, you might be empowered to discipline and call out kids for making homophobic remarks. And you should. Immediately letting a teen know that his comment is inappropriate helps curb this behavior and it establishes an atmosphere that your library is a hate-free zone where prejudice of any sort is not tolerated.

Worries that a Teacher Will Object to LGBTQ Material

When presenting books to classes, no matter what they are about, you should let the teachers know about the titles ahead of time. If they express any concern over content or language, consider saving certain titles for another time. With some teachers, you may need to take baby steps to warm them up to queer material. Rather than start off on the wrong foot, it's more important to form a productive and comfortable relationship with a teacher so that he or she will continue to ask you to visit the class year after year. Remember, teachers are in command of their classes, and they have the right to know what kinds of materials you'll present. If they don't want you to present a queer book, they may have a very good reason why. For instance, a New York City high school teacher asked Jack Martin not to present his *Boy Meet Boy* booktalk because the teacher had been working very hard to decrease the amount of verbal homophobia in his class and he was worried this booktalk might incite students to shout epithets at other classmates. Even though Jack personally thought it would help the class to hear the booktalk, he didn't want to question the teacher's authority or his ability to predict the class's response, so he substituted another title.

Worries that Other People Will Complain About LGBTQ Material

By letting teachers know what types of materials you'll be presenting to their classes, you are letting them make the choice. This, in turn, gives you recourse if a principal or parent later complains about your presentation. Remember, teachers—not you—are charged with making decisions regarding what materials to provide to their students in the classroom. In communities where queer people are highly visible and queer books widely read, it's often unnecessary to flag queer content. That said, you know your community best and whether or not you'll need to single out queer books when talking to a teacher ahead of time.

Worries that You'll Be Accused of "Recruiting" Teens to the "Gay Lifestyle"

This simply isn't true. By having LGBTQ materials in your library you're not endorsing anything, much less recruiting people to a particular so-called "lifestyle": you're simply satisfying the needs of your community. As we've said throughout our book, queer teens are a part of your community, visible or not. And sometimes teens might surprise you at just how visible they are. Sara Ryan, a YA author and teen services specialist at the Multnomah County Library in Portland, Oregon, shared this anecdote in an April 2005 e-mail: "One time I was booktalking at a middle school and was surprised and impressed to see a seventh grade girl wearing freedom rings and a T-shirt that read 'I don't do boys'!"

MAKING THE TEEN-LIBRARY CONNECTION WORK

So far, this book has explored who queer teens are today, examined the types of materials that are available specifically for them, and offered some advice on how to design programs and booktalks that are guaranteed to excite teens and encourage them to participate in your library. As noted several times, encouraging teens to participate is the best way that we, as librarians, can help them develop into healthy, productive adults and community members. Another theme throughout this book has been the importance of creating a hate-free zone in your library, a space where straight and LGBTQ teens alike can attain peace of mind. In the remainder of this chapter, all these concepts are drawn together into a strategic plan, offering a series of self-evaluation questions that rate your service to LGBTQ teens, paired with goals and suggestions for improvement.

Questions and recommendations are grouped into three general areas: (1) representing the population; (2) creating a safe space; and (3) encouraging participation. Although participation is singled out as a separate category, you can empower teens to take action in every aspect of library service. Also keep in mind that you can always take things a step further. It's one level if your teen advisory group participates in planning a program, another level if they execute the program themselves and promote it among their friends, and it's a whole new dimension if they take a program into the larger community. You should always be thinking of ways to elevate your programs and services to these higher levels of participation to help teens build assets.

REPRESENTING THE POPULATION

Q: How can you ensure the presence of LGBTQ materials in your library?
A: Talk to your library's administrators and show them that queer youth exist in your community and in the library. Add a clause to your collection development plan about the importance of collecting materials that represent your community's diversity along the lines of race, ethnicity, age, religion, sexual orientation, and gender expression. Ask your teen advisory group to write letters to your administrators and board of trustees to ensure that such a clause is included within your library's collection development plan. Meet with local queer community groups

and ask them to do the same. Ask them how they think your library can better serve their population.

Q: What is the proportion of LGBTQ materials in relation to non-LGBTQ materials in your library? Do you have items that represent not just gay kids, but lesbians, bisexuals, trans, and questioning teens, too?

A: Conduct an inventory of your library's queer-themed YA materials and note which sex or sexual orientation is represented. Identify gaps in your collection and acquire books that feature lesbian, bisexual, and trans characters in addition to gay boys. Also be on the lookout for books that feature queer youth of color.

Q: Do you collect only LGBTQ-themed fiction?

A: Focus on collecting LGBTQ materials in a variety of formats, including nonfiction, graphic novels, music, film, TV on DVD, and other multimedia.

Q: Do you offer representations of real queer people?

A: Purchase a collection of coming out stories. Purchase biographies and memoirs of queer people. Commission a collection of coming out stories written by your patrons and other teens in the community; print it and donate copies to local schools and agencies; host a publishing party at your library and put the publication on your library's home page. Create a series of coming out podcasts.

Q: Where do you search for new queer materials to acquire for your collection?

A: Survey your patrons. Read journals such as *Kirkus Reviews* and *School Library Journal*, as well as queer periodicals such as *Out* and *The Advocate*, to find reviews of queer-themed books. Read your community's local queer newspaper.

Q: How accessible are LGBTQ materials in your library? Are they hidden behind the desk; buried deep in stacks; kept behind locked cases; shelved in the adult area; or are they on full view?

A: Rescue queer YA items from the adult collection. Establish a library "Queer Zone" that permanently and openly houses all of your LGBTQ materials in the YA room. Enabling teens to access this without adult assistance protects their privacy and helps increase their self-sufficiency.

Q: How often do you display LGBTQ titles? How does this compare to other types of displays: more frequently, or less? Do you only display LGBTQ titles during Pride Month?

A: Offer a variety of LGBTQ displays throughout the year, not just during Pride Month, and make sure to include queer materials as part of other displays when appropriate, such as for Valentine's Day. Make sure to include LGBTQ titles in your "staff picks" displays: By doing so, you'll send a signal that you're tolerant of queer people and that you can knowledgeably assist LGBTQ teens in finding appropriate material.

Q: What types of materials do you include in LGBTQ displays—only books?

A: In addition to novels, promote less obvious forms of queer creative expression: Arrange a display of queer playwrights, politicians, musicians, and poets. Be sure to include nonfiction, graphic novels, CDs, DVDs, and a variety of other multimedia items.

Q: Does your library offer contact information for local and national queer community groups? Do you have a queer section of your library's home page, or a list of queer organizations and Web sites displayed in your library?

A: Post pamphlets and flyers that describe both local and national organizations that focus on LGBTQ topics including health and wellness and parent support groups. Create a special Web page listing queer resources and bibliographies.

Q: How effectively are you visually representing queer youth in your library: Are there any images of queer people in your library?

A: Create a list of LGBTQ-themed materials that might be useful for homework assignments, including titles on health and wellness, homophobia, and biographies of celebrated queer people. Post this list in your library and on its home page. Create an LGBTQ caucus of its teen advisory group or a gay-straight alliance. Advertise it in your library and on your library's home page. Elect a member of this group to be the YA room's LGBTQ ambassador within the library and beyond it. Start a teen library newsletter that features a special column for LGBTQ books and events. Post it on the Internet or distribute it as a zine.

Q: Do you design programs specifically to draw an LGBTQ audience?

A: Create an online survey or an anonymous suggestion box in your reading room to ask your patrons what kind of LGBTQ-related programming they'd like to see in your library. Publish the results on your library's Web site. Ask your LGBTQ teen advisory group caucus or your gay-straight alliance to develop a schedule of queer programming for Pride Month.

Q: Do you invite queer presenters—authors, artists, members of the community—to your teen programs? Can gay-straight alliances from nearby schools, and similar groups such as PFLAG, meet in your library and sponsor events there?

A: Ensure that your library's meeting room policy does not specifically discourage LGBTQ-related groups from using the facility. Meet with a local queer community group to brainstorm what programming they might be able to offer in your library. Invite queer authors, or authors of queer-themed books, to speak in your library. Design flyers advertising your LGBTQ programs and post them on your library's bulletin board and Web site. Have your teen advisory group post the flyer in their schools and give it to their friends.

Q: Have community members challenged the presence of LGBTQ materials or programs in your library? How have you handled these challenges?

A: Defend open access and intellectual freedom. If a community member is concerned about the presence of LGBTQ books and programs in your library, try to find common ground. Explain that your library collects materials to serve all members of the community, including queer people. Make this person go through the official challenge process, don't just acquiesce to their demands. Make noise and attract attention—don't take censorship quietly.

CREATING A SAFE SPACE

Q: Are there out youth in your library? How safe do they feel there?

A: Start a discussion in your teen advisory group about what it's like to be a queer teenager in the world today. Ask them to describe the tolerance level in their schools, among their friends, and in the library. Create an LGBTQ-related survey so teens can offer ideas for how to improve the atmosphere in your library, as well as queer materials and programs your library should offer.

Q: How often do you hear the kids in your library use the expression "that's so gay," or other homophobic remarks?

A: Immediately call out patrons when they make homophobic comments such as "that's so gay." Enforce the rules and show teens your library does not tolerate any forms of homophobia. Display "No Name Calling" or "Hate-Free Zone" posters on the walls of your library; distribute these flyers to schools and post them on your library's home page. Develop a plan with your teen advisory group for combating homophobic comments. Contact other young adult librarians in the country, via listserv or e-mail, to ask what they do to combat homophobia. Contact the Gay, Lesbian and Straight Education Network and other national groups; have your teen advisory group make the contact.

Q: Do you have an action team to address LGBTQ concerns in your library?

A: Create an LGBTQ caucus of your teen advisory group, or a gay-straight alliance. Elect a member to become the LGBTQ ambassador within the library and beyond it.

Q: When patrons ask for help finding a good book or a "different kind of love story," how do you present LGBTQ materials to them?

A: When performing readers' advisory, be sure to place a variety of materials—straight *and* queer—into a patron's hands and let her decide which titles interest her. At the end of your conversation, instead of simply pointing to the location of a queer-themed book in the stacks, walk the patron to that location and take the book off the shelf for her. Explain to her that she can find other materials like the book she's holding in the same shelf location. If a teen asks for a specific LGBTQ title that your library lacks, ask her to fill out a request form. Order the title and then make sure that she is the first person to get her hands on the book when it arrives.

Q: How do you protect the privacy of teens who ask for LGBTQ materials?

A: Respect LGBTQ teens' need for privacy by allowing them to peruse materials in a carrel or cubicle away from the general population of your reading room. Be alert to hints that they feel uncomfortable, and lower your voice or wait until others move out of earshot if necessary. If it's permitted in your library, set up a way for teens to text message you or chat online for readers' advisory and reference questions.

Q: Do patrons feel comfortable borrowing LGBTQ materials?

A: Bend your library's circulation rules to allow teens to borrow LGBTQ materials on an honor system to respect their privacy.

Q: Do you promote LGBTQ materials during high school class visits?

A: Present LGBTQ booktalks during class visits: Show both straight and queer teens that you offer these resources in your library. Mention your library's request form to students and tell them they can request whatever kinds of materials they would like: adventure stories, music, science fiction and fantasy, biographies, *and* LGBTQ books.

Q: How often do you talk to your community's LGBTQ teens? Do you actively seek them out and let them know they're welcome in your library?

A: Visit local LGBTQ advocates and agencies in your community, or check out other national agencies online, and ask how you can work together. Ask queer teens in your community what kinds of LGBTQ programs they'd like to see at your library and then implement these programs and promote them in town. Initiate a listserv discussion with other young adult librarians around the country to see how they reach LGBTQ audiences for after-school programs.

ENCOURAGING PARTICIPATION

Q: Do you have up-to-date and popular titles in your collection, and who identifies new LGBTQ materials to include in your library's collection?

A: Create a topical survey for library materials. Include a section in which teen readers can indicate if they want materials for LGBTQ audiences. Distribute the questionnaires to patrons; create an anonymous suggestion box; create an anonymous online survey. Ask your teen advisory group to develop a list of their favorite LGBTQ titles to distribute to their friends and schools. Contact local queer groups to see what they would like to see in your library.

Q: Do you know if your queer YA patrons feel that they have a say in what happens in the library?

A: Create a survey to gauge how well your patrons think you're meeting the needs of LGBTQ teens: Ask about everything from materials and programming, to reference service and general atmosphere. Ask for suggestions on how to improve. Distribute the survey to patrons; provide an anonymous suggestion box or an online survey. Post the results along with an action plan with goals for improvement.

Q: Can LGBTQ teens meet with their peers in your library, and/or with librarians, to discuss issues that are important to them? Does your library have its own gay-straight alliance or queer caucus of its teen advisory board?

A: Start your own library gay-straight alliance, or initiate an LGBTQ caucus within its teen advisory board. Have this group be the one that surveys patrons to gauge the library's LGBTQ service; have it present the results to your library's administrators and trustees. Ask this team to suggest their favorite LGBTQ books, movies, and music to add to your library's collection, as well as queer-themed workshops they'd like to see in the library. Working with the team, organize a night at the library on which the teen advisory group or gay-straight alliance can talk to parents about the needs of LGBTQ teens. With your team, create an LGBTQ site on your library's home page. Empower your team by asking them to become the front line for combating homophobia in the library. Ask your team to make a list of five things they think the library can do to help LGBTQ teens in their town.

8 FINDING AND IMPLEMENTING THE RIGHT PACE FOR CHANGE

INTRODUCTION

Regardless of the size of your community, regardless of what it looks like politically, and regardless of your library's budget, the guiding principle presented here is that every library, large and small, public libraries and school libraries, should offer LGBTQ materials that are suitable for YA audiences: a minimum of ten titles. The first ten titles listed in Chapter 10 are ideal. As noted several times throughout our book, queer and straight teens alike want and need these materials in their local library. It's simply not good enough to rely on a regional system to fill in the gaps in a branch or small library collection. Interlibrary loans take time, and it takes guts—more guts than some teens have—to request them.

That said, some of you may not be able to build and program the ideal queer YA collection. Accordingly, this chapter provides you with a framework for deciding how to provide LGBTQ materials and services that will work best in your community or your school. There are four suggested speeds—"Red Light," "Yellow Light," "Green Light," and "School Zone"—at which to move. Within each one are four different areas: collection development; designing programs; booktalking (even though it's part of programming, it's treated separately in order to offer specific tips); and establishing a welcoming atmosphere within your library. At the end of this chapter, there is a visual matrix that matches these four speeds to the sample programs and booktalks that you will find in Part II of this book. Keep in mind, too, that Chapter 9 contains complete reviews of all the books we list in this chapter.

To help you determine which plan is right for you, each one begins by offering characteristics of libraries and communities that fit the bill for the plan. You know your own library best, so feel free to modify these suggestions if you feel that they are unnecessary in your circumstances. Also, keep in mind that virtually any program can be tweaked to give it a queer twist; conversely, even the queerest program can be straightened for more closeted audiences. And, finally, remember that each teen is unique. This sounds obvious, and maybe even hokey, but even if you live in a stereotypically conservative town you might be surprised to encounter out and proud teens in your library. Likewise, even if you live in queer havens such as Provincetown, Massachusetts, you will still encounter closeted teens and homophobia. No matter where you are, be prepared to roll with the punches and give all the teens in your library the respectful, thorough service they deserve.

MOVING FORWARD
SPEED 1—RED LIGHT

Is your library small, or a branch within a system, with limited shelf space and a limited budget? Do you only have a children's collection and an adult collection—no YA collection as such? Does your library currently have only an outdated handful of queer-themed YA books, or none at all? Have you ever had a teen ask you for LGBTQ materials? Can you name any out teens whom you know? Have other libraries nearby, or maybe the local high school, been challenged because they carried LGBTQ-themed books? Has yours? Do you live in a rural, conservative area of the country? If you answered "yes" to any of these questions, then try our Red Light plan.

RED LIGHT—COLLECTION DEVELOPMENT

In terms of collection development, you can pursue one of two paths. If your community is really conservative and you anticipate a backlash if you acquire anything too bold, choose books that don't draw too much attention to their LGBTQ content: namely, books that have queer secondary characters. For a list of suitable titles, refer to Chapter 10. Your second option is to acquire titles that represent a diverse cross-section of LGBTQ life: Pick one gay novel, one lesbian novel, one bisexual novel, and a trans book. For lists of YA titles based on the characters' sexual orientation, see Chapter 10. Acquire the titles on these lists, place them in circulation, and track them. If they do well, continue adding more.

RED LIGHT—PROGRAMMING

When it comes to programming, subtlety is key. Stick to displays that focus on diversity in its broadest sense, rather than ones with an all-queer theme, and title these displays in a way that heightens their universality. For instance, instead of offering the "Did You Know They Were Gay?" display in Chapter 12, retitle the display something like "Celebrate Diversity" and feature a range of different materials including African American and Jewish novels, as well as books with LGBTQ content. Another obvious place to showcase a queer title would be in a display for Banned Books Week. Finally, if you think it can fly without raising too many eyebrows, choose an LGBTQ title to discuss during a meeting of your library's teen book discussion group, assuming you have one. Feel free to choose whether or not you mention that a character is queer—you can describe a book in any way you choose. If you're subtle but persistent, over time the message that your library offers LGBTQ materials will filter to the right audience, i.e., queer teens, without setting off a panic that you're pushing a queer agenda.

RED LIGHT—BOOKTALKING

Slip a queer-themed title into your booktalking routine, but do it in a way that doesn't call attention to its presence at all. Admittedly, this isn't an out and proud method of promoting queer-themed books, but if you're in a conservative region, or in a highly volatile classroom, this may the best and only choice you have. Choose a book with an exciting plot and talk about the plot in universal terms without revealing the LGBTQ characters or content. Once you've hooked the kids on a plot, their interests will be piqued enough to read the book regardless of the characters' sexual identity. Fiction titles with secondary queer characters are a great choice for this type of booktalk, but you could even talk about a title that features a queer protagonist if you focus on other elements aside from the character's sexual identity. For instance, you could describe the lesbian novel *Orphea Proud* as a book in which an orphaned girl is unhappy living with her abusive brother, so she gets sent away to live with two older aunts whom she's never met. Or, you could booktalk *The Realm of Possibility*, a prose-poem with multiple characters of diverse sexual identities, also leaving out the queer content entirely.

RED LIGHT—ATMOSPHERE

Discretion is paramount when handling LGBTQ concerns during the reference interview and readers' advisory. For instance, be alert to subtle cues that teens send when they are seeking "different" kinds of love stories. Also, unless teens openly ask you for queer materials, without regard to who else is within earshot, protect their privacy by finding a more secluded part of the reading room where you can chat. If a teen requests it, let him or her check out queer books concealed by a different cover or use the honor system. Similarly, as the library may be the only place where teens can browse the Internet privately, include one or two LGBTQ Web sites in a list of resources that teens can find online (refer to Chapter 4 for suggestions).

Finally, in terms of the atmosphere you create in your library, display "safe zone" posters and other signs that convey the message your library is a space in which bullying of all kinds—including homophobia—is not permitted. If you hear kids using homophobic slurs, including "that's so gay," don't let them get away with it. Invisible or not, there are LGBTQ teens in your library; they, and others, find these remarks offensive. Refer to Chapter 3 for more tips.

MOVING FORWARD
SPEED 2—YELLOW LIGHT

You already have a few queer-themed YA books in your collection. You'd like to add some more and you have the budget to do it, but you're not sure which ones to get. You'd really like to start promoting your collection of LGBTQ books to teens in the library and during school visits, but you don't know where to begin. You live in a medium-sized, reasonably tolerant community, but your town lacks an annual Pride celebration—in other words, the queer community isn't that big or maybe it's still a little closeted. There are a couple of out teens who visit your library, but you sense they're not entirely comfortable being there and that you're not giving them the best readers' advisory and reference service possible. Does this sound like your library and your community? If you said "yes," then try the Yellow Light plan.

YELLOW LIGHT—COLLECTION DEVELOPMENT

If you already have a few queer-themed YA titles in your collection, focus on filling in the gaps by making sure that your collection represents the complete cross-section of LGBTQ readers; also focus on acquiring nonfiction and non-print materials. For suggestions, refer to the lists in Chapter 10. As always, the best tool to help you identify gaps in your collection will be surveying your patrons. Depending on how many out or queer-friendly teens there are, you could either design a questionnaire specifically devoted to LGBTQ materials, or simply add a few LGBTQ questions to your general reader surveys. As you go about acquiring new titles, be sure to track their circulation. This will be a great yardstick to determine which types of books your patrons like best and it will help you make the case for acquiring more. Finally, if you don't have one already, write a clause to insert into your library's collection development plan that says your institution does not discriminate on the basis of sexual orientation and gender expression.

YELLOW LIGHT—PROGRAMMING

Your LGBTQ programming will be a queer take on traditional library programming. For instance, offer an LGBTQ book discussion group, or have your teens write and publish a queer-themed zine. In terms of displays, you should definitely have a Pride Month display of your LGBTQ titles—if you don't have one already—and you might consider displays that are tied to other important days on the queer calendar, such as National Coming Out Day. If your library hosts author visits and readings, be sure to invite queer authors and the authors of LGBTQ books. You might even consider starting a library gay-straight alliance, or a gay-straight caucus of your teen advisory group.

YELLOW LIGHT—BOOKTALKING

Include a few LGBTQ titles in the stack of books you booktalk in your library and while conducting visits to local high schools. Just a few titles will suffice, and be sure to act as casually with these books as you do for all the others you bring. Choose a queer title with an exciting plot and describe that plot, revealing an LGBTQ twist at the end. Most often, this twist increases the audience's intrigue about the book. The *Hard Love* booktalk—actually classified in the Red Light category—is an excellent example of this. Typically, when a classroom full of teens hears the last line, which reveals that the book's main character, a straight boy, is lusting after a lesbian, audiences usually start to hoot and holler "Dawg!" or "Dang!" You know they want to read the book now! *Hard Love* works in Yellow Light settings because it is told from the point of view of a straight character who describes a queer secondary character. But you could also choose a racier Green Light title, such as *Leave Myself Behind*, and tone down its queer elements. *Leave Myself Behind*'s plot unfolds as a mystery, which makes it ideal for booktalking. By the time you get to the last few sentences of your presentation, in which you reveal the protagonist's sexual orientation, your audience won't even notice because they'll be dying to know how the mystery ends.

YELLOW LIGHT—ATMOSPHERE

Liberal or conservative, small city or large, you should always respect teens' privacy and be alert to subtle cues that they may be sending as they approach the desk for readers' advisory and reference help. Also, include an LGBTQ title in the stack of books you hand to a teen during readers' advisory. In terms of general atmosphere, ensure that your library is a safe space, free of all homophobic comments. Do this by displaying posters that say "Safe Space," and by calling out kids who make homophobic comments. Finally, make sure that LGBTQ items are easy to find in your library by posting bibliographies in the YA room or on your library's Web site.

MOVING FORWARD
SPEED 3—GREEN LIGHT

Your library is large, and so is your community—or, even if your town and your library are small, they have very large hearts. There's a queer part of town, a queer community center, maybe even a queer teen center, and your annual Pride parade draws thousands of participants and happy spectators. You can boast that your library's YA reading room—and yes, you actually have a special YA room—has plenty of LGBTQ titles, and every June you proudly display titles during Pride Month. But you know there's still more you can do to program LGBTQ books in your library and in school visits. And, in the interest of assembling the highest quality collection possible, you want to see if you're missing any LGBTQ titles. In fact, your queer patrons are asking for it: fresh programming and new, exciting materials. You want to do all this, but you don't have the time to design an off-the-wall program from scratch, nor can you read every new queer book that comes out because there just so many of them now. Sound like you? Our Green Light plan may be able to help.

GREEN LIGHT—COLLECTION DEVELOPMENT

Chances are, you already have a good collection of LGBTQ resources. But, just to be sure, use the lists in Chapter 10 as a yardstick to help you identify and fill any remaining gaps. Your main goal will be to stay on top of new materials as they are published. Do this by reading reviews in library and youth-related journals, and by reading queer periodicals including *Out* and *The Advocate*. Also be sure to survey your patrons, either with a queer-specific questionnaire or a detailed set of questions included in your general surveys, to see what they want—and be sure to satisfy their requests. As always, track your circulation to gauge where the biggest demand lies, where to weed your collection, and to demonstrate how successful your collection is. If you're tapped out of YA titles, begin to acquire suitable adult books—or, at the very least, compile booklists of suitable titles available in your library's adult collections and make these lists available to teens in the YA room or online. This will be particularly helpful if you're looking to beef up the nonfiction and non-print areas of your collection. For tips on how to do this, refer to Chapter 6. At this point, you've already built a collection, so your main task is maintaining it.

GREEN LIGHT—PROGRAMMING

Push the envelope as far as you think it will go: Design programs that are out and proud, guaranteed to attract a large group of teens regardless of their sexual identity. Two rules of thumb to keep in mind: Any program you dream up can be given a queer twist, and to attract a specifically queer audience you can always partner with queer community centers and/or advertise your programs with local high school gay-straight alliances. Although you're free to make programs as out as you and your teens want, be sure to include an angle for straight teens as well. Your library is a tolerant place, but you don't want to let "diversity" morph into exclusivity. Thus, create a gay-straight alliance or a queer subcommittee of your teen advisory board: both to empower teens, and to bring the different constituencies together. And, as always, remember that you can tone down the queerness in your programs if necessary, by changing the title or through careful advertising.

GREEN LIGHT—BOOKTALKING

If queer visibility is high in your library, or in the school where you're booktalking, you should let your booktalks be as out as you want them to be and offer as many LGBTQ titles as you like. This is when you can present titles such as *Boy Meets Boy* (notice our booktalk uses the word "gay" at least half a dozen times!), *Kings & Queens: Queers at the Prom*, and even *GLBTQ: The Survival Guide for Queer and Questioning Teens*. In Green Light settings you're already preaching to the converted. Thus, you should try to present as wide a range of queer titles as possible: something for gay boys, for lesbians, and all of the letters represented in the LGBTQ acronym.

GREEN LIGHT—ATMOSPHERE

If you have a gay-straight alliance in your library, or a queer caucus of your teen advisory group, let them self-police the YA room to keep it free of hate speech and homophobia. Not only will this empower teens to take ownership of their space, it will be more effective than if you, the librarian, are the "bad cop." We're not saying that you should let the YA room degenerate into *Lord of the Flies*, because you will obviously need to intervene in some circumstances, but letting teens establish the room's atmosphere helps them participate in your library directly and acquire developmental assets. Be sure to display lists of community centers and Web sites, the local queer community newspaper, and other resources. As noted earlier, Kevin Jennings, the founder of the Gay, Lesbian and Straight Education Network, has observed that this is the generation that "gets it" (Cloud, 2005: 45).

Today's teens are coming to the library for information about the queer community near them and across the country, so be sure to provide it. But, as always, be aware that some kids will be reluctant to talk openly about LGBTQ issues. Thus, when conducting readers' advisory and reference interviews, you'll encounter out and proud teens who confidently ask you for help finding the next Julie Anne Peters novel, but you'll also encounter the shy girl who asks for a "different" kind of love story. We're not living in a gaytopia yet, so be alert to subtle cues and always respect teens' privacy.

MOVING FORWARD
SPEED 4—SCHOOL ZONE

School libraries are an active battleground for would-be censors, particularly those who seek to ban books with LGBTQ content. Although school libraries sometimes seem like an entirely different species, it's important to remember that they're libraries, just like any other. This means that they're subject to the same "Library Bill of Rights," as laid out by the American Library Association—namely, they should represent a diversity of voices, including those of LGBTQ teens. The biggest difference, really, is that a school library assumes the extra mantle of serving its school and the school's curricular needs (Reichman, 1993).

SCHOOL ZONE—COLLECTION DEVELOPMENT

The document "Free Access to Libraries for Minors: An Interpretation of the Library Bill of Rights" contains a key directive that forms the basis for how you should approach including LGBTQ materials in your school library collection:

> Librarians and governing bodies should maintain that parents—and only parents—have the right and the responsibility to restrict the access of their children—and only their children—to library resources. Parents who do not want their children to have access to certain library services, materials, or facilities should so advise their children. Librarians and library governing bodies cannot assume the role of parents or the functions of parental authority in the private relationship between parent and child. (ALA, 1974)

The responsibility for shielding children from certain materials belongs to parents and their children, not to you, the librarian. In other words, you should not exclude certain items—such as queer-themed books—simply because a few parents complain. If parents want their children to stay away from LGBTQ books, it is their responsibility to make sure this happens. Your responsibility is to follow your library's collections development policy and to maintain as balanced a collection as possible (Reichman, 1993).

As Henry Reichman observed in *Censorship and Selection: Issues and Answers for Schools*, your best defense against would-be censors is to have a collection development plan in place and ready to go ahead of time—a document that outlines your library's purpose and its relation to the school, i.e., how it supports the school's curriculum and its studies (Reichman, 1993). In schools, collection development plans are generally formulated using input from librarians, school administrators, and district boards. Given that there are a number of opinionated stakeholders involved in this process, many of whom may be pushing an exclusionary agenda, your role as the librarian is to ensure that the plan contains language broad enough for you to maintain a balanced collection. The justification for this is simple: You are in a school, a place of learning where students should be free to explore diverse opinions.

The problem with would-be censors is that they often fail to understand how a school library differs from a classroom, and nervous school librarians allow this confusion to get in the way of maintaining a balanced collection (Whelan, 2006). In a school library, students should have the opportunity to explore a range of diverse opinions and "vast realms of knowledge"; in a classroom, by contrast, the teacher's goal is to impart specific curricular information (Reichman, 1993:22). A school library, in other words, can and should contain LGBTQ materials, whereas a classroom may not need them. Censors often falsely assume that if a school library contains a book, this means that the book will be used for instruction. But while many books in the library are indeed there for curricular reasons, some are there purely for enjoyment. Most school libraries have special budgets to purchase books for students' recreational reading (Whelan, 2006). This fact alone should be all the justification you need in acquiring LGBTQ-themed items. As we've said several times throughout our book, queer and questioning teens are everywhere—as are straight allies—and they deserve to find themselves represented in school library collections.

Two final words of advice about ensuring the presence of LGBTQ books in a school library's collection. To guard against any single person's retaining the sole power to remove a book from the collection, you should ensure that your collection development plan mandates that a committee will make any final decisions regarding the removal of books. This committee should include you, representatives from the faculty and administration, and even district administrators. The final piece of advice is simply this: Don't let fear get in the way of doing your job well. As former American Library Association President Ann Symons told *School Library Journal*, your best strategy is "building the collection you feel you need and dealing [with the controversy] later" (Whelan, 2006:48). Aside from these school-specific tips, advice for building an LGBTQ collection in a school library is the same as the Yellow Light advice offered earlier in this chapter.

SCHOOL ZONE—PROGRAMMING

If you're a school librarian, helping students with their homework probably doesn't leave much time for designing elaborate programs. That said, we can still suggest a few ideas that won't take much of your time to execute and will still get the message across that your library is an open place where students can explore different viewpoints. The best way to do this will be through displays, such as the first series offered in Chapter 12. When you're designing these displays, don't be afraid to use the words "gay" or "LGBTQ" as much as possible. The same goes for when you promote new books in the library. "Make frequent announcements on the school's intercom about any new or interesting books so kids will get used to hearing the word 'gay,'" a school librarian in Kansas told *School Library Journal* (Whelan, 2006:48). Kids use the word "gay" all the time, but often in a negative way. Here's your chance to present LGBTQ themes in a positive, normal light.

SCHOOL ZONE—BOOKTALKING

Just as if you were a public librarian, include an LGBTQ-themed title or two in the mix of books that you present for classes. Refer to the Yellow Light booktalking section for more advice and specific techniques.

SCHOOL ZONE—ATMOSPHERE

To help queer and questioning students feel more at home in your library—and raise the awareness level of all other students—post bibliographies of your library's LGBTQ titles, as well as queer YA titles available at the nearby public library. Also, you might want to extend a hand to your school's gay-straight alliance, if it has one, and make your library available as a meeting space for this group, and in the interest of fairness, you should extend this invitation to all other extracurricular clubs. If your school lacks a GSA, perhaps you might want to be the faculty sponsor who helps get one off the ground. As you would in a public library, respect teens' privacy and never make any assumptions about who they are. You also want to send the message that your library is a safe space in which disrespectful language, including homophobic comments, is not tolerated. Be aware, too, that in a school you have added responsibilities: As noted in Chapter 3, your school can be held liable if you or other faculty members fail to intervene when a studier is being bullied on the basis of actual or perceived sexual orientation (Cianciotto and Cahill, 2003).

How Fast Can You Go in Your Community or School?		
	Suggested Programs in Chapter 12	**Suggested Booktalks in Chapter 11**
Red Light	▼ Lovely in Lavender ▼ Bet You Didn't Know... ▼ Straight Allies Display ▼ Did You Know They Were Gay? ▼ "We're Here, We're Queer, We're Banned Books!" Display	▼ *Hard Love*, by Ellen Wittlinger ▼ *Donorboy*, by Brendan Halprin
Yellow Light	▼ Pride Month Display ▼ National Coming Out Day Display ▼ Start Your Own LGBTQ Book Discussion Group ▼ Create Your Own Queer Book Soundtrack ▼ Create Your Own Queer Library Zine ▼ Create Your Own Queer Graphic Novel ▼ Queer TV Night / Coffee House at Your Library ▼ Create Your Own LGBTQ Web Page	▼ *My Heartbeat*, by Garret Freymann-Weyr ▼ *Orphea Proud*, by Sharon Dennis Wyeth
Green Light	▼ Build a Library Gay-Straight Alliance ▼ Queer Eye for the Straight Guy...or Librarian ▼ Create Your Own Coming Out Podcast ▼ Check Out the Circulating Queer ▼ Host Your Own Anti-Prom	▼ *Leave Myself Behind*, by Bart Yates ▼ *Boy Meets Boy*, by David Levithan
School Zone	▼ Bet You Didn't Know... ▼ Straight Allies Display ▼ Did You Know They Were Gay? ▼ "We're Here, We're Queer, We're Banned Books!" Display ▼ Pride Month Display ▼ National Coming Out Day Display	▼ *Hard Love*, by Ellen Wittlinger ▼ *My Heartbeat*, by Garret Freymann-Weyr

11 RECOMMENDED LGBTQ MATERIALS AND PROGRAMS

9 AN ESSENTIAL CORE COLLECTION OF LGBTQ FICTION, NONFICTION, AND NON-PRINT ITEMS

INTRODUCTION

In theory, building a queer YA collection is as simple as buying all of the roughly 200 novels with LGBTQ characters published since 1969. But this would be impractical due to obvious constraints, such as space and budget—not to mention the fact that many older titles are out of print, while others are simply not worth owning. Plus, novels are only part of the picture. This is the true value of this chapter. There are certain queer-themed materials that any YA collection worth its salt should include, and to that end, this chapter offers you an annotated, alphabetical bibliography of fifty items—fiction, nonfiction, graphic novels, periodicals, films, and television programs on DVD—that constitute the ideal queer YA core collection. Each item is discussed at length, showing you what's important about it, where it falls within the larger canon, and whether or not an author has written sequels. In many cases, you will find what other librarians, reviewers, teens, and authors have said about the title. For details such as the publisher's name and date, please refer to the Bibliography at the end of the book.

First, a word about how these materials were selected. Since the overall number of LGBTQ titles published for YA audiences is modest, all could easily be included, but the goal was not to provide a comprehensive catalog. Indeed, others have already done so. If you are interested in such a study, see Michael Cart and Christine Jenkins' *The Heart Has Its Reasons*, which is sure to become the definitive critical study of queer teen lit. Published in 2006, it supplies an annotated bibliography of every queer-themed YA novel published between 1969 and 2004: all 187 of them (Cart and Jenkins, 2006). Other good annotated bibliographies, which have the benefit of including nonfiction items and adult books, are Frances Ann Day's *Lesbian and Gay Voices*, published in 2000, and the Gay, Lesbian and Straight Education Network's list of books suitable for school settings, available online at www.glsen.org/cgi-bin/iowa/educator/booklink/index. html.

The criteria for selecting the following items were: (1) strong personal opinions that any collection should have these items; (2) validation of these opinions by other librarians, reviewers, and, most important, teens;

and (3) these items are still in print and teens are actively reading them *now*. As to this last point, focusing on newer materials runs the risk that this core collection may soon grow outdated. In a sense, there could be no better sign that queer YA lit has matured than if today's "best" materials soon seem quaint. That said, these recommended books, films, etc., are all good enough to stand the test of time.

One final note about the annotation system. In this chapter you'll notice that the name of each item is followed by symbols that help you understand, in one glance, its queer content; these pictures are our "Queer-O-Meter" ratings. Similar to visual aids found in restaurant guidebooks, the Queer-O-Meter quickly conveys the type of LGBTQ themes along three dimensions: a queer character's sexual identity; whether or not this character is the protagonist or a secondary character (such as a relative or best friend); and the amount of sexual content. Why care about whether or not the queer character takes the lead role? For too long, queer characters have played second fiddle. As noted in Chapter 6, the first-person voice helps readers identify more closely with a character—something that queer and questioning teens especially crave. Why care about the amount of sex in a book? Many people don't, actually, but some communities care very much. Sexual content is famously difficult to rate, but the scale simplifies it into three categories: "None to Mild," which means there's no sexual content or that any such content is restricted to a kiss or two; "Medium," which means there's a fair bit of kissing, maybe the suggestion of more; and "Strong," which includes everything beyond kissing. The sexual content may be queer or heterosexual; the ratings don't discriminate between the two.

AN ANNOTATED BIBLIOGRAPHY OF FIFTY BOOKS AND OTHER MATERIALS

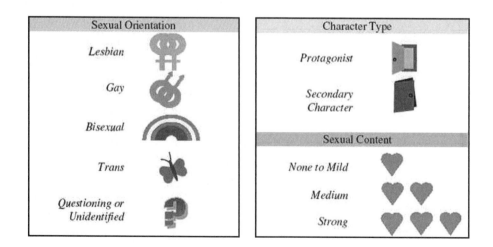

ABSOLUTELY, POSITIVELY NOT . . ., BY DAVID LAROCHELLE

In this light-hearted comedy of a teen novel, Minnesotan Steven square dances with his mother, hides a stash of International Male catalogs under his bed, and lusts over his gym teacher, but remains convinced that there is no way he could possibly ever be gay. Readers know he's completely mistaken in this conviction, of course, and they will laugh their way through his steadfastly conscientious attempts at disproving their assumptions: He sits with the jocks, dodges his best friend Rachel's hints about his sexuality, steals an outdated book from the library on deviant male sexual behavior (the best part is that the librarian lets him get away with it!), and makes a hilarious attempt at purchasing a *Playboy* magazine. When he finally comes clean and admits that he's gay, his best friend blabs the news to the world, including her parents, and immediately urges him to start the school's first gay-straight alliance (GSA). Amidst all the hilarity, though, there remains Steven's discomfort with saying the words "I am gay," and his uncertainty at becoming the school's first token gay guy, much less starting a GSA. What LaRochelle's novel shows librarians—as friends, family members, and mentors of LGBTQ people—is that even though we may be more than ready to accept someone's sexuality, the person in question, like Steven, may not yet be comfortable with it. Nevertheless, *Absolutely, Positively Not . . .* is mostly a fun, easy-to-read coming out story perfect for younger readers, aged twelve to fifteen.

THE ADVOCATE

The Advocate bills itself as "the national gay & lesbian newsmagazine," but truthfully it covers news and viewpoints from all corners of the queer landscape. Published on a biweekly basis, this slender periodical is essentially the all-queer version of mainstream newsmagazines such as *Time* and *Newsweek.* Though aimed at an adult audience, its articles are written in an easy style, complemented by plenty of sidebars, photos, and other fun doodads that make it teen-friendly. Also, one of the magazine's regular departments is "Generation Q," which includes news from high schools and colleges nationwide, as well as profiles of queer teens and twenty-somethings. (There's also a companion Web site, www.advocate.com/genq.) This periodical's teen-friendliness quotient is further boosted by the fact that, although *The Advocate* is technically a "news" magazine, the bulk of its coverage focuses on popular culture that teens avidly follow. And, unlike other adult queer periodicals that profile pop culture, *The Advocate*'s sexual content is kept to a bare minimum—no pun intended—so it can be readily recommended that your YA room subscribe to it. It would be great to include *YGA* (Young Gay America), a Canadian periodical dedicated exclusively to queer teens, alongside *The Advocate*, but as of this writing, *YGA* is on a publishing hiatus.

AM I BLUE? COMING OUT FROM THE SILENCE, ED. BY MARION DANE BAUER

This groundbreaking short story collection from 1994 features sixteen original LGBTQ-themed works from acclaimed authors including Lois Lowry, Bruce Coville, Francesca Lia Block, William Sleator, Jane Yolen, M. E. Kerr, Gregory Maguire, and others. Its mostly quietly paced stories focus on LGBTQ youth forming an identity: sometimes by seeing other queer people, sometimes through conversations with friends, sometimes in brief romantic interludes with friends, boyfriends, or girlfriends. Primarily, the stories are about gay boys and lesbian girls, though trans characters populate the background of Francesca Lia Block's fiery "Winnie and Tommy" story, about a boyfriend and girlfriend who travel to San Francisco for a weekend. Tommy remarks, "The most beautiful people are the ones that don't look like one race or even one sex." Jane Yolen's lesbian fantasy "Blood Sister" remains one of the few of its kind. Meanwhile, readers breathe a sigh of relief when they discover that seventeen-year-old David, in James Cross Gilbin's subtly erotic "Three Mondays in July," finds a mentor—not a lover—in a thirty-eight-year-old man he spies skinny-dipping on the beach.

Perhaps the collection's most memorable story is its title piece, "Am I Blue?" by Bruce Coville, in a which a young male victim of homophobia wishes he had a secret power that would allow him to tell whether or not a person was gay: the ultimate form of gaydar. Then, blam!, along comes a fairy godfather named Melvin, dressed in loafers and chinos, who gives him three wishes. As soon as the main character—whose name we never learn—gets his wish granted, he begins to see that everyone who has even the smallest homosexual tendencies becomes colored by various shades of blue: Some are dark vivid blue, others are paler. What Coville's story shows is that people's sexualities are as varied as the color of their skins, and that we should think twice before deciding who is queer, who isn't, who's right, and who's wrong. The stories in *Am I Blue?*, despite their age, remain timeless—and though they lack some of the in-your-face impact common in more recent LGBTQ YA lit, kids still read them.

ANNIE ON MY MIND, BY NANCY GARDEN

In this groundbreaking, now classic 1982 novel by Nancy Garden, two teenage girls, Liza and Annie, meet at the Metropolitan Museum of Art in New York City and fall in love. And nothing irrevocably terrible happens. No dogs die. No queer characters are killed in car crashes. Instead, the two girls fall in love and have a magical time together. But Garden's book is not without drama. Liza and Annie hook up one afternoon while cat-sitting for a pair of teachers—who also happen to be lesbians—and get caught when another teacher unexpectedly looks in on the house. In the rocky aftermath of this scene, the lesbian teachers are dismissed from school, and Liza faces a homophobic-tinged disciplinary hearing. Fortunately, this drama doesn't diminish the fact that the heart of this novel is a love story—and it ends happily. Indeed, *Annie on My Mind* blazed a path for writers such as Francesca Lia Block, David Levithan, and Alex Sanchez to pen happy queer love stories. To contemporary eyes, Garden's novel reads somewhat stiffly in comparison to newer LGBTQ teen lit, and indeed kids are more interested in newer books such as *Keeping You a Secret*, *Kissing Kate*, *Geography Club*, and *Boy Meets Boy*. That said, *Annie on My Mind* still resonates and deserves a place in a well-rounded collection.

BEAUTIFUL THING, DIRECTED BY HETTIE MACDONALD

Set against the backdrop of a grim public housing project populated by typical English eccentrics, this 1995 film from Britain unexpectedly explodes with life and optimism. Its soundtrack, the sunny California music of Mama Cass, has a lot to do with this, but it's the characters' resilience that truly makes the film shine. *Beautiful Thing* is partly a coming-of-age story, partly a coming out tale, but it's mainly all romance. Its lead character, high school student Jamie, awakens to the fact that he's gay—and in love with his next door neighbor, the jocky, soccer-playing Ste. Jamie handles his personal realization with aplomb, reading gay magazines and seeking the community of a nearby gay bar, and he builds up the courage to ask if Ste feels the same way. Happily, Ste does, but he fears that coming out would only aggravate matters with his abusive father and bullying older brother. The boys' romance is sweetly depicted but the film's setting has just enough grittiness, not to mention complicated dynamics between Jamie and his fierce single-parent mother, Sandra, to keep it real. The film's ending? No need to spoil it, but suffice to say the ending expresses exactly what Mama Cass sings: "It's Getting Better." This film is rated R, but this seems undeserved. There are a few curse words, to be sure, but the only flash of nudity lasts less than a second and is confined to Ste's bare buttocks: Hence the reason why *Beautiful Thing* has only one heart in its Queer-O-Meter rating and why it is highly recommended for your YA collection.

BEND, DON'T SHATTER: POETS ON THE BEGINNING OF DESIRE, ED. BY T. COLE RACHEL AND RITA D. COSTELLO

Love, crushes, desire, obsession, withheld affections, and unrequited queer longings are all described in this excellent volume of LGBTQ poems, written mostly by poets whose names you may not recognize. The poems' subjects range from a young queer cowboy who refuses to yield to gay stereotyping, to a girl who overhears the conversations of the people around her as they observe her and her girlfriend interact. The language ranges from mild to strong, and while there is some sexual content it is always eloquently and thoughtfully written. For this reason, *Bend, Don't Shatter* is suited for older teens, but mature tweens will be savvy enough to grasp the poems' meanings and enjoy them. This volume gives equal treatment to both gay and lesbian desires, and while bisexual and transgender voices figure less prominently, this collection—one of the few of its kind—helps fill most LGBTQ gaps in YA poetry collections.

THE BERMUDEZ TRIANGLE, BY MAUREEN JOHNSON

Three childhood best friends, Nina, Avery, and Mel, spend their first summer apart in what proves to be the most surprising reinterpretation of the popular teen girl novel since *The Sisterhood of the Traveling Pants*. Nina leaves to attend a summer program near Stanford, leaving Avery and Mel on their own, temporarily breaking their triangle of friendship. And triangle is definitely the operative word. Nina, Avery, and Mel chant to their triangle power, meaning the power of the three girls' friendship. Tellingly, the triangle metaphor resurfaces in the shape of an upside-down pink triangle, which is a symbol of the queer rights movement. Unbeknownst to Nina, Avery, and Mel hook up and begin to explore a new, romantic dimension of their relationship. When Nina returns, Avery and Mel are secretive about their summer adventure, and only when Nina catches them making out in a dressing room do they come clean. Avery freaks out and disappears from the relationship altogether. Mel, meanwhile, comes to terms with being a lesbian and spends much of the novel pining for Avery, until Nina finally begins to work on patching the friends' triangle back together. Johnson's novel is not only fun, it's full of genuine insight into the exploratory nature of teen sexuality. And sadly, at least in Avery's case, the book is also full of the realistic pain that often comes during the aftermath of such explorations. Sometimes people realize they have correctly self-identified, and other times they're wrong. In Avery's case, she's wrong. It's this realism and Johnson's talent for creating fully believable characters that ensures any teen girl, queer or straight, will enjoy reading *The Bermudez Triangle*.

BOY MEETS BOY, BY DAVID LEVITHAN

In a gaytopian universe where boys come out of the closet in kindergarten and the high school's star quarterback doubles as the cross-dressing homecoming queen, love at first sight takes on an entirely new meaning when cerebral sophomore Paul falls head over heels for the ethereally green-eyed Noah. Their feelings are mutual, and the two form a romantically intellectual relationship that is magical and unique enough to stand beside even the most star-crossed of YA lovers. But their romance is threatened by a series of misunderstandings, and Paul finds he must devise a scheme swoon-worthy enough to win his true love back. Levithan's focused sense of energy and whimsy—similar to early Francesca Lia Block—mixes with likeable, well-rounded characters to make a fantastic, well-written novel that prophesizes a hate-free world where two teenaged boys can meet and fall in love without fear of persecution. Critics hailed *Boy Meets Boy* as the most important gay teen book since *Annie on My Mind* and a revolution in teen lit. Levithan's storytelling mastery bridges the gap between "traditional" love stories and the "gay" love story. *Boy Meets Boy* is the unique kind of title you can give a teen and know that it will be enjoyed, regardless of a reader's sexual orientation. The book's title suggests it's an out-and-out gay love story, but Levithan's writing transcends whatever prejudices readers may have when it comes to the multifaceted nature of love, surpassing expectations and assumptions about sexuality. The love story in *Boy Meets Boy* is a universal tale—and that's why it works.

Although it's a drastically different book and should not be construed as a sequel, Levithan's novel *Wide Awake*, released in 2006, may resonate with some readers who enjoyed the fantastical elements of *Boy Meets Boy*. The newer book imagines a not-too-distant future in which a gay Jewish man, Duncan, is elected president of the United States—and the nation's "First Partner" is a multiracial guy named Jimmy. *Wide Awake* is a fairy-tale of sorts, but one that's not too far outside the realm of possibility. Speaking at the American Library Association's June 2006 conference,

Levithan said that he wrote *Wide Awake* as a "protest song" against what he described as a rising tide of intolerance in this country—intolerance for people of other religions and sexual orientations.

BUFFY THE VAMPIRE SLAYER

Every teenager can sympathize with feeling alienated from the other kids at school. Even "popular" kids, who outwardly look like they're part of the in crowd, inwardly feel that they're different. Well, it turns out that California Valley girl Buffy Summers is different. Really different. She's the latest incarnation of a spirit as old as time: the Vampire Slayer, whose sacred duty is to battle the undead every night, despite the fact that all Buffy wants is to go shopping. For seven television seasons, beginning in 1997, Buffy and her best friends Willow and Xander slay all manner of evil demons as well as their own personal ones. To this end, during season four Willow comes to realize that not only is she a gifted witch, she's also a lesbian. Season five, the queerest of them all, sees Willow romantically and happily involved with another witch named Tara. Buffy and Xander could care less about who Willow loves; indeed, they can sympathize with feeling like love is sometimes taboo. Xander falls head over heels for a former man-hating demon, while Buffy's soulmate turns out to be a vampire named Angel.

In real life, queer teens probably don't battle bloodsucking corpses on a nightly basis, but they certainly share Buffy's feelings of alienation and no doubt recognize her attempts to resist an innate part of herself—in Buffy's case, being the Slayer, in the case of queer teens, their sexual orientation. Obviously, queer teens can also sympathize with Willow. Although *Buffy* concluded its initial run in 2003, it continues to air in syndication, and the full series is available on DVD. It's popular with all teens, not just Goths and fantasy fans, and it even appeals to adults. This universal appeal is simple. Like the best science fiction, the warped and fanciful extremes of Buffy's world help us to explore the moral dimensions of our own.

CLAY'S WAY, BY BLAIR MASTBAUM

Hawaiian skater-punk Sam longs to wrap his arms around closeted, cool surfer dude Clay. All it takes is one meeting for Clay to fall for Sam, but when Sam discovers Clay has a girl on the side, his jealousy gets in the way. What began as a sweetly innocent romance quickly turns into a personality clash and tug of war. Sam is forced to recognize the limits of his romantic expectations and his crushingly nihilistic personality. His anger and frustration explode as he deals with his disinterested parents and romantic disappointment, and he often copes by resorting to self-mutilation. Twenty-something first-time novelist Blair Mastbaum perfectly blends the double-edged pleasure and pain of first love, the unpredictable angst of youth, and the skater surfer culture, setting it against the backdrop of the ethnically diverse Hawaiian landscape. The cover features a full-color photograph of a hot shirtless guy, guaranteeing it will appeal, at the very least, to gay boys and straight girls. But its skater subculture topic and blatantly demonstrative teen angst broaden its appeal to other audiences.

DANGEROUS ANGELS: THE WEETZIE BAT BOOKS, BY FRANCESCA LIA BLOCK

Set in a hazy, whirlwind, fairytale-like Los Angeles, where plastic kitsch is cool and convertibles and pink sunglasses reign, nouveau punk girl Weetzie Bat meets Dirk, the best-looking guy in school with a "shoe-polish-black" Mohawk. They become friends, and during what seems to be a datelike jaunt to San Francisco, Dirk outs himself to Weetzie, flatly informing her that he's gay. Weetzie doesn't bat an eyelash when she says "It doesn't matter one bit, honey-honey," and then the two go off duck-hunting together. Ducks are what Weetzie calls boys. She calls her dream guy Secret Agent Lover Man. Sure enough, in this magical setting where anything is possible, Weetzie and Dirk meet the guys of their dreams: Weetize meets a guy in a trench coat who's actually named My Secret Agent Lover Man, and Dirk meets a guy who's named Duck. The four move in together and live happily ever after.

What sets Block's first novel, *Weetzie Bat*, apart from all the rest in the *Dangerous Angels* series isn't just her explosively lush setting or her wild, energetic style, but the fact that she essentially wrote the first teen novel in which two gay boys not only fall in love, they live happily ever after—all packed into less than 100 pages. Moreover, Weetzie's immediate acceptance of Dirk's sexuality stands as a benchmark in teen literature that friends can be okay with friends who are gay—that it is possible to come out of the closet with happy results. As a novel, *Weetzie Bat*'s magical realism gives queer teen readers hope that a place like Weetzie and Dirk's Los Angeles does exist, or will exist, and that's what makes this 1989 book still one of the most important queer teen novels out there.

For more queer adventures in magical Los Angeles, check out other books in the *Dangerous Angels* series. *Missing Angel Juan* features young adult literature's first acknowledged trans secondary character. *Baby Be-Bop*, meanwhile, follows Dirk's pre-Weetzie life: how he lived with his grandmother and coped with being gay. One particular passage in this thorny book describes how Dirk hardens against the homophobic world as he stares into the mirror and shaves his hair into a Mohawk; indeed, *Baby Be-Bop*'s plot focuses on Dirk, who is attacked by a gang of angry punk thugs who beat him to a pulp. Dirk barely makes it home, and when he does, he passes out into a near-coma in which he discovers the life his parents once led.

DARE, TRUTH OR PROMISE, BY PAULA BOOCK

Steadfast fencer Willa first meets feisty actress Louie while making coleslaw at a local burger joint. Sparks fly when their eyes meet, and before long the two are tossed headfirst into the throes of love. Their sweetly portrayed love scenes beam with genuine sexual chemistry, and Boock packs every chapter with sharply outlined scenes that are not only exciting to read, but whose settings capture the mood of whatever seems to be going on between the two girls in love. Louie's parents come between the girls, and strangely enough, Louie, normally headstrong and outspoken, seems to obey their orders that she avoid Willa. A car wreck finally shakes her into reality, and unlike in past queer YA lit, the crash actually brings the two girls back together. The story concludes with Willa and Louie at a restaurant, in love, and joking how they wished they had enough money to afford a hotel room together for the night. Perhaps that's what makes this novel succeed so well!—that these two strong, unique heroines can crack such sexually loaded jokes so comfortably, yet so knowingly and wisely de-stigmatizing their relationship and inspiring hope that one day two girls such as Louie and Willa can fall in love and stay together. Heck, even their priest says it's okay. Though getting on in years, and still confined to hardcover, this New Zealand import continues to entertain U.S. teen audiences—who may not even need to use its helpful glossary of Kiwi slang.

DELIVER US FROM EVIE, BY M. E. KERR

On a farm in rural Missouri, sixteen-year-old Parr faces the fact that the rumors about his sister, Evie, being a lesbian are true. When Evie begins taking off on long weekend excursions with the daughter of the town's banker, Parr begins to worry that she'll abandon the family, leaving him to take care of the farm and his parents, scuttling his own lifelong dream to leave the farm and attend college. In a harebrained attempt to pair Evie with the family's lughead farmhand, Cord, Parr agrees to hang a sign from the town's silo decreeing that Evie is a lesbian. Kerr's lively writing style is at times humorous but always cuts straight to the chase. Young lesbians will commend Evie's strength of character in her refusals to change her appearance, her interests, and her romantic inclinations. At the same time, all readers can empathize with Parr's fear that he may be trapped in the farming life unless he somehow manages to convince Evie to stay home—and with his mounting guilt at publicly betraying her trust. First published in 1994, *Deliver Us from Evie* was revolutionary in its direct portrayal of Evie as a lesbian unafraid and unwavering in who she is (although in the end, her relationship with Patsy is relegated to secretive holiday weekends). The book was also notable for its frank portrayal of how the town reacts to a lesbian in its midst: Parr and Cord, for instance, wonder aloud "what do two girls do together?" at the book's midpoint. *Deliver Us from Evie* is no longer the most popular LGBTQ title with teen readers, but teens living in more conservative, rural communities no doubt recognize themselves in this easy-to-read, eye-opening story about a young man who must come to terms not just with his sister's sexuality, but with his own place in the world.

EERIE QUEERIE SERIES, BY SHURI SHIOZU

Graphic novels today are more than just superhero adventures; they're realistic, nuanced stories that really are novels in graphic form. Manga, a Japanese strain of graphic novels that leads the market in the United States, contains many queer characters and queer subgenres—the *Eerie Queerie* series falls into the *shonen-ai*, or "boy's love," subgenre. In a humorous manner, *Eerie Queerie* follows the lives of Mitsuo, a beautiful male high school theater student, and Hasunama, a former member of the school's theater club who has a crush on Mitsuo, as the pair explore the supernatural world of ghosts, hauntings, and possessions. In a typical plotline from the series' second volume, Mitsuo is possessed by a ghost in the middle of a play rehearsal and Hasunama must save his friend and the theater. This plot may seem thin, but the meat of this Manga lies in Hasunama's devoutly clandestine pursuit of Mituso—and in Mituso's completely clueless responses to his advances. Mituso still doesn't get it when Hasunama just magically appears in Mitsuo's bed one night—will Hasunama ever get his man? Stay tuned to find out. Popular with all Manga fans, this series is now up to four volumes, and adds breadth to any YA collection, LGBTQ or otherwise.

EMPRESS OF THE WORLD, BY SARA RYAN

Nic, short for Nicola, Lancaster, doesn't know what to expect when she enrolls at the Siegel Institute Summer Program for Gifted Youth, aside from the fact that the other teens there will be geniuses and there will probably be a lot of competition among them. What she doesn't know—since she usually likes guys—is that she'll fall in love with a girl named Battle who's also in the program. It takes a while for the relationship to get going, and what's amusing is that Nic and Battle's other friends at the program think they're a couple before the two girls actually get together. Following in the footsteps of M. E. Kerr's *"Hello," I Lied*, Ryan has penned one of the small handful of teen titles with a bisexual protagonist. The first half of the book follows Nic as she tangles with liking both boys and girls. At the book's halfway point, the two girls hook up and strike a fairly physical relationship, making it to first, second, and third bases. Despite some later dramatics—Battle appears to be hooking up with Isaac, another guy in their circle of friends—the book ends with the two girls walking away hand-in-hand. Ryan's book balances just the right amount of drama with romance such that teen girls of all sexual orientations enjoy it.

FROM THE NOTEBOOKS OF MELANIN SUN, BY JACQUELINE WOODSON

Author Jacqueline Woodson has never shied away from homosexuality, especially in *The House You Pass on the Way*, but her novel *From the Notebooks of Melanin Sun* thrusts a truckload of LGBTQ issues into the forefront. Melanin Sun, an almost-fourteen-year-old African American boy living in Brooklyn, New York, learns that his mother has a girlfriend, who is white. Not only must Melanin Sun come to terms with the fact that his mother is a lesbian, but he also must accept her girlfriend, Kristin, into his own circle of primarily African American friends and family members. Melanin's mom takes him to the beach to reveal her secret, and when the words are uttered, Melanin flashes back to a book he read once about a white boy whose dad took him out in a boat on the lake to come out of the closet—A. M. Holmes's celebrated adult novel, *Jack*. Melanin's reaction to his mom's news is rough; he begs her not to be a "dyke" and refuses to talk to her on the ride home. But he starts to see things differently when a nosy member of the community reports that his mom may be unfit—as a lesbian—to take care of him. And when Kristin takes him to the beach for a talk, Melanin begins to feel "something melting out of him," opening the door for Kristin to come into his heart and his life. Woodson's novel is well-written and jam-packed with important themes about race, sexuality, acceptance, prejudice, hatred, and love. It proposes that differences can be overcome if only people would sit and talk to one another, and that conversations can eliminate hatred and fear and replace them with enlightenment. *From the Notebooks of Melanin Sun* won the Coretta Scott King Honor Book award, and in 2006 Woodson received YALSA's coveted Margaret A. Edwards Award. Woodson must keep these kinds of novels coming!

THE FULL SPECTRUM: A NEW GENERATION OF WRITING ABOUT GAY, LESBIAN, BISEXUAL, TRANSGENDER, QUESTIONING, AND OTHER IDENTITIES, ED. BY DAVID LEVITHAN AND BILLY MERRELL

When teens approach the information desk inquiring about real stories about coming out and coming to terms with anything remotely LGBTQ, this is the book you should give them. Included are forty stories of coming out, coping, falling in and out of love, fighting homophobia, celebrating, and more. All the stories are written by new, previously unpublished young authors, many of them teens. Editors' notes tell us that each of the submissions was received anonymously through a Web site called Queerthology.com, and that proceeds from the book's sale go to support the Gay, Lesbian and Straight Education Network. There are stories about girls falling for girls, boys falling for boys, boys and girls feeling uncomfortable in their own skins, victims of abuse at the hands of their boyfriends, girlfriends, friends, and parents. Also of note is the fact that, to date, this is the most solid contribution of trans writings to the world of young adult literature. And, unlike similar works before it, many of *The Full Spectrum*'s pieces search for a balance between homosexuality and religion. Each of the stories, poems, memories, and photographs in this book represent a unique facet of the LGBTQ experience as it stands today—its ups, downs, celebrations, traumas, dreams, and realities.

GEOGRAPHY CLUB, BY BRENT HARTINGER

Closeted junior Russel Middlebrook discovers that his online gay chat buddy is none other than the uber-hot high school baseball star, Kevin Land. After several clandestine meetings in a nearby park, the two boys—along with Russel's bisexual best friend, Min, and her girlfriend, Therese—form an after-school club for queer students. So that its purpose will be safe from prying straight eyes, they name their group "Geography Club," which they figure will repel all normal teens. Problems arise, of course, when a straight girl expresses interest in joining an actual geography club. Humorous, in-your-face, with just enough sexuality, Hartinger's first novel features well-rounded, realistic characters involved in believable enough scenarios to inspire many teenagers to form their own "geography" clubs at school—and it's no surprise that *Geography Club* is often the first book that GSAs read together. Much of this book's merit stems from its inclusiveness. It depicts a broad cross-section of sexual orientations. Also important, queer characters become empowered enough to unite with straight students and form a gay-straight alliance, discovering that they're not alone, even in the straight world, and that they can create their own niche. The book's tremendous appeal is surprising. Simply everyone reads it, queer or straight.

With its titillating cover, high dramatics, and steamy romance triangles, *Order of the Poison Oak* might score big with teens hankering for a sequel to *Geography Club*. It focuses on Russel, who hopes to escape his identity as the token gay guy by spending the summer as a counselor in a camp for burn victims. Hartinger is now working on a third book, making this series a trilogy, called *Split Screen: Attack of the Soul-Sucking Brain Zombies/Bride of the Soul-Sucking Brain Zombies*. It's due out in early 2007.

GINGERBREAD, BY RACHEL COHN

Headstrong go-getter Cyd Charisse got pretty messed up in boarding school. Not only did she get caught selling drugs for her sleazoid boyfriend, Justin, she aborted his child—which, of course, her parents don't know. But when Cyd returns home and violates curfew one too many times while hanging out with her new surfer-punk boyfriend, Shrimp, her parents feel they have no choice but to send her to New York City to stay with her bio-dad, Frank, whom she hasn't seen since she was five. Just before Cyd leaves, Shrimp dumps her after they fight about some minor mutual indiscretions. In New York, Cyd finds bio-dad Frank to be a disappointment—and he does nothing to curb her hell-raising ways. But the city's twenty-four-hour energy, and working at her gay half-brother's Greenwich Village coffee shop, help distract Cyd from thinking about Shrimp and worrying about Justin. Named an ALA Best Book for Young Adults as well as a Quick Pick in 2003, *Gingerbread* grabs teens' attention from the first page and doesn't let up. Teens identify with Cyd's daring curiosity, her eagerness to reinvent herself, and her sometimes flawed, always electric personality. Although Cyd comes across like a hellion, underneath her tough surface she really isn't. Though her gay brother is only a minor character, Cyd's unquestioning acceptance of his relationship with his partner shows that younger people are more accepting of differences than we think they are.

Shrimp, the sequel to *Gingerbread*, finds Cyd Charisse back in San Francisco seeking the lowdown on her ex-boyfriend Shrimp. Along the way she meets tough bisexual Helen, whose conservative family runs an Asian restaurant beneath their apartment. With Helen's help, Cyd—now self-christened CC—tries to win back Shrimp's affection. She also learns that Autumn, the object of Shrimp's erstwhile indiscretion, is really a lesbian and has a crush on Helen. Part romance, part road trip to self-discovery, and despite its 272-page length, *Shrimp* is almost more popular than *Gingerbread*. Cohn's writing is spot-on, capturing its hip, streetwise heroine's whiplash sarcasm and bewitching sense of humor. *Shrimp* will definitely grab attention and amaze teen readers of all ages. *Cupcake*, the third installment, finds Cyd Charisse back in New York City, sharing an apartment with her gay brother and looking after Max, a grouchy old gay man who lives next door. If every teenager who read Cohn's trilogy would embrace diversity and change as easily as Cyd Charisse, the world would definitely be a better place.

GLBTQ: THE SURVIVAL GUIDE FOR QUEER AND QUESTIONING TEENS, BY KELLY HUEGEL

Finally, the queer YA manual you've been waiting for: everything you wanted to know about how to come out, how to deal with homophobia, whom to contact for help, how to date, how to make decisions about sex and your sexuality, how to stay healthy, and an entire chapter devoted to trans teens. Huegel's manual is concise and full of practical, real-world advice. We especially like the section on homophobia, which gives advice on how to respond to a homophobic joke or when someone says, "But you don't look gay." Huegel also addresses what to do when homophobia becomes full-fledged harassment. She lists organizations that can help and other informational resources. Her advice for teens ranges from planning when and how to come out to your parents, to how to respond to their reactions. Plus, there's a section on how to form a gay-straight alliance at school; a section on dating, which helps answer the question of who pays on a gay date; and a nondidactic section on practicing safe sex, for when teens feel that they are ready for it. The trans section features psychological definitions of transgender, intersexed, and crossdressing; it also offers a list of questions that teens can ponder if they feel that they may be trans; it describes the transitioning process and talks about how to change your name; and it supplies a list of organizations where teens can seek help or advice from experts on gender-related issues. Huegel's book covers all the LGBTQ bases, and the book's catchy cover, easy-to-follow language, boldface print, text boxes, sidebars, and conversational tone will make it a hit not just with your queer and questioning audience, but with straight teens who want to know more about their queer friends, family, and acquaintances. *GLBTQ* is also a great resource for librarians to learn about what goes on behind the faces of queer teens and how we can give them the help and encouragement they need.

HARD LOVE, BY ELLEN WITTLINGER

John, a sixteen-year-old loner, blames his sour personality on his parents' divorce—and their apparent desire to have nothing to do with him. John's father can barely sustain a conversation with him, and his mother recoils in horror whenever he happens to come into contact with her. Plus, since he's always en route to visit one parent or the other, John never gets a chance to meet new friends—much less friends who share his love of zines. Whenever he visits his dad in Boston, John drops off copies of his own zine, *Bananafish*, at Tower Records and checks out the others left on the magazine racks there: particularly *Escape Velocity*, his favorite, written by someone named Marisol. John vows to meet the mysterious Marisol and stakes out Tower Records every day until she arrives. Already in love with her zine, John falls head over heels in love with Marisol at first sight. With so much in common—dysfunctional families, separated parents, and zines—John can't help it, even though Marisol says right away that she's a lesbian. Engaging, existential, and poignant, *Hard Love* cuts straight to the quick with raw emotion. Wittlinger's characters wobble on the brink of adulthood, eager to shed their old skins in search of a world beyond the sheltered one created by their parents—a world where they can be accepted as themselves. And for John, if he can find someone with whom to share that discovery—even if she's not interested in him romantically—that makes it all the more exciting. A perennial favorite among teens and teachers, *Hard Love* was a 2000 Printz Honor Book. Wittlinger creates a balanced love story from John's search for acceptance and romance: a romance that cannot be consummated. This tension drives the book, keeping teens hooked while persuading them to think about love in relationship to sexual orientation.

HEART ON MY SLEEVE, BY ELLEN WITTLINGER

Romantic sparks fly when soon-to-be-senior Chloe meets Julian on a summer college visit. After spending a romantic weekend together, the two vow to stay in touch throughout the following school year until they meet again to start their freshman year of college. Wittlinger relates their sometimes flaky, sometimes funny, always engaging correspondence through e-mail, postcards, instant messaging, and letters. The result is a well-conceived web of communication with excellent characterization featuring Chloe, Julian, and their friends and families. But Wittlinger's novel isn't without drama that has real depth to it. Just when readers think Chloe's hunky-dory world is all roses, a single e-mail or three seconds of IM-ing can change everything, as when Chloe's sister, Genevieve, comes out as a lesbian and forces her to come to terms with it. Wittlinger's characters are always on the threshold of change, whether they're moving to another state or coming out of the closet. Wittlinger uproots characters from their tiny, insular worlds and plunges them into completely new environments, allowing them to gain perspective on their place in the world. Chloe has always lived in a world that's perfect—perfect friends, perfect parents, perfect boyfriend—but when she meets Julian, she catches a glimpse of a life that is foreign to her. Suddenly she finds herself eager to shed her skin and reinvent herself. Her sister's coming out plays a large role in her new expanded worldview, and Chloe comes to realize that things aren't always what they seem. Given its perspective, this book has crossover appeal to the straight friends and family of queer teens.

THE HOOKUP ARTIST, BY TUCKER SHAW

On the heels of Brian Sloan's post-gay comedy *A Really Nice Prom Mess*, Tucker Shaw takes the baton with his latest novel, a queer take on the matchmaker love story. Lucas, the school's friendly, gay matchmaker has a habit of finding dates for all of his best girl friends, but usually winds up empty-handed when it comes to finding a guy for himself. When Lucas and his best friend, Cate, lay eyes on Derek, the hot new guy in town, Lucas vows to set Cate up with him. But Derek seems to be making more passes at Lucas than at Cate, and drama soon ensues between the two best friends. Shaw's writing is superbly streamlined and full of catty one-liners traded like barbs back and forth between Lucas, Cate, and their hootchie friend Sonja. While the novel is mostly comedic, there are serious elements at work, such as what happens to Lucas and Cate's friendship after Derek's two-timing is exposed. And when Lucas makes his affections for Derek public, he is beaten and called "faggot" by Vince, Cate's bully of an ex-boyfriend. In an especially revealing scene afterward, Lucas says to Sonja: "I'm alone in this. No one gets me. I have nowhere to go. My friends can't understand me.

People at school just think I'm fine all the time. They think they're okay with the gay thing. But calling a guy a 'faggot' is the worst thing you can call him." Sonja replies that she understands, because she's been dubbed the school slut; she knows what harassment feels like. While Lucas realizes she can't completely understand his dilemma, he takes to heart that her anger at being harassed cuts as deeply as his own. In a final twist, Cate and Sonja set Lucas up on a date with the last person he expected was gay; the novel ends, leaving it open for readers to interpret whether or not this date will be a success. *The Hook-Up Artist* moves quickly but plumbs unexpected depths. Shaw embeds his themes of friendship, homophobia, sexuality, trust, dedication, and love so deeply that readers will believe they are just reading a whirlwind of a mixed up matchmaking story. The result is a multifaceted take on what it's like to self-identify as a gay teenager, how others think of you, and what to do when reality rears its ugly head.

HOW I LEARNED TO SNAP: A SMALL-TOWN COMING-OF-AGE COMING-OUT STORY, BY KIRK READ

Unabashed, up-front, and uncensored, Kirk Read's vignette-style autobiography twists our perceptions of what it was like growing up gay in the Reagan-era South. Hilarious, sardonic, and witty, this Sedaris-like memoir reinvents the gay coming-of-age story by refusing to focus on the isolation and sorrow of its hero. Instead, Read embraces the differences that make him an outsider with infectious optimism and buoyant confidence: outing himself to his high school by authoring and performing in a gay-themed play, and coaching a little league soccer team. Uncompromising and full of attitude, just like the punk rock mantras that Read lives by, *How I Learned to Snap* serves as an ultimatum for acceptance and tolerance. Best suited for older teens, this memoir is sure to stimulate thought-provoking discussions, which is exactly what Read intended. Although the book contains some material that librarians in conservative communities might want to take a second look at, the themes it addresses, such as bringing a same-sex date to school dances, safe sex, and maintaining strong parental relationships, are extremely important and relevant to all kids. Few books—especially teen nonfiction—address them with such candor. In a September 2003 e-mail, author Kirk Read said of his book: "I want young gay characters to be more than vessels for coming out narratives. Not all young gay people go through hell, and even when they do it's often less of a gay hell than it is an adolescent hell."

THE INCREDIBLY TRUE ADVENTURE OF TWO GIRLS IN LOVE, DIRECTED BY MARIA MAGGENTI

"I've never done this before," Evie whispers to Randi, her very first girl-friend, as they kiss for the very first time. The pair couldn't be more different. Evie, an African American girl who hangs with the popular crowd in high school, comes from a wealthy family that expects her to pursue a career in medicine. Randi, meanwhile, is an outcast in every sense of the word: An openly out lesbian, she works at a gas station, lives with her two moms, and has been having an affair with a married woman. But the two girls find common ground, and even learn to overcome the disappointment when Evie's former "best" friends desert her, and their romance continues to blossom until one morning when Evie's mom discovers the pair entangled in each other's arms. Blithe and frolicsome, but not without some drama, Maria Maggenti's *The Incredibly True Adventure of Two Girls in Love* is exactly the kind of film that lesbian teen girls might love to see. It features strong, rebellious female protagonists who struggle with real teen issues in a high school setting that teens will recognize. There is a fairly racy sex scene, and the film often suffers from the constraints of its indie, shoestring budget, but these are our only caveats in recommending *The Incredibly True Adventure*—it makes an excellent companion to the gay British film *Beautiful Thing*.

JACK, BY A. M. HOLMES

Jack's parents are divorced, and when his father takes him out into the middle of a lake in a rowboat to reveal that he is in love with his best friend and roommate, Jack feels slapped in the face with betrayal. Holmes's story portrays Jack's coming to terms with his father's homosexuality, his own feelings of abandonment by his father, and levels of homophobia that burble to the surface in conversations with his friends at school. What's most interesting about books such as *Jack* and *From the Notebooks of Melanin Sun*, which also features a queer parent, is how the two main characters—both straight—themselves begin to feel the stigma of homophobia once they discover the truth about their parents. For instance, they become attuned to casual homophobia at school, such as the often heard expressions "faggot" and "dyke." These novels uproot a character's position in the mainstream—they may have hung out with the popular crowd, they themselves may have even used homophobic slurs—and drop them into the world of the stigmatized. When news of his father's homosexuality spreads around town, Jack himself is called "faggot" numerous times by his classmates. His feelings of isolation and grief, which stem from these incidents, bring him closer to his father and Jack finds that he must walk in his father's shoes to understand what kind of life his father leads, and why he must be strong for him. First published in the 1980s, this now classic adult book still resonates with teen audiences because the voice is so true, as is Jack's angst-ridden, wry, sarcastic sense of humor. And, like *From the Notebooks of Melanin Sun*, this book remains essential reading for straight teens with queer family members.

KEEPING YOU A SECRET, BY JULIE ANNE PETERS

Even today, in the dawn of what could be the "post-gay" society prophesized by those who study teen sexuality, coming out can turn a kid's life upside down. Holland Jaeger, a popular member of the high school's swim team, sees her world upended when she summons the courage to admit to herself that she's in love with the new girl in school, the proudly out Cece. But admitting their love to her mother is an entirely different matter, and when Holland stands by it, her mother kicks Holland out of the house and prevents her from seeing her family again. And that's only the beginning of the homophobia that Holland encounters. But Holland is a survivor, and she discovers that she has more allies than she imagined. Although *Keeping You a Secret* isn't exactly light-hearted reading, Peters injects just the right amount of humor into Holland's sarcastic, nihilist voice. It's these touches that prevent the book from falling into the didactic trap of a problem novel. Indeed, kids nationwide have written to Peters expressing their gratitude at how much *Keeping You a Secret* has helped them.

Peters had been writing for ten years before she even considered authoring a queer YA book. Then, one day in 1999, she and her editor, Megan Tingley, were having lunch and Peters happened to mention that she and her partner were celebrating their twenty-fifth anniversary. Tingley suggested that Peters write a lesbian teen romance novel. Peters was nervous about this, to say the least. In a June 2004 interview, she said, "I said to her, 'What? Are you insane? Do you have a death wish for me?' I had so many fears because I live in Colorado and it's tough living in Colorado; you can't be an out gay person there. This would be a global outing for me, and that was scary." But Peters reluctantly agreed to give it a try. When *Keeping You a Secret* was finally published in 2003, Peters was afraid of getting hate mail. She was overjoyed, therefore, to receive letters that contained only praise and words of gratitude.

KISSING KATE, BY LAUREN MYRACLE

Kate and Lissa were inseparable best friends for four years, until one night at a party Kate had too much to drink and seduced Lissa. The next day she behaved like nothing had happened between them, and claimed that they both must've been really drunk. Thing is, though, Lissa wasn't drunk at all—and actually found herself enjoying what it felt like kissing her best friend. When Kate's hand slid up her shirt it was unlike anything she had ever felt in her entire life. Myracle's straightforward, crunchy granola story picks up after this party, with Lissa and Kate now ignoring each other. Kate has a new dolt of a boyfriend, and Lissa now spends her time avoiding Kate, reading up on lucid dreaming, working at a restaurant called Entrées on Trays, and making friends with Ariel, a girl who claims to have been abducted by aliens. Despite these distractions, Lissa finds that she can't get Kate out of her mind. Kate wants to remain friends with Lissa, but can't seem to realize that Lissa might actually be in love with her and that Lissa's feelings are valid, even "normal"—much less that she can return Lissa's affection. What stands out about *Kissing Kate* is its heroine's growing realization that she might be a lesbian, and her courage to make her best friend see this, no matter what the consequences are. While the book's hippie elements may distract and seem hokey, *Kissing Kate* solidly moves away from the predictable coming out story and plants readers deeply into the mind of the main character as she begins accepting what she already knows must be true. And when Lissa's new friend Ariel accepts her in the end, the story gets even jucier, making this book one of the more successful ones with lesbian characters—and, to boot, it's popular among teen readers straight and queer alike.

KINGS & QUEENS: QUEERS AT THE PROM, BY DAVID BOYER

In this eye-opening, one-of-a-kind photography book, Boyer examines the history of queers at the prom. Divided into four sections—titled, what else, Freshmen, Sophomores, Juniors, and Seniors—Boyer begins his chronology in 2003 at the progressive Harvey Milk School for queer teens in New York City. Working backward through the decades, Boyer highlights the prom memories of everyday queer people and unsung queer heroes, with an eye to the overall perception of queer people at a given point in time. Their diverse, real-life stories range from awkward and painful, to celebratory and inspirational. The book mixes history, popular culture, biography, and bad fashion.

If nothing else, it will be well-thumbed-through just for the photos, many of which are hilariously awful. Most important, as more and more queer teens summon the courage to attend their own proms with whomever they choose, *Kings & Queens* presents a timely look at the prom concept and how it has evolved to fit—or not fit, as the case may be—changing social conventions.

LEAVE MYSELF BEHIND, BY BART YATES

Noah, a seventeen-year-old smart aleck, always knew his mother was crazy. But when the pair move from Chicago to an old Victorian house in a small town in New Hampshire, her behavior seems to get worse. The first signs of insanity are triggered when she and Noah begin remodeling the house and they discover mason jars hidden in the walls. The jars contain clothing, toys, jewelry: pieces of a past life that suggest a grisly, fifty-year-old murder of a mother and child. The mystery fuels Noah's mother's downward spiral of crazed obsession, and the chaos mounts when Noah finds himself falling in love with J.D., the guy next door. While Noah's mother accepts his sexuality instantly, J.D.'s parents, on the other hand, kick J.D. out of the house and he moves in with Noah. The mental instability of Noah's mother escalates into mania, and soon she is tearing down every wall in the house—as fast as Noah rebuilds them—desperate to find more clues about the previous residents. Yates combines an emotional coming out story with an intellectual thriller that coalesces into an intense, multilayered novel that's twisted enough to satisfy even the straightest of teen readers. Engaging, sophisticated, and literary, *Leave Myself Behind* contains enough sexual action to make its adolescent male characters ring true. Readers also latch onto Noah's sense of alienation from himself, from his mother, and from the rest of the world. As he falls in love with J.D., it's exciting to watch his own internal defenses crumble, along with the walls of his mother's house. Published as an adult book, *Leave Myself Behind* was a 2004 Alex Award winner.

LUCKY, BY EDDIE DE OLIVEIRA

In this British novel, nineteen-year-old bisexual, soccer-playing Sam Smith can't help but fall hard for the fearless and daring Toby, who also likes both girls and boys. Their budding romantic relationship sparks after a dreamy first date to London, but soon tailspins when Toby meets Emma, a sassy, independent girl who both boys find attractive. Toby begins spending more and more time with Emma, leaving Sam—who still has eyes for

Toby *and* Emma—as the angry and uncomfortable third wheel on their dates. De Oliveira's first novel cleverly sets Sam's seething jealousy of Toby and Emma against his own angst over coming out. Although the book begins slowly, readers who make it past the first eighty pages are rewarded with a meaningful and fast-paced story that explores the many facets of teen love and friendship, and the wafer-thin lines that exist between the two. To date, few YA titles delve this deeply into bisexuality, making *Lucky* an important addition to any collection. The characters are well drawn and quirky enough to catch the interest of teen readers, and *Lucky* has enough grit, romantic twists, and sports to sustain their attention.

LUNA: A NOVEL, BY JULIE ANNE PETERS

Fifteen-year-old Regan is haunted by her older brother's dual personality. By day he is Liam, her studious older brother; at night, he dons makeup and clothing to transform into his true self, a girl named Luna. Keeping Liam's secret is hard enough for Regan, but when Liam asks her to help him make the transformation permanent, she wonders where it will end. Regan increasingly sacrifices her own life at home and in school to help her brother in any way possible. Her dedication to him, although it often hurts, makes Regan an admirable and universally appealing character. The first teen novel to address transgender issues in more than just passing, *Luna* and its subject matter is a must-have for any YA collection because, to date, it is the only book like it. For this reason, *Luna* is a smash hit with teens around the country—but all teens can relate to Regan's selfless desire to help and protect a family member. When it comes to *Luna*'s power, Jamie, a trans teen, said this in a July 2004 interview at The New York Public Library: "This is the first book I read, a novel anyway, with trans issues in it. It kind of makes me feel that I have a place in the world, because I feel separate from everything, and reading just takes me away to a different place and I can just kind of find myself."

MAMA'S BOY, PREACHER'S SON: A MEMOIR, BY KEVIN JENNINGS

Kevin Jennings, founder of the Gay, Lesbian and Straight Education Network (GLSEN), was raised in a North Carolina trailer park by his evangelical preacher father and his hard-working mother, a woman who never made it through high school. His life, one of poverty, sports, deep-seated racism, and homophobia, is drastically changed when his father dies in a swimming pool accident on Jennings's eighth birthday. The family is plunged even further into poverty, and Jennings begins to question his religious upbringing—not to mention wonder and worry about his sexuality. For the next few years, Jennings, chubby, never an accomplished sportsman nor as assertive as the other boys in school, soon becomes the brunt of homophobic torment, and, like so many other LGBTQ teens, spends each morning plotting how to avoid bullying during the rest of the school day. But Jennings survives. After transferring to two different schools, he goes on to Harvard University, where he studies history. From there, much to the chagrin of his mother, Jennings decides to teach, most successfully at the prestigious Concord School in Massachusetts, where his coming out in a school assembly sparked the gay-straight alliance movement that GLSEN leads, now some 3,000 chapters strong. Teenagers, teachers, and parents will be moved by this straightforward, conversationally told, autobiographical tale about a man shaped by his adolescence and by the teenagers in the schools where he teaches. Jennings addresses issues such as the fear of losing his job because of his sexuality, heterocentrism in schools, and queer people's larger fight for equal rights. Most inspiring is Jennings' work with teens: He discovers, not unlike Ritch Savin-Williams in *The New Gay Teenager*, that today's teens are quite possibly the most tolerant generation yet in accepting and embracing all forms of diversity.

MY HEARTBEAT, BY GARRET FREYMANN-WEYR

Ellen, a precocious fourteen-year-old Manhattanite, has always been in love with James, the best friend of her brother, Linc. The three are usually inseparable, but when Ellen hears rumors that Linc and James's relationship is more than "just friends," she asks whether or not it's true. Linc reacts badly and storms out of the friendship, leaving James and Ellen with a lot of time on their hands—time for James to discuss his true feelings about Linc, and then fall in love with Ellen. *My Heartbeat*'s twisted love triangle touches on all aspects of love and relationships between siblings and friends, as well as the mutable boundaries between heterosexuality, bisexuality, and homosexuality. This novel proves that love knows no boundaries and that even a self-professed guy-who-likes-guys can fall for a girl. Freymann-Weyr's streamlined novel packs an unexpected emotional wallop as the characters work through their relationships with each other and discover their own emerging, multifaceted identities. Whether it's because teens can identify with what it's like to have a crush, or because they understand what it's like to be isolated from a sibling, readers simply love this book. One of the most poignant things we've ever heard a teen say was spoken when Freymann-Weyr met with a group of teens at The New York Public Library in 2002. A girl said that had been kicked out of her house because she was pregnant and that she hadn't seen her brother in more than a year; she told Freymann-Weyr that she intimately knew the pain of Ellen's alienation.

MY SO-CALLED LIFE

My So-Called Life, which aired for only half a season between 1994 and 1995, is still considered by many to be the most accurate, if angst-ridden, fictional portrayal of adolescence on television. Told from the point of view of Angela Chase, a heterosexual high school sophomore, the show's nineteen episodes chronicled what it's like to sever comfortable ties with old friends in pursuit of a newer, slightly more dangerous crowd—and the parental resistance that accompanies this transformation. Among Angela's new friends are Rickie, a.k.a., Enrique, a gay boy just beginning to come out of the closet. Rickie is forced to leave home and is taken in by a teacher—who also happens to be gay—but viewers never learn what happens next since, sadly, the show was canceled. Rickie was the first regular queer teen character to appear on a network drama, and for an entire generation of queer teens, he was their first glimpse of someone like them on TV. The ABC television network abruptly cancelled the show, however, after advertisers became nervous about its content, sparking heartfelt protests of teenaged fans that made national headlines. Today, networks probably wouldn't think twice about the show's content—an unintended legacy and proof of the progress that queers have made in entering mainstream popular culture. But the show's most enduring legacy may be that although it's now more than ten years old, *My So-Called Life* remains as powerful and fresh today as it was when it first aired. It still resonates with teens both queer and straight, all of whom hear something of themselves in Angela's angst.

NICK & NORAH'S INFINITE PLAYLIST, BY RACHEL COHN AND DAVID LEVITHAN

Neither Nick nor Norah are queer. Moreover, the plot of this novel takes these two through one reckless, energy-filled night on the town as they discover themselves and each other amongst the skyscrapers of New York City. But what matters to us in this whirlwind story, in which the f___ word appears multiple times on nearly every page, are the gay boys who infiltrate the book's eclectic scheme of secondary characters and linger in the background, picking up the pieces, holding life together as Nick and Norah explore it. These secondary gay characters even manage to find love between each other, and other band members; Nick, it turns out, is the only straight guy in an all-queer punk band. *Nick & Norah* opens after Nick has broken up with the love of his life, Tris. When he spots her at the concert where his band is playing, he begs Norah to be his girlfriend for the next five minutes to make Tris jealous. The plan works. Tris is dumbfounded. A kiss seals the deal as Nick and Norah crash into each other, and pull away, for the rest of the evening. Meanwhile, the boys in Nick's band meet, kiss, hook up, and save the day. Levithan and Cohn create the same "post-gay" universe of *Boy Meets Boy*: a place exploding with magical energy, where queer teens go about their lives unfettered by "coming out" and are simply on a quest for love. The queer characters may not be in the novel's foreground, but they can exist and coexist with their friends in a world that is safe, accepting, and full of adventure just around the corner.

ORPHEA PROUD, BY SHARON DENNIS WYETH

At an open mike before a live audience, sixteen-year-old African American Orphea Proud shares her life story while her cousin Raymor paints murals inspired by her delivery. Orphea recounts the death of her parents, an event that left her in the care of her domineering and abusive older stepbrother, Rupert. Upon discovering Orphea's blossoming lesbian romance with a childhood friend, Rupert dumps her into the backwoods arms of their good-natured, elderly aunts. In the country, Orphea finds the solace to transform her anger and sadness into poetry, while at the same time discovering her heritage and befriending her slightly batty white cousin, Raymor, who lives across the street. Beautifully written as a monologue interspersed with Orphea's poetry, *Orphea Proud* embeds racial and gender issues within a powerful story of survival and trust. The book's action-packed beginning carries enough drama to hook even the most reluctant reader: In less than forty pages, Orphea's parents die, she suffers abuse at the hands of her brother, and her girlfriend is killed in a car accident. It almost makes coming out seem like a breeze. *Orphea Proud* isn't just about being queer, it's about overcoming challenges, reflecting upon them, and turning pain, sorrow, and angst into something beautiful. We'd be remiss not to acknowledge that there's an important queer character who dies in *Orphea Proud*—in a car crash, no less. And, in grand old form, this wreck happens after a dramatic coming out scene. Fortunately, however, this character's death is nothing personal; she's one of many people who die, and their deaths have nothing to do with sexuality. The proud protagonist, Orphea Proud, survives.

THE PERKS OF BEING A WALLFLOWER, BY STEPHEN CHBOSKY

This novel, originally for adults but hugely popular with teens, is Chbosky's classic tale of a high-schooler named Charlie and his attempts to discover, communicate with, and participate in the world around him and the people he encounters along the way. Charlie's story unfolds through personal letters he's written to an anonymous person he calls, simply, his "friend." Indeed, readers soon suspect that Charlie is most likely not the storyteller's real name, but in fact a pen name to protect his real identity. Whatever the case, his letters are funny, sad, and sweet—made even more so by Charlie's dedication and desperation in hurling his thoughts, dreams, fears, and hopes into this anonymous void that frees him to write whatever he pleases. Along the way, Charlie meets another boy he first names "Nothing," but soon reveals to be named Patrick. Patrick, who is gay and in love with the football team's quarterback, adopts Charlie into his circle of friends that includes Patrick's sister, on whom Charlie develops a major crush.

For the purposes of our discussion it's the relationship between Charlie and Patrick that is most significant. Charlie never bats an eyelash when it comes to Patrick's sexuality and his acceptance is almost childlike, which fits his invisible wallflower persona. Charlie has been cut off from the world, and almost like a baby discovering something for the first time, he becomes both fascinated by and enamored with Patrick: not necessarily in a romantic way, but interested nonetheless. He buys Patrick a book about Harvey Milk, a pioneering gay politician; he makes Patrick a mix tape; and he plays Rocky in a screening of the *Rocky Horror Picture Show*. Ultimately, Charlie and Patrick do share a moment of physical contact—a kiss—but it's a mistaken moment on both parts and each easily moves on with their friendship intact. Chbosky's portrayal of Charlie is perhaps the first multilayered depiction of the chameleonlike nature of contemporary teenage sexual identities. Understandably, therefore, teens of all ages, races, and sexual orientations continue to enjoy this novel, evidenced by the fact that although it was published in 1999, *Perks* still makes the top ten list of most challenged books.

POSTCARDS FROM NO MAN'S LAND, BY AIDAN CHAMBERS

Travel broadens the mind in more ways than one. The strangeness and anonymity of a new place is liberating, providing an anonymous laboratory where we can reinvent ourselves; the distance from home, meanwhile, gives us the perfect vantage point from which to reexamine our lives. Jacob, a reclusive teen, experiences the benefits of travel to their fullest when he leaves his home in Britain to stay with Geertrui, an elderly Dutch woman who knew Jacob's grandfather while he was stationed in Holland during World War II. *Postcards* opens with a scene that many travelers will recognize as Jacob sits in a Dutch café, getting his bearings and vainly searching for something familiar—such as the flirtatious advances of a beautiful woman. The woman, whose name is Ton, chats with Jacob and when she gets up to leave, bestowing the briefest of kisses on his lips, she simultaneously shares a secret that throws Jacob for a loop. She is actually a he.

Ton's gender-bender is only the first of many secrets in this multilayered novel that alternates between the present day and events during the Second World War, as relayed to Jacob by Geertrui. By the end of the book, Jacob not only understands his family in an entirely new light—it turns out that his grandfather was more than just friends with Geertrui—he also manages to shake his antisocial leanings. And, to boot, in a subtle, entirely believable way that captures the complexity of modern teenage sexuality, Jacob questions his sexual orientation: remaining open to Ton while falling in love with a girl named Hille. Winner of the Carnegie Medal as well as the Printz award in 1999, this novel remains popular with sophisticated teen readers today. Although the historical layering sometimes slows its pace, *Postcards*'s plot unravels like a good mystery that keeps readers hooked to the end.

PRETTY THINGS, BY SARRA MANNING

Four unlikely friends get trapped in a love triangle, or love square as the case would be. Brie, a fashionista type who lives up to her fancy cheese first name, harbors a deep crush on her indie rock, gay best friend, Charlie. But Charlie, of course, has a crush on a Marlboro man–like, womanizing, two-timing guy named Walker. And Walker, whom readers discover is actually a much sweeter guy than the other characters perceive him to be, is head over heels in love with Daisy, a deadpan, man-hating lesbian who hates Walker, Brie, and pretty much anyone who isn't queer. Together, these four are trapped in a summer stock production of Shakespeare's *Taming of the Shrew*, with Brie as Kate and Walker as Petruchio. Fur flies when Walker begins to pursue Daisy and, despite her protests, in one amazing scene on a road trip, the pair hook up and fall in love. Incredibly, their love forms the heart of *Pretty Things*.

Sarra Manning, who also authored the popular *Guitar Girl*, convincingly describes Walker and Daisy's wonderment at the transitory nature of love and sexuality—especially when Daisy answers Brie's question about whether she's gay, straight, bisexual . . . "or what?" Daisy replies, "I'm all of the above. I'm none of the above. I'm a lesbian who likes kissing Walker, even though he hates the ground I walk on. I'm me and I'm still trying to figure out what and who the hell I am. When I figure it out, I'll get back to you." The book, of course, is a take on Shakespeare's story about the hapless gadabout romantic male lead who falls hard for a stone-cold-angry female and has to convince her that she loves him. The novel ends with Brie, Daisy, Walker, and Charlie, all drunk and contemplating the nature of love, friendship, and how their summer expectations were completely different from what actually unfolded. Kids enjoy this book not just because it's a funny read, but because it realistically captures what teens, unlike many adults, are willing to admit: Love knows no boundaries, so attempting to categorize and label it is impossible.

RAINBOW BOYS TRILOGY, BY ALEX SANCHEZ

Like a high school PG-13 version of the television program *Queer as Folk*, Alex Sanchez's *Rainbow Boys* follows the lives of three gay teen boys as they come out, fall in and out of love, and make plans for college. Jason Carrilo, the good-looking popular jock, has a girlfriend but secretly has the hots for Kyle, the quiet, friendly star of the swim team. And Nelson, the out-and-proud loudmouth, secretly longs for Kyle. Coming out, safe sex, STDs, and parental relationships are only a few of the issues that Sanchez addresses—and helpfully pairs with a resource guide at the book's end. Light-hearted, fun, and informative, *Rainbow Boys* is exactly the kind of romance that many queer teens have been wanting for decades. Make no mistake, the book is out and proud. Its cover, featuring a trio of handsome lads worthy of an Abercombie and Fitch catalog, appeals to gay boys and straight girls alike.

 Rainbow High, the second book in the trilogy, sees the triumvirate navigate their way through senior year of high school. Jason and Kyle's romance blossoms as Jason's conservative, religious family learns to accept it, while Nelson has an AIDS scare—and then, ironically, falls in love with an HIV-positive college student. In *Rainbow Road*, which takes place the summer after their senior year, the three chums embark on a zigzag drive from Washington, D.C., to Los Angeles, where Jason has been asked to speak at the opening of a new gay high school. As expected, 2,700 miles of madcap drama, histrionics, and romantic interludes ensue in this final and most enjoyable book of the trilogy. Although the sexual content of the first two books is fairly mild, *Rainbow Road* does feature a few starkly drawn— by YA standards, at least—sexual encounters between Kyle and Jason.

A REALLY NICE PROM MESS, BY BRIAN SLOAN

Cameron's prom plans with his closeted heartthrob boyfriend, Shane, are thwarted by his irritated beard date; a hot Russian drug dealer; a deaf, underaged go-go dancer; and a chunky strip-teasing straight jock. And it all takes place in less than twelve hours. Brian Sloan's hilarious, page-turner first novel races through Cameron's disaster-prone evening. Just when you think the shameless, button-pushing humor has reached its apex, Sloan pulls another ridiculous stunt out of his cache and pushes the book even further over the top. But *Prom Mess* is more than just slapstick humor. Sloan's wit and ability to spit out ironically double-edged one-liners subtly unmasks Cameron's growing realization that a world does exist beyond the confines of high school, the prom, and his closeted jerk of a boyfriend. Although this is a coming out drama, much to Cameron's surprise no one cares that he or Shane are gay—in fact, Shane's best friend, Ian, whom Cameron was most worried about, performs a strip-tease at a gay bar to help him recover his lost tuxedo. Even the beard doesn't care that Cameron is gay—she's just upset that she won't be getting any action on prom night from her date. All kids, regardless of their sexual identity, love this book. Straight boys see the cover, think it's about a heterosexual prom disaster, and by the time they get to the gay revelation, they can't stop reading—just one of the reasons why *Prom Mess* was named a Quick Pick in 2006.

THE REALM OF POSSIBILITY, BY DAVID LEVITHAN

"Here is what I know about the realm of possibility—it is always expanding, and it is never what you think it is." So ponders Jed, a young man about to celebrate his one-year anniversary with his boyfriend, Daniel. Meanwhile, Peter, a kind-hearted jock, fights to hoist his girlfriend, Mary, out of her eating disorder rut. And Diana, a bitter songwriter, composes ballads for the girlfriend she can never have. Similar to E. R. Frank's *Life Is Funny*, Levithan's second novel weaves in and out of the interconnected lives of these teens and fourteen others, illustrating the many facets of love and the different realms of possibility it can inhabit. Characters emerge in a poem told from their point of view, submerge, and then resurface in another character's story. Lives are torn apart, then pieced back together again by relationships that are simultaneously singular and plural—all fully realized through Levithan's minimalist, prose-poem style. As a whole, *The Realm of Possibility* effortlessly conveys the interconnectedness of humans, the varying degrees of bonds that hold us together, and the overwhelming and transitory nature of love that makes it all possible. Unlike Levithan's breathtaking *Boy Meets Boy*, this book isn't all queer, but its equal treatment of all forms of love makes a subtle and important statement about differences and acceptance. Although its unique style appeals mainly to sophisticated readers, all teenagers should find at least one aspect of themselves in the myriad characters represented here.

SO HARD TO SAY, BY ALEX SANCHEZ

In Alex Sanchez's first foray into tween fiction, we are introduced to fourteen-year-old Xio, a headstrong, vivacious Latina who loves three things: talking, chocolate, and beautiful, blond Frederick, the new student in her southern California high school. Xio yanks Frederick into her circle of friends and lays on the flirtation pretty thick. But Frederick, who hails from Wisconsin, is shy in this new environment and doesn't know what to make of her moves—especially since he's beginning to question his own sexuality. And it doesn't help that Frederick can't keep his own eyes off Victor, the hot captain of the soccer team. Xio's frustration with Frederick's evasiveness grows, as does her determination to make him hers, until it culminates in a big, juicy smooch that she plants on him while they're both ironically standing in a closet. In *So Hard to Say*, Sanchez steps away from the melodrama of his *Rainbow Boys* trilogy and creates strong, life-like characters on the brink of discovery. Its exploration of universal issues such as friendship ensures this book's appeal to readers of all ages and sexual orientations, but *So Hard to Say* was actually one of the first LGBTQ books written expressly for ages eight to twelve. Its special appeal to this audience, plus its strong portrayals of Latino youth, make this book a must-have for any collection.

TALKING IN THE DARK: A POETRY MEMOIR, BY BILLY MERRELL

Divorce, coming out, father-son dynamics, first love, first sexual experience, and first HIV test are only a few of the issues woven between the lines of Billy Merrell's intricate and well-conceived poetry memoir. The understated narrative is subtly revealed through Merrell's emotional and intellectual discovery embedded within a series of sharply individualized images that are lucid, honest, and open. *Talking in the Dark* capably stands on its own as both a gay coming-of-age memoir and as a volume of queer poetry. Some readers may find it hard to believe that in central Florida, on the edge of the Bible Belt, Merrell's coming out could be accepted so easily by his family and schoolmates—but it's exactly this remarkable story that makes *Talking in the Dark* essential reading. At age twenty-three, Merrell proves that queer youth can come out safely even in conservative regions of the United States. More important, he illustrates that queerness is only a small part of a person's personality, and that underneath the surface, boundaries between queer and straight aren't as rigid as some may think. In describing his memoir in a September 2003 e-mail, twenty-three-year-old Billy Merrell said: "In the book, I struggle with believing in love, having faith in relationships. I date someone and am dumped. It is typical stuff—none of which is necessarily characteristic of homosexuality. And the struggles of the narrator should come across as universal struggles."

A TALE OF TWO SUMMERS, BY BRIAN SLOAN

Two childhood best friends, Hal and Chuck, spend their first summer apart. Chuck, who is straight, goes to theater camp. Hal, who is gay, stays home. The two vow to stay in touch by keeping a private blog where they record their adventures, thoughts, hopes, and dreams. Both boys hope to lose their virginity over the summer, and they do: Hal with a French exchange student named Henri, and Chuck with MK, a cool girl in his theater program. Their conversations are frank and thoughtful as they describe their romantic and sexual experiences in genuine boyspeak. In fact, Chuck and Hal's blogs are exactly the types of conversations that all straight and gay boys should have with one another. They leave no stone unturned, covering everything from what happens during gay sex versus straight sex, why straight boys are obsessed with breasts, and why many gay boys, like Hal, can't help but check out other boys' rear assets. They even discuss what happened between Hal and Chuck that caused a rift of awkwardness to fall between them on New Year's Eve—which the reader assumes was an ill-advised moment of flirting. The differences and similarities between gay and straight men are brought to the forefront in a humorous, in-your-face manner, and the characters remain steadfast friends throughout. It's this friendship that forms the heart of Sloan's book, proving that gay boys and straight boys can overcome their differences and prejudices and still remain best friends. As a result, the book has something for boys both gay and straight. We can only hope that someone writes the equivalent novel for lesbians and straight girls. More of these frank conversations between straight and queer teens need to happen in literature and in real life.

TOTALLY JOE, BY JAMES HOWE

A companion to *The Misfits*, one of James Howe's earlier novels, *Totally Joe* focuses on the life of thirteen-year-old Joe Bunch, who came out of the closet in the first book and, with his friends, started a "No Name-Calling-Day" in school. *Totally Joe* unfolds as an alpha-biography, a writing assignment for Joe's English class. According to this assignment's rules, the writer must pen an A-to-Z account of his or her life and crown each entry with an Oprah-like life lesson at the chapter's conclusion. Thus, readers tumble through the hilarious up-and-down days of Joe, who sometimes wishes he were named JoDan. We see him with his first crush and boyfriend, Colin (that would be chapter three, the letter C, of course). We see him as a victim of homophobic epithets from school bullies. We see him form a gay-straight alliance at school with his friends, which eventually defeats the bullies. And, in the last chapter, we see Joe on the threshold of a new relationship with a guy named Zachary.

The importance of this hilarious and poignant novel lies in its title, *Totally Joe*: Joe, the protagonist, reveals himself candidly and honestly through Howe's diary-like framework, and readers watch him come into his own as a self-actualized, down-to-earth, funny, happy, strong gay teen. Not that the novel is all happy, of course, but what makes *Totally Joe* so realistic are the moments of crisis in which Joe must confront not just his enemies but what they say to him and how it hurts him. Howe describes these moments with such sharp insight and clarity that any reader—teen or adult, queer or straight—will surely appreciate the creativity of Joe and his plight to stay happy and healthy, despite the undercurrent of homophobia that threatens to upset his happy world. Published in 2006, *Totally Joe* immediately became an important contribution to the growing handful of queer-themed books for tween audiences.

WHAT HAPPENED TO LANI GARVER?, BY CAROL PLUM-UCCI

Effeminate, angelic Lani Garver arrives on sleepy Hackett Island simultaneously bewildering and fascinating Claire MacKenzie, a leukemia survivor currently battling an eating disorder. As Lani, pronounced "Lonny," guides Claire through the metamorphosis of self-discovery, his androgynous appearance and confrontational personality make him an excellent candidate for ridicule, torment, and the unavoidable hate crime that will change both characters' lives forever. As in her Printz Honor

Book, *The Body of Christopher Creed*, Plum-Ucci examines the psychological concept of "convenient recollection," whereby characters believe the lies they tell themselves, blurring the lines between reality and the supernatural, fact and superstition. Told from Claire's point of view, *What Happened to Lani Garver?* captures the awe and horror of small-town gossip as Lani ventures forth into their close-knit and close-minded territory. Readers watch with growing dread as the town unites against him, and, over Claire's protests, drives him out in an ending that leaves readers guessing.

Whether Lani is a boy or a girl, transgendered, gay, or straight, isn't the point. What matters instead is that Lani symbolizes the plight of all outcasts—outcasts by appearance, ideology, and religion. Plum-Ucci injects Lani with each and all of these archetypes and illustrates how the mob mentality of a small town can snowball from wonder, to shock, and eventually to hate. Lani becomes, in essence, a martyr for all outcasts. If this sounds heavy-handed, it isn't. The novel is a suspenseful page-turner, written in tightly controlled prose with rich characterizations. Teen readers admire Lani's outspokenness just as much as they admire Claire's growing guts to fight not just for herself, but for others.

WHEN I KNEW, ED. BY ROBERT TRACHTENBERG

Notable queers and unsung queer heroes alike share their sometimes humorous, sometimes touching coming out stories in a simple, easy-to-read, picture book format that invites readers to browse rather than read the entire work from cover to cover. Trachtenberg loosely groups the anecdotes into four types: when I knew; when my parents knew; when everyone else knew; and coming out. This compilation of overwhelmingly positive memories illustrates to teen readers and their friends that perhaps the coming out process may not be nearly as painful as popular culture implies. The book's vignette style, moreover, is ideal for short attention spans and reluctant readers. Stories vary in length from one sentence to four pages, but regardless of length each one packs a wallop.

THE WORLD OF NORMAL BOYS, BY K. M. SOEHNLEIN

For most of his life, freshman Robin Mackenzie has lived by everyone else's rules; he's the dutiful son of his meat-and-potatoes dad, and he enjoys taking day trips with his mom into New York City. But when

Robin's obnoxious younger brother unexpectedly dies, his family's membrane begins to disintegrate, and Robin finds that the only way he can cope is to get out of the house. He falls into a sordid love triangle with two other outcasts, Todd and Scott, but their lack of interest in emotional connection or affection leave Robin feeling empty and used. With his mother on the road to alcoholism and his father ever more emotionally distant, Robin soon finds himself further away from normality than he ever could have imagined. Set in 1978 suburban New Jersey, Soehnlein's well-written and poignant coming-of-age story insightfully traces Robin's escape from the world of normal boys and re-emergence as an experienced, thoughtful young adult capable of moving forward from his family's tragedy. Although written for adults, *World of Normal Boys* appeals to teens because it reads as a mature, fleshed-out version of the typical gay teen novel.

10 MATERIAL LISTS ARRANGED BY TOPIC

INTRODUCTION

Perhaps you don't have time to read all the way through the reviews in Chapter 9 and you need to find a book quickly. If that's the case, flip to this chapter and peruse our lists of top titles. You can use these lists either as a series of benchmarks, to gauge how representative your existing collection is when it comes to LGBTQ themes, or you can use them as an on-the-fly guide when a patron asks for books or other materials with queer themes. The lists are organized thematically to cover the full spectrum of LGBTQ topics: a list of novels for boys who like boys; girls who like girls; teens with queer siblings; parents of queer kids; books with surprise queer endings; adult nonfiction that might be suitable for teens, etc. There are lists of both fiction and nonfiction titles, as well as lists of graphic novels, television programs, films, periodicals, and other non-print items. And, whereas the core collection outlined in Chapter 9 contains only fifty items, here you will find many additional suggestions. To help you cross-reference, we've placed an asterisk next to titles that appear in our core collection.

These lists contain selected materials that are currently available and, more important, that teens actually enjoy; they are not comprehensive. Materials are listed alphabetically; thus these are not a ranking of the "best" items within each category. Many titles appear on more than one list. As always, for complete citations refer to the Bibliography. Finally, the very first list is the most important in this chapter, and perhaps in the entire book: It contains ten titles that any YA collection, no matter how large or small, should contain. This list is a mixture of classic books and new ones, fiction and nonfiction, and it represents all facets of sexual orientation. Think of it as the core of a core collection.

THIRTY-FOUR CATEGORIZED LISTS OF BOOKS AND OTHER MATERIALS

TEN BOOKS IF YOU CAN ONLY HAVE TEN LGBTQ BOOKS IN YOUR LIBRARY

▼ *Annie on My Mind*, by Nancy Garden*
▼ *Boy Meets Boy*, by David Levithan*
▼ *Dangerous Angels: The Weetzie Bat Books*, by Francesca Lia Block*
▼ *From the Notebooks of Melanin Sun*, by Jacqueline Woodson*
▼ *The Full Spectrum: A New Generation of Writing about Gay, Lesbian, Bisexual, Transgender, Questioning and Other Identities*, ed. by David Levithan and Billy Merrell*
▼ *Geography Club*, by Brent Hartinger*
▼ *Hard Love*, by Ellen Wittlinger*
▼ *GLBTQ: The Survival Guide for Queer and Questioning Teens*, by Kelly Huegel*
▼ *Luna: A Novel*, by Julie Anne Peters*
▼ *Rainbow Boys, Rainbow High, Rainbow Road*, by Alex Sanchez*

FICTION FOR BOYS WHO LIKE BOYS: THE GAY TEEN MALE PROTAGONIST

▼ *Absolutely, Positively Not . . .*, by David LaRochelle*
▼ *Boy Meets Boy*, by David Levithan*
▼ *Clay's Way*, by Blair Mastbaum*
▼ *Geography Club*, by Brent Hartinger*
▼ *The Hookup Artist*, by Tucker Shaw*
▼ *Leave Myself Behind*, by Bart Yates*
▼ *Rainbow Boys, Rainbow High, Rainbow Road*, by Alex Sanchez*
▼ *A Really Nice Prom Mess*, by Brian Sloan*
▼ *A Tale of Two Summers*, by Brian Sloan*
▼ *The World of Normal Boys*, by K.M. Soehnlein*

FICTION FOR GIRLS WHO LIKE GIRLS: THE LESBIAN TEEN PROTAGONIST

▼ *Annie on My Mind*, by Nancy Garden*
▼ *The Bermudez Triangle*, by Maureen Johnson*
▼ *Dare Truth or Promise*, by Paula Boock*
▼ *Deliver Us from Evie*, by M. E. Kerr*

▼ *Keeping You a Secret*, by Julie Anne Peters*
▼ *Kissing Kate*, by Lauren Myracle*
▼ *Kissing the Witch: Old Tales in New Skins*, by Emma Donague
▼ *Hard Love*, by Ellen Wittlinger*
▼ *The House You Pass on the Way*, by Jacqueline Woodson
▼ *Orphea Proud*, by Sharon Dennis Wyeth*

FICTION WITH BISEXUAL CHARACTERS

▼ *Geography Club*, by Brent Hartinger*
▼ *Empress of the World*, by Sara Ryan*
▼ *"Hello," I Lied*, by M. E. Kerr
▼ *Lucky*, by Eddie de Oliveira*
▼ *My Heartbeat*, by Garret Freymann-Weyr*
▼ *Pretty Things*, by Sarra Manning*
▼ *Postcards from No Man's Land*, by Aidan Chambers*

FICTION WITH TRANS, CROSS-DRESSING, OR ANDROGYNOUS CHARACTERS

▼ *Born Confused*, by Tanuja Desai Hidier
▼ *Boy Meets Boy*, by David Levithan*
▼ *Boy2Girl,* by Terrence Blacker
▼ *The Flip Side*, by Andrew Matthews
▼ *Luna: A Novel*, by Julie Anne Peters*
▼ *Missing Angel Juan (Dangerous Angels: The Weetzie Bat Books),* by Francesca Lia Block
▼ *Postcards from No Man's Land*, by Aidan Chambers*
▼ *Rainbow Road*, by Alex Sanchez*
▼ *The Realm of Possibility*, by David Levithan*
▼ "The Welcome," by Emma Donague (a short story in Michael Cart's *Love & Sex* anthology)
▼ *What Happened to Lani Garver?*, by Carol Plum-Ucci*
▼ *What Night Brings*, by Carla Trujillo

FICTION FOR QUESTIONING TEENS

▼ *The Bermudez Triangle*, by Maureen Johnson*
▼ *Far from Xanadu*, by Julie Anne Peters
▼ *My Heartbeat*, by Garret Freymann-Weyr*
▼ *The Perks of Being a Wallflower*, by Stephen Chbosky*
▼ *Postcards from No Man's Land*, by Aidan Chambers*
▼ *Pretty Things*, by Sarra Manning*

▼ *Sexy*, by Joyce Carol Oates
▼ *So Hard to Say*, Alex Sanchez*

FICTION FOR YOUNGER TEENS

▼ *Absolutely, Positively Not . . .*, by David LaRochelle*
▼ *The Misfits*, by James Howe
▼ *So Hard to Say*, by Alex Sanchez*
▼ *Sonny's House of Spies*, by George Ella Lyon
▼ *Totally Joe*, by James Howe*

FICTION WITH MULTIPLE QUEER CHARACTERS

▼ *Geography Club*, by Brent Hartinger*
▼ *Pretty Things*, by Sarra Manning*
▼ *Rainbow Boys, Rainbow High, Rainbow Road*, by Alex Sanchez*
▼ *The Realm of Possibility*, by David Levithan*
▼ *Wide Awake,* by David Levithan

FICTION WITH QUEER SECONDARY CHARACTERS

▼ *Alt Ed*, by Catherine Atkins
▼ *Born Confused*, by Tanuja Desai-Hidier
▼ *Dangerous Angels: The Weetzie Bat Books*, by Francesca Lia Block*
▼ *Eight Seconds*, by Jean Ferris
▼ *From the Notebooks of Melanin Sun*, by Jacqueline Woodson*
▼ *Getting It*, by Alex Sanchez
▼ *Gingerbread, Shrimp,* and *Cupcake*, by Rachel Cohn*
▼ *Heart on My Sleeve*, by Ellen Wittlinger*
▼ *Keesha's House*, by Helen Frost
▼ *My Heartbeat*, by Garret Freymann-Weyr*
▼ *Nick & Norah's Infinite Playlist*, by Rachel Cohn and David Levithan*
▼ *One of Those Hideous Books Where the Mother Dies*, by Sonya Sones
▼ *The Perks of Being a Wallflower*, by Stephen Chbosky*
▼ *True Believer*, by Virginia Euwer Wolfe

FICTION WITH STRAIGHT TEENS WHO HAVE QUEER FRIENDS

▼ *Absolutely, Positively Not . . .*, by David LaRochelle*
▼ *The Bermudez Triangle*, by Maureen Johnson*
▼ *Dangerous Angels: The Weetzie Bat Books*, by Francesca Lia Block*

▼ *Getting It*, by Alex Sanchez
▼ *The Hookup Artist,* by Tucker Shaw*
▼ *The Misfits*, by James Howe
▼ *Nick & Norah's Infinite Playlist*, by Rachel Cohn and David Levithan*
▼ *The Perks of Being a Wallflower*, by Stephen Chbosky*
▼ *Pretty Things*, by Sarra Manning*
▼ *Shrimp*, by Rachel Cohn*
▼ *Sorcerers of the Nightwing*, by Geoffrey Huntington
▼ *A Tale of Two Summers*, by Brian Sloan*

FICTION WITH UNEXPECTED QUEER TWISTS AND CHARACTERS

▼ *Gossip Girl* series, by Cecily von Ziegesar
▼ *Heart On My Sleeve*, by Ellen Wittlinger*
▼ *Ironman*, by Chris Crutcher
▼ *One of Those Hideous Books Where the Mother Dies*, by Sonya Sones
▼ *Pop Princess*, by Rachel Cohn
▼ *The Princess Diaries* series, by Meg Cabot
▼ *Sloppy Firsts*, by Megan McCafferty

QUEER YA CLASSICS STILL IN PRINT

▼ *Am I Blue? Coming Out from the Silence*, ed. by Marion Dane Bauer*
▼ *Annie on My Mind*, by Nancy Garden*
▼ *The Arizona Kid*, by Ron Koertge
▼ *Deliver Us from Evie*, by M. E. Kerr*
▼ *Eight Seconds*, by Jean Ferris
▼ *Jack*, by A. M. Holmes*
▼ *Night Kites*, by M. E. Kerr
▼ *Peter*, by Kate Walker
▼ *Dangerous Angels: The Weetzie Bat Books*, by Francesca Lia Block*

AWARD-WINNING QUEER YA FICTION

▼ *Am I Blue? Coming Out from the Silence*, ed. by Marion Dane Bauer*
▼ *Annie on My Mind,* by Nancy Garden*
▼ *Boy Meets Boy*, by David Levithan*
▼ *Dangerous Angels: The Weetzie Bat Books*, by Francesca Lia Block*
▼ *Deliver Us from Evie*, by M. E. Kerr*
▼ *Dream Boy*, by Jim Grimsley
▼ *From the Notebooks of Melanin Sun*, by Jacqueline Woodson*
▼ *Keesha's House*, by Helen Frost

▼ *My Heartbeat*, by Garret Freymann-Weyr*
▼ *Postcards from No Man's Land*, by Aidan Chambers*
▼ *A Really Nice Prom Mess*, by Brian Sloan*
▼ *So Hard to Say*, by Alex Sanchez*

NONFICTION: LGBTQ LIFE

▼ *The Advocate College Guide for LGBT Students*, by Shane L. Windmeyer
▼ *GLBTQ: The Survival Guide for Queer and Questioning Teens*, by Kelly Huegel*
▼ *The Full Spectrum: A New Generation of Writing about Gay, Lesbian, Bisexual, Transgender, Questioning and Other Identities*, ed. by David Levithan and Billy Merrell*
▼ *Growing up Gay In America: Informative and Practical Advice for Teen Guys Questioning Their Sexuality and Growing up Gay*, by Jason Rich
▼ *How It Feels to Have a Gay or Lesbian Parent: A Book by Kids for Kids of All Ages*, by Judith E. Snow
▼ *Kings & Queens: Queers at the Prom*, by David Boyer*
▼ *Love Makes a Family: Portraits of Lesbian, Gay, Bisexual, and Transgender Parents and Their Families*, by Gigi Kaeser, photographer, and Peggy Gillespie, ed.
▼ *Queer Facts: The Greatest Gay and Lesbian Trivia Book Ever*, by Michelle Baker and Stephen Tropiano
▼ *Revolutionary Voices: A Multicultural Queer Youth Anthology*, ed. by Amy Sonnie
▼ *When I Knew*, ed. by Robert Trachtenberg*

ADULT QUEER FICTION CROSSOVER TITLES FOR TEENS

▼ *Bastard out of Carolina*, Dorothy Allison
▼ *A Boy's Own Story*, by Edmund White
▼ *Donorboy*, by Brendan Halprin*
▼ *Dream Boy*, by Jim Grimsley
▼ *Leave Myself Behind*, by Bart Yates*
▼ *The Perks of Being a Wallflower*, by Stephen Chbosky*
▼ *Rubyfruit Jungle*, by Rita Mae Brown
▼ *The World of Normal Boys*, by K.M. Soehnlein*
▼ *The Year of Ice*, by Brian Malloy

ALL-TIME QUEER FICTION CLASSICS FOR ADULTS

▼ *The Agony and the Ecstasy*, by Irving Stone
▼ *A Boy's Own Story*, by Edmund White

▼ *The City and the Pillar,* by Gore Vidal
▼ *The Color Purple*, by Alice Walker
▼ *The Front Runner*, by Patricia Nell Warren
▼ *Giovanni's Room*, by James Baldwin
▼ *Maurice*, by E.M. Forster
▼ *The Picture of Dorian Gray*, by Oscar Wilde
▼ *Rubyfruit Jungle*, by Rita Mae Brown
▼ *The Swimming Pool Library*, by Alan Hollinghurst
▼ *Tales of the City* series, by Armistead Maupin

QUEER FANTASY AND SCI-FI BOOKS

▼ *Bending the Landscape*, ed. by Nicola Griffeth
▼ *Kissing the Witch: Old Tales in New Skins*, by Emma Donague
▼ *Swordpoint*, by Ellen Kushner

PEOPLE OF COLOR IN QUEER YA FICTION

▼ *Born Confused*, by Tanuja Desai-Hidier
▼ *The Dear One*, by Jacqueline Woodson
▼ *From the Notebooks of Melanin Sun*, by Jacqueline Woodson
▼ *Geography Club*, by Brent Hartinger*
▼ *Getting It*, by Alex Sanchez
▼ *Hard Love,* by Ellen Wittlinger*
▼ *The House You Pass on the Way*, by Jacqueline Woodson
▼ *Name Me Nobody*, by Lois Ann Yamanaka
▼ *Orphea Proud*, by Sharon Dennis Wyeth*
▼ *Ruby*, by Rosa Guy
▼ *So Hard to Say*, by Alex Sanchez*
▼ *Sunday You Learn How to Box*, by Bil Wright
▼ *True Believer*, by Virginia Euwer Wolfe
▼ *What Night Brings*, by Carla Trujillo

QUEERS IN VERSE

▼ *Bend, Don't Shatter: Poets on the Beginning of Desire*, ed. by T. Cole Rachel and Rita D. Costello*
▼ *Howl and Other Poems*, by Allen Ginsberg
▼ *The Full Spectrum: A New Generation of Writing about Gay, Lesbian, Bisexual, Transgender, Questioning and Other Identities*, ed. by David Levithan and Billy Merrell*
▼ *Leaves of Grass*, by Walt Whitman
▼ *One of Those Hideous Books Where the Mother Dies*, by Sonya Sones

▼ *The Realm of Possibility*, by David Levithan*
▼ *Talking in the Dark: A Poetry Memoir*, by Billy Merrell*
▼ *True Believer*, by Virginia Euwer Wolfe

GRAPHIC NOVELS

▼ *Les Bijoux* series, by Eun-Ha Jo and Park Sang Sun
▼ *Cardcaptor Sakura* series, by Clamp
▼ *Eerie Queerie* series, by Shuri Shiozu*
▼ *Enigma*, by Peter Milligan
▼ *Green Lantern: Brother's Keeper*, by Judd Winick
▼ *Pedro and Me*, by Judd Winick
▼ *Potential*, *Awkward*, and *Definition*, by Ariel Schrag
▼ *Sailor Moon* series, by Naoko Takeuchi
▼ *Shade the Changing Man*, by Peter Milligan
▼ *Stuck Rubber Baby*, by Howard Kruse

CHILDREN'S PICTURE BOOKS

▼ *And Tango Makes Three*, by Peter Parnell
▼ *Daddy's Roommate*, by Michael Willhoite
▼ *Heather Has Two Mommies*, by Leslea Newman
▼ *How My Family Came to Be: Daddy, Papa, and Me*, by Andrew Aldrich
▼ *Jack & Jim*, by Kitty Crowther
▼ *King & King*, by Linda de Haan and Stern Nijland
▼ *One Dad, Two Dads, Brown Dads, Blue Dads*, by Johnny Valentine
▼ *The Sissy Duckling*, by Harvey Fierstein

BOOKS ABOUT SEX AND SEXUALITY

▼ *Changing Bodies, Changing Lives: A Book for Teens on Sex and Relationships*, by Ruth Bell
▼ *GLBTQ: The Survival Guide for Queer and Questioning Teens*, by Kelly Huegel*
▼ *The Lesbian Health Book: Caring for Ourselves*, by Jocelyn White and Marissa Martinez
▼ *Love and Sex: 10 Stories of Desire*, ed. by Michael Cart
▼ *The Underground Guide to Teenage Sexuality*, by Michael J. Basso

FICTION TITLES WITH HOMOPHOBIA

▼ *Baby Be Bop (Dangerous Angels: The Weetzie Bat Books)*, by Francesca Lia Block*

▼ *Deliver Us from Evie*, by M. E. Kerr*
▼ *Dream Boy*, by Jim Grimsley
▼ *The Hookup Artist*, by Tucker Shaw*
▼ *Keeping You a Secret*, by Julie Anne Peters*
▼ *The Misfits*, by James Howe
▼ *Orphea Proud*, by Sharon Dennis Wyeth*
▼ *What Happened to Lani Garver?*, by Carol Plum-Ucci*

FICTION IN WHICH STRAIGHT FALLS FOR QUEER, OR VICE VERSA

▼ *Hard Love*, by Ellen Wittlinger*
▼ *Pretty Things*, Sarra Manning*
▼ *The Realm of Possibility*, by David Levithan*
▼ *Sloppy Firsts*, by Megan McCafferty
▼ *So Hard to Say*, by Alex Sanchez*

SHORT STORIES AND SHORT STORY COLLECTIONS

▼ *Am I Blue? Coming Out from the Silence*, by Marion Jane Bauer*
▼ *Athletic Shorts*, by Chris Crutcher
▼ *Growing up Gay*, by Bennett L. Singer
▼ *Kissing the Witch: Old Tales in New Skins*, by Emma Donague
▼ *Love & Sex: Ten Stories of Desire*, ed. by Michael Cart
▼ *Necessary Noise: Stories about Our Families as They Really Are*, ed. by Michael Cart
▼ *Not the Only One: Lesbian and Gay Fiction for Teens*, ed. by Jane Summer
▼ *One Hot Second: Stories of Desire*, ed. by Cathy Young
▼ *Sixteen: Stories about That Sweet and Bitter Birthday*, ed. by Megan McCafferty

MEMOIRS AND BIOGRAPHIES WRITTEN FOR YA AUDIENCES

▼ *Adrienne Rich*, by Amy Sickles, (Chelsea House series)
▼ *Allen Ginsberg*, by Neil Heims (Chelsea House series)
▼ *Andy Warhol: Prince of Pop*, by Jan Greenberg and Sandra Jordan
▼ *James Baldwin*, by Randall Kenan (Chelsea House series)
▼ *James Baldwin: Voice From Harlem*, by Ted Gottfried
▼ *Oscar Wilde*, by Jeff Nunokawa, (Chelsea House series)
▼ *Sappho*, by Jane McIntosh Snyder (Chelsea House series)
▼ *Talking in the Dark: A Poetry Memoir*, by Billy Merrell*

▼ *Walt Whitman*, by Arnie Kantrowitz (Chelsea House series)
▼ *Young, Black and Determined: A Biography of Lorraine Hansberry*, by Patricia C. McKissack and Frederick L. McKissack

MEMOIRS AND BIOGRAPHIES WRITTEN FOR ADULTS

▼ *The Best Little Boy in the World*, by Andrew Tobias and John Reid
▼ *Funny Thing Is*, by Ellen DeGeneres
▼ *How I Learned to Snap*, by Kirk Read*
▼ *I Have Chosen to Stay and Fight*, by Margaret Cho
▼ *I Know Why the Caged Bird Sings*, by Maya Angelou
▼ *I'm the One That I Want*, by Margaret Cho
▼ *The Intimate World of Abraham Lincoln*, by C. A. Tripp
▼ *Mama's Boy, Preacher's Son: A Memoir*, by Kevin Jennings
▼ *Naked*, by David Sedaris
▼ *Name All the Animals*, by Allison Smith
▼ *Running with Scissors*, by Augusten Burroughs

PERIODICALS

▼ *The Advocate**
▼ *www.oasismag.com*
▼ *Out*
▼ *XY*
▼ *YGA*

FILMS

▼ *Beautiful Thing**
▼ *Boys Don't Cry*
▼ *Boys Life* series
▼ *Brokeback Mountain*
▼ *But I'm a Cheerleader*
▼ *The Celluloid Closet*
▼ *Edge of Seventeen*
▼ *Hedwig and the Angry Inch*
▼ *The Incredibly True Adventure of Two Girls in Love**
▼ *The Laramie Project*
▼ *Lilies*
▼ *The Lost Language of Cranes*
▼ *Ma Vie en Rose*
▼ *The Times of Harvey Milk*
▼ *Wild Reeds*

TELEVISION

- ▼ *Buffy the Vampire Slayer**
- ▼ *Dawson's Creek*
- ▼ *The L Word*
- ▼ *My So-Called Life**
- ▼ *Queer as Folk*
- ▼ *Queer Eye for the Straight Guy*
- ▼ *Will & Grace*

MUSIC

- ▼ Ani DiFranco
- ▼ David Bowie
- ▼ The Homosexuals
- ▼ Indigo Girls
- ▼ Janis Joplin
- ▼ Jason and deMarco
- ▼ *The L Word* soundtracks
- ▼ K. D. Lang
- ▼ The Magnetic Fields
- ▼ Melissa Etheridge
- ▼ Morrissey
- ▼ Pansy Division
- ▼ *Queer as Folk* soundtracks
- ▼ Sigur Ros
- ▼ The Smiths
- ▼ Rufus Wainwright

FICTION FOR TEENS WITH QUEER PARENTS

- ▼ *Athletic Shorts*, by Chris Crutcher
- ▼ *Between Mom and Jo*, by Julie Anne Peters
- ▼ *Donorboy*, by Brendan Halprin*
- ▼ *From the Notebooks of Melanin Sun*, by Jacqueline Woodson*
- ▼ *Jack*, by A. M. Holmes*
- ▼ *Out of the Shadows*, by Sue Hines
- ▼ *Sonny's House of Spies*, by George Ella Lyon

BOOKS FOR PARENTS WITH QUEER TEENS

- ▼ *Always My Child: A Parent's Guide to Understanding Your Gay, Lesbian, Bisexual, Transgendered or Questioning Son or Daughter*, ed. by Kevin Jennings and Pat Shapiro

▼ *Everyday Activism: A Handbook for Lesbian, Gay, and Bisexual People and Their Allies*, by Michael R. Stevenson and Jeanine C. Cogan
▼ *Family Outing*, by Chastity Bono
▼ *GLBTQ: The Survival Guide for Queer and Questioning Teens*, by Kelly Huegel*
▼ *How Homophobia Hurts Children: Nurturing Diversity at Home, at School, and in the Community*, by Jean M. Baker, PhD
▼ *Losing Matt Shepard: Life and Politics in the Aftermath of Anti-Gay Murder*, by Beth Loffreda
▼ *Mama's Boy, Preacher's Son: A Memoir*, by Kevin Jennings*
▼ *The New Gay Teenager*, by Ritch Savin-Williams
▼ *Straight Parents, Gay Children: Keeping Families Together*, by Robert A. Bernstein
▼ *When I Knew*, by Robert Trachtenberg*

FICTION FOR TEENS WITH QUEER SIBLINGS

▼ *Deliver Us from Evie*, by M. E. Kerr*
▼ *Gingerbread*, *Shrimp*, and *Cupcake*, by Rachel Cohn*
▼ *Heart on My Sleeve*, by Ellen Wittlinger*
▼ *My Heartbeart*, by Garret Freymann-Weyr*
▼ *Luna: A Novel*, by Julie Anne Peters*

11 COMPELLING LGBTQ BOOKTALKS

INTRODUCTION

Tips for booktalking queer materials appeared in Chapter 7, and this chapter offers six examples to get you thinking—sample LGBTQ booktalks, all guaranteed crowd-pleasers. You could perform them verbatim, but you'll probably want to change the words and content to suit your personal voice and style. The more you make a booktalk your own, the more convincing and enticing it will be. So, feel free to use these samples as inspiration and adapt them so that they work for you. The following six booktalks encompass a range of queer-themed novels: some with gay protagonists, others with lesbians, and some books in which the queer character is a friend or relative of the straight protagonist. All of these titles are also reviewed in Chapter 9, so be sure to cross-reference for additional information—but, as recommended in Chapter 7, you should read these books for yourself. For complete citations, refer to the Bibliography.

SIX SAMPLE BOOKTALKS

HARD LOVE, BY ELLEN WITTLINGER

John gets lots of tough love. He's used to being a loner. Since his parents' divorce he stays at home in Darlington, Massachusetts, with his mom and whatever washed-up boyfriend she's managed to acquire. Weekends are spent in Boston with his dad, who somehow always manages to have pressing commitments on Saturday and Sunday nights: charity benefits, literary events, parties given by important people he can't afford to miss. Every week. What a joke. Of course he thinks he makes up for all of it by taking John to dinner every Friday night, when he's forced to spend one painful silent hour face-to-face with his only son. Once dinner's over, John barely gets a glimpse of his dad until he gets back in the Saab on Sunday night for the drive back to Darlington.

So John has lots of free time on weekends and it's one particular weekend he finds himself wandering around Tower Records, flipping through the magazine racks, stumbling on the section where the zines are kept: Homemade magazines that were written by other teenagers who just wrote down their lives, photocopied at Kinko's, and put out for anyone who's interested to read.

John zeroes in on a zine called *Escape Velocity*, written by someone named Marisol, who wrote about walking in the cemetery and imagining old dead families still arguing with each other underground. She made up her own list of Shakespearean insults. She wrote a hilarious article called "Why My Mother Still Has a Dorothy Hamill Haircut."

And then John reads a title-less piece—a kind of free-form poetic want-ad—about how her name means "bitter sun" in Spanish but that she wasn't bitter because that was a waste of time. And how her birth parents were Puerto Rican but her adoptive white mom named her after her heritage. And how her dad was a Cuban college professor. And how she was a writer who was looking for love. The poem, in a way, was her creed—a creed that John couldn't get out of his mind.

Escape Velocity haunts John until he can get back to Tower Records for the second issue. On the day it's scheduled to arrive, he waits there for Marisol to deliver it. They meet. She tries to blow him off, but he's persistent. He convinces her to get coffee. They talk about zines. They talk about their lives. John can't stop himself from falling for her.

They start spending time together. Every weekend that John goes to Boston, he hangs out with Marisol. He finds himself looking forward to visiting his dad every week because he gets to see her. And before he knows it he's head over heels in love with Marisol. Which is more than tough. It's hard, especially because Marisol's a lesbian.

DONORBOY, BY BRENDAN HALPRIN

Here's how Rosalind was conceived: Fifteen years ago, in Boston, a guy named Sean took the Red Line to the Green Line. He got off at Brookline Village and walked into this eight-story glass box of a building. He took the elevator to the fourth floor, and walked into Fertility Solutions, suite 416. He signed in with the receptionist, and then a nurse named Angela, who reeked of cigarette smoke and wore about a dozen gold rings on every finger, escorted him to the donation room. She handed him a clear plastic cup with a blue lid. Sean went into the hospital room, placed the donation into the cup, replaced the lid, and returned the cup to Angela— quite possibly the most embarrassing moment of his life. A month later, Rosalind's mom Sandy called to say that her partner Eva was pregnant. Thus, Rosalind was conceived.

Sean never laid eyes on her until fifteen years later. Her two moms are killed in an automobile accident. Her aunt—a friend of her mom's and probably the closest of kin—can't afford a lawyer to win the custody battle. Her grandmother thinks she's too old to take care of her.

The last person she wants to turn to is Sean, the biological father whom she didn't even know existed. She's never seen him before, never talked to him, never even thought about him. So even though Sean's trying really hard to be a good father and do the right things, buy the right groceries, send her to the right schools—do everything he can to make Rosalind feel at home in the wake of her tragedy—she still can't really see him as anything but a donorboy.

MY HEARTBEAT, BY GARRET FREYMANN-WEYR

"Everyone in the world has a different way of looking at the same thing." So Ellen's mother says.

Ellen loves her big brother, Linc, the piano-playing track star. She also loves his best friend, James. In fact, she's totally head over heels in love with James. And he knows it. James likes to tease her by saying stuff like, "When you grow out of it, you'll break my heart." But Ellen knows she'll never grow out of it. She'll always love James in that way—just as much as, if not more than, she loves her brother—and she can't really help it that her cheeks flush bright red when she sees him.

The three are inseparable. Linc and James are always together both at home and school, and Ellen spends most of her spare time with them. But even though she's constantly around them, it's not like she really knows them all that well. Not in a complete way. Linc and James had their own secrets like normal best friends. The secrets didn't occupy Ellen so much as they mystified her—and during the first few days of ninth grade, she discovered that every other freshman girl felt the same.

Ellen has always been a loner, so it's strange that on her first day of school she's flooded with girls who want to be her friend. Girls who treat Ellen like a celebrity because her brother and his best friend are the hottest seniors in school. Girls who grill her about Linc and James.

"How close are you and Linc?"

"You must know James really well."

"Tell James I said 'Hi.'"

Usually the questions are pretty innocent and leave Ellen wondering why the girls don't ask her brother and James these questions themselves. But one day Ellen's new friend Adena asks her an uncomfortable one:

"Linc and James, they're a couple, right?"

Immediately Ellen feels lost. That thought never occurred to her. And the truth is, as much time as Ellen spends with them, she really doesn't know. Taking her mother's advice, Ellen decides to ask Linc herself. The question first goes over like a joke. She asks them "Are you a couple?"

"A couple of what?" Linc says, "Geniuses?"

James says, "That's not what she meant."

"I know what she meant," Linc replies, and then he doesn't say anything. His silence is the only answer Ellen needs to her question: mistake, big, big mistake. So big that Linc stalks out of James's apartment, leaving Ellen and James alone.

That same night, Ellen discovers that James wants to love Linc, but her brother's not ready to deal with that or any of the other issues that go along with it. And truthfully neither of them are really sure if they're gay or not. In fact, James, who admits his love for Linc, says that girls do interest him—he's just never met the right one.

Ellen immediately knows that she is the right girl, and with Linc slamming the door on the both of them, she and James begin spending more and more time alone together. Time for Ellen to try and rebuild her relationship with her brother. Time for Ellen's parents to reveal the secrets behind Linc's angry silence. Time that causes Ellen's heart to beat faster and faster for James. Ellen falls harder than ever for James, and yet longs to be closer to Linc. And as every step brings Ellen closer to James, those same steps widen the gulf between her and Linc. But what happens when James falls for Ellen too?

ORPHEA PROUD, BY SHARON DENNIS WYETH

Orphea Proud's dad died of a heart attack. Her mom died of brain cancer soon after. That same year, she went color-blind, moved in with her older brother, Rupert, and his wife, Ruby, and met her best friend in Lissa.

Orphea, who's black, and Lissa, who's white, were inseparable. They shared peanut butter and jelly sandwiches in the lunchroom. They did science projects together. The listened to the same music, rap and folk. They were at each other's houses all the time making cakes, learning to dance, having sleepovers.

But by age sixteen, the sleepovers had morphed into something else. At sixteen they stopped getting up at the crack of dawn. Instead they stayed in bed together, watching the snowfall outside, touching each other, kissing, laughing.

Early one morning they were so busy Orphea didn't hear Rupert knocking on the door. Without waiting, he opened the door and stood there, staring at the two girls tangled in each other's arms. For a second Orphea and Lissa were frozen. Then Rupert lurched across the room, grabbed Orphea by the hair, and threw her across the room. Lissa slipped out the door as Rupert slammed Orphea's head into the wall over and over and over again, telling her she was surely going to hell for this.

Orphea heard Lissa's van revving up in the street outside. It sounded like she was having trouble getting out of the parking space because of all the snow. Her tires spun, and then she peeled off into the dark. That was the last time Orphea ever saw her.

Three hours later, Rupert and Ruby tell her that Lissa's van skidded off the road. She'd been injured. Her spleen ruptured. She had died almost instantaneously.

Orphea lasted in school for about three weeks after the funeral, pretending to be there when really she wasn't. She disappeared, answering anyone who spoke to her with a mechanical nod and tilt of her mouth. She shaved her head. She took a safety pin and carved the word "Fool" into her arm, because that was what she felt like—a fool. She washed back a handful of pills with vodka, but it only made her sick.

Rupert and Ruby decided the only place that was safe was Virginia: a town called Handsome Crossing where her mom was born and raised on Proud Road, a street that was named after her family. Rupert tied up Orphea, gagged her, drove her to Virginia, and dumped her in front of Proud Store, owned by her two great aunts and the only business in town.

But Orphea was smart. She knew she was going nowhere fast living with her brother and she didn't have much to lose. She knew that sometimes you have to take a few steps backward before you can you move forward. And something Lissa once told her stuck in her head: "It's your movie, you might as well write the script."

This is the script. *Orphea Proud*, by Sharon Dennis Wyeth.

LEAVE MYSELF BEHIND, BY BART YATES

Noah never wanted a different mother. He just wanted his mother to be different.

Get in line, right?

Because anyone who tells you he doesn't have mixed feelings about his mother is either stupid or a liar. Granted, Noah's mom, Virginia, is a special case, like living with a myth. She's only half human: The rest is equal parts wolverine, hyena, goddess, and rutting goat. In other words, she's a poet. A psycho-poet.

How else could Noah rationalize her yelling at him, "No means no, you little shit," then hurling a spackling knife at his head? Thankfully, the knife missed and hit the plaster wall behind him, which crumbled and fell into a heap on the floor.

See, Noah and his mom just moved from Chicago to this giant Victorian house in the very tiny town of Oakland, New Hampshire. He wants to get a temporary job before school starts—it'll be his senior year—but his mom won't let him until he gets the new house remodeled. The house is a mess: plaster dust, nails, boards, spackle, paint cans, caulking guns, and a bunch of boxes. Getting it in shape sounds easy enough, but in the middle of tearing down and repairing the walls, Noah begins to discover old mason jars hidden in the plaster. Sometimes they contain poems. Sometimes pieces of jewelry. Sometimes articles of clothing.

At first, Noah and his mom think nothing of the jars and the oddities they contain. But when they hear of the previous homeowner's wife, who mysteriously disappeared decades before along with her child, Noah's mom becomes more and more obsessed with the relics. She maniacally begins to tear away at every wall in the house to find any clue that might lead to the woman's disappearance. And every wall Noah reconstructs, she bashes back down again. And with every wall she pulls down, Noah feels the weak threads of his own life tearing away at the seams, piece by piece, as he watches her obsession with the mystery grow along with her deeper descent into insanity.

He needs it like a hole in his head, but in the midst of everything Noah realizes he can't stop thinking about J.D., his neighbor, who unfortunately has a girlfriend but still holds his gaze—especially when they're alone together.

Inevitably, what lies behind the walls in Noah's house isn't just boards and plaster, but a secret strong and dangerous enough to force him and his mother over the edge. Permanently.

BOY MEETS BOY, BY DAVID LEVITHAN

Once upon a time in a world far, far away—well, as far as New Jersey can get—there lived a boy named Paul, who came out of the closet . . . in kindergarten.

"Paul is definitely gay, and has a very good sense of self." At least that's what his kindergarten teacher wrote on his report card. When he read it, he asked his teacher for some clarification: "Am I definitely gay?"

Mrs. Benchley looked at him and nodded. Paul thought for a moment, and pointed to the painting corner, where Greg Easton was wrestling on the ground with Ted Halpern.

"Is Greg gay?" he asked.

Mrs. Benchley replied: "No. At least, not yet."

Interesting. Paul found it all very interesting. "But what I feel is right, right?"

"For you, yes," Mrs. Benchley told him. "What you feel is absolutely right for you. Always remember that."

Paul soon became the first openly gay class president in the history of Ms. Farquar's third-grade class, running on the platform "Vote for me! I'm gay!" His only opponent was Ted Halpern, who first chose "Vote for me! I'm not gay" for his platform. Then he considered "You can't vote for him, he's gay!" But finally decided on "Don't vote for the fag," which unfortunately lost him the race. While Ted racked up only the close-minded, lint-head vote, Paul took the girl vote, the open-minded guy vote, the third-grade closet case vote, and the Ted-hater vote. It was a total blowout.

In sixth grade, he formed a gay-straight alliance with his friends to teach all the straight kids how to dance.

In eighth grade he started a food column in the local paper, called "Dining Out."

All in all it seems junior high is pretty fun and not so out of the ordinary. He has the usual series of crushes, confusions, and intensities. But then in his sophomore year of high school he attends a concert at the local bookstore and notices a pile of books that have fallen from the shelf. He bends down to pick them up and spots the coolest pair of sneakers he's ever seen standing near the pile. Attached to them is the coolest guy he's ever seen. His hair points in ten different directions. His eyes are kind of close together, and so green you could almost dive into them. There's a birthmark on his neck shaped like a comma. He's holding a book out to Paul called *Migraines Are Only in Your Mind*. Suddenly Paul becomes aware of his untucked shirt, his unsteady breathing, his heartbeat.

"I'm Paul."

"I'm Noah."

And suddenly everything gets complicated.

Boy meets boy. Boy loses boy. Boy has to figure out how to get boy back.

12 SUCCESSFUL LGBTQ PROGRAMS

INTRODUCTION

This chapter offers eighteen LGBTQ-themed programs guaranteed to generate teen excitement in your library. As noted in Chapter 7, programs are listed here in order of how openly queer they are, but you can always adjust them to suit your library. Likewise, be sure to let teens know that these programs are open to people of any sexual identity—you don't have to be queer, in other words, to participate. For each of the following programs you are given a list of materials, instructions on how to execute the program, and a bibliography that you can tie into the display or activity. Titles with an asterisk next to them are profiled in Chapter 9. Also keep in mind that each of the title lists in Chapter 10 make great themes around which you could create a display. Finally, remember that even though these programs are designed to be led by you without the help of outside expertise, if you do bring in a professional presenter or special guest, this could be a fantastic opportunity for teens to interact with the queer community.

EIGHTEEN STEP-BY-STEP PROGRAMS

LOVELY IN LAVENDER

What You Will Need

- ▼ Lavender-colored labels
- ▼ Clear book tape
- ▼ All of your LGBTQ fiction titles

How to Make It Happen

The lavender label initiative is a subtle, yet effective method of displaying LGBTQ materials without any flashy rainbow flags or hot pink triangles. The initiative is very simple. First, make an inventory of queer-friendly materials in your library. Once you've inventoried your titles, apply a lavender label—small or large, round or square—onto the spine of each book, CD, DVD, periodical, graphic novel, etc. Then, cover the label with heavy, clear book tape so it doesn't peel. Finally, re-shelve the item where you found it. You're done!

Secretive? Yes. Closeted? Partially. Subversive? Most definitely. By marking your LGBTQ titles and re-shelving them in your regular collection, though, you've set in motion a learning process on the part of your patrons. It's up to you to reveal the system's secret to the brave teen who asks for books about gay people, or the student researching LGBTQ people. After identifying one or two queer-themed titles in your catalog and making the mental connection that these materials all have a lavender label, other teens will soon figure out what the color lavender signifies. And, by the way, lavender has been associated with queer people since the ancient Greeks, who used the word "omofylofilos" to refer to the lavender plant as well as gay men.

In more conservative communities, like the one where this idea originated, lavender labels are a great way for librarians to help their LGBTQ teen population without tipping off homophobic members of the public. Lavender labels work best with fiction, graphic novels, and non-print items, because they tend not to feature detailed catalog entries and subject headings that reveal their LGBTQ content. Conversely, you shouldn't need to label your nonfiction collection because the catalog probably already indicates subject headings—and the titles of these books generally contain queer clues, too. One final note: While this program is ideal for public libraries, school librarians may feel more reticent about enacting it given that schools often seek to present books without any distinguishing characteristics, the idea being that students of all reading levels and backgrounds will be encouraged to explore without a hint of bias. That said, our "Lavender Labels" program complies with the American Library Association's guidelines about labels and ratings systems in that it is neither prejudicial nor restrictive—rather, it is a neutral locating aid (ALA, 1951).

BET YOU DIDN'T KNOW . . .

What You Will Need

- ▼ Signage and exhibit materials such as banners, pictures, and magazine cut-outs
- ▼ Paper, tape, glue, stapler, markers, pens, cut-out lettering, etc.

▼ Display space

▼ Books with LGBTQ secondary characters

Title Tie-Ins

▼ *Dangerous Angels: The Weetzie Bat Books*, by Francesca Lia Block*

▼ *From the Notebooks of Melanin Sun*, by Jaqueline Woodson*

▼ *Gingerbread*, *Shrimp*, and *Cupcake*, by Rachel Cohn*

▼ *Heart on My Sleeve*, by Ellen Wittlinger*

▼ *One of Those Hideous Books Where the Mother Dies*, by Sonya Sones

▼ *The Perks of Being a Wallflower*, by Stephen Chbosky*

▼ *Pretty Things*, by Sarra Manning*

▼ *The Realm of Possibility*, by David Levithan*

▼ *Sorcerers of the Nightwing*, by Geoffrey Huntington

▼ *True Believer*, by Virginia Euwer Wolff

How to Make It Happen

Titles such as *Boy Meets Boy*, *Kissing Kate*, *Rainbow Boys*, and *Annie on My Mind* are pretty far out of the literary closet—their titles give you a fairly good idea of their contents—and they all feature protagonists who are LGBTQ. But what about the books with secondary queer characters, like a gay sibling or lesbian best friend? These titles are often harder to find because fiction cataloging rarely mentions a secondary character's sexual orientation. Here's an idea for a display that puts these titles in the limelight, bringing those unsung queer heroes to the forefront. It's perfect for the teen who's already read titles featuring LGBTQ protagonists, and even better for teens who want—or need—to broaden their horizons when it comes to queer life. In conservative areas, this display is an inconspicuous way to promote not-so-queer titles that boast a lavender lining. Come up with a snappy display title such as: "Bet You Didn't Know . . ."; "Out on the Sidelines"; "In the Outfield"; "Out Offstage."

STRAIGHT ALLIES DISPLAY

What You Will Need

▼ Books about celebrated straight allies, fiction titles with straight friends of queer characters, or straight parents of queer kids

▼ Signage and exhibit materials such as banners, pictures, and magazine cut-outs

▼ Paper, tape, glue, stapler, markers, pens, cut-out lettering, etc.

▼ Display space

Title Tie-Ins

▼ *Dangerous Angels: The Weetzie Bat Books*, by Francesca Lia Block*

▼ *From the Notebooks of Melanin Sun*, by Jacqueline Woodson*

▼ *Geography Club*, by Brent Hartinger*

▼ *Gingerbread*, *Shrimp*, and *Cupcake*, by Rachel Cohn*

▼ *Hard Love*, by Ellen Wittlinger*

▼ *Nick & Norah's Infinite Playlist*, by Rachel Cohn and David Levithan*

▼ *The Perks of Being a Wallflower*, by Stephen Chbosky*

▼ A *Tale of Two Summers*, by Brian Sloan*

How to Make It Happen

The emergence of gay-straight alliances in high schools across the country is heightening the profile of people who are "straight but not narrow," i.e., the straight allies of queer people. The point of this display is not to segregate enlightened straight people from homophobes, but to show queer teens that they have straight allies in the public spotlight and close to home. A display featuring straight allies could include pictures and biographies of people including:

▼ Halle Berry, actor

▼ Tina Fey, comedy writer and actor

▼ Matthew Fox, actor

▼ Jake Gyllenhaal, actor

▼ Lisa Kudrow, actor

▼ Heath Ledger, actor

▼ Bill Maher, talk show host

▼ Gavin Newsom, mayor of San Francisco

▼ Yoko Ono, musician and artist

▼ Gwyneth Paltrow, actor

- ▼ Peter Sarsgaard, actor
- ▼ Rev. Al Sharpton, African American religious leader
- ▼ Jon Stewart, political satirist
- ▼ Shania Twain, singer
- ▼ Kanye West, musician
- ▼ Trisha Yearwood, musician
- ▼ Neil Young, musician

As you've probably noticed from this list, many of these people are Hollywood celebrities—but that virtually guarantees your teens will know who they are. To find more straight allies, check out *The Advocate*, a gay and lesbian periodical that runs a regular department called "Big Gay Following." *The Advocate*, in fact, is where we found many of the people that we listed above.

You might also include fiction titles that feature supportive friends of queer characters including Charlie in *Perks of Being a Wallflower*; Weetzie in the *Dangerous Angels* series; Cyd Charisse in *Gingerbread*, *Shrimp*, and *Cupcake*; Nick and Norah of *Nick & Norah's Infinite Playlist*; and Melanin Sun of *From the Notebooks of Melanin Sun*. Including pictures of YA authors is a good idea, too. Unlike Hollywood celebrities, authors are in the public eye less and so their sexual orientation is less publicized. That said, one source for this information is the book *Lesbian and Gay Voices: An Annotated Bibliography and Guide to Literature for Children and Young Adults*, by Frances Ann Day, which contains revealing author profiles. While you're at it, why not put a picture of your library among with the rest of the signage—just to reinforce the message that you are proud to serve your LGBTQ patrons.

DID YOU KNOW THEY WERE GAY?

What You Will Need

- ▼ Pictures of famous queer people from magazines, etc.
- ▼ Paper, tape, glue, stapler, markers, pens, cut-out lettering, etc.
- ▼ Display space
- ▼ Books about or by famous queer people

Title Tie-Ins

- ▼ *Andy Warhol: Prince of Pop*, by Jan Greenberg
- ▼ *Leaves of Grass*, by Walt Whitman

▼ *James Baldwin: Voice from Harlem*, by Ted Gottfried

▼ *When I Knew*, ed. by Robert Trachtenberg*

▼ *Young, Black and Determined: A Biography of Lorraine Hansberry*, by Patricia L McKissak and Frederick L McKissack

How to Make It Happen

Hopefully your library is able to set up Pride displays during the month of June, just as it celebrates Black History Month and Women's History Month. This display is a nice departure from the average pile of fiction books, short stories, and issue-related series about homophobia. "Did You Know They Were Gay?" highlights famous queer people: James Baldwin, Lance Bass, Margaret Cho, Robert Rauschenberg, Maurice Sendak, Sheryl Swoopes, George Takei, and Andy Warhol, among many others. Its purpose is to help queer teens learn about their roots and help straight teens realize that queer people are everywhere. *GLBTQ: The Survival Guide for Queer and Questioning Teens* offers a fabulous list of queer historical figures as well as current role models. Also check out www.glbtq.com, the online encyclopedia of queer culture. Whoever you feature, try to include photos of these people to accompany the books in the display. If your library or media center is out and proud, your public will probably be okay with a display title like "Did You Know They Were Gay?" If you're in a more conservative community, though, you might shorten it to something like "Did You Know . . .", or "Discover Your Roots." The latter title is perfect for libraries in ultraconservative areas because using the word "roots" allows you to mix other themes into the display such as African American history and women's history.

An interesting twist on the "Did You Know . . ." display might be to include a section of well-known people who have queer family members. You can also do Title Tie-Ins to biographies, memoirs, and other nonfiction works profiling these straight folk. Call this display something like "All in the Family." Lists of queer family members are harder to come by, but queer publications such as *The Advocate* often highlight them. Here's a few suggestions to get you started:

▼ Vice President Dick Cheney, whose daughter, Mary, is a lesbian.

▼ Cher, whose daughter, Chastity, is a lesbian.

▼ Former Speaker of the House Newt Gingrich, whose half-sister, Candace, is a lesbian.

▼ Rev. Al Sharpton, the African American religious and political leader, who has a lesbian sister.

▼ Hip-hop artist Kanye West, who has a gay cousin. In 2005, West went on MTV to call for an end to homophobia: "Not just hip-hop, but America just discriminates. And I wanna just, to come on TV and just tell my rappers, just tell my friends, 'Yo, stop it'" (Associated Press, 2005).

Some of the people on this list, such as Dick Cheney and Newt Gingrich, are less than supportive of equal rights for queer people. Including them in this display, however, underscores the point that LGBTQ people really are everywhere.

"WE'RE HERE, WE'RE QUEER, WE'RE BANNED BOOKS!" DISPLAY

What You Will Need

▼ A list of banned queer-themed books and banned books with queer characters, with these titles highlighted in pink or lavender

▼ A selection of the books that have been banned

▼ Copies of the First Amendment to the Constitution of the United States

▼ Quotes from queer books that resulted in these books' being banned

▼ Exhibit materials such as brown paper jackets or "banned" labels to cover the titles of books on display, or quotes from the books that people often challenge

▼ Paper, tape, glue, stapler, markers, pens, cut-out lettering, etc.

▼ Display space

Title Tie-Ins

▼ *Annie on My Mind*, by Nancy Garden*
▼ *The Color Purple*, by Alice Walker
▼ *Geography Club*, by Brent Hartinger*
▼ *I Know Why the Caged Bird Sings*, by Maya Angelou
▼ *Jack*, by A. M. Holmes*
▼ *Leaves of Grass*, by Walt Whitman
▼ *The Perks of Being a Wallflower*, by Stephen Chbosky*

How to Make It Happen

We hope that most libraries highlight the importance of the First Amendment by offering displays during Banned Books Week. The American Library Association, which sponsors the week, compiles a list of the top ten most challenged books of each year. With that in mind, we suggest this twist on the traditional banned books program. Group the titles in your display according to the reasons why they are banned including religion, strong language, sexuality, and homosexuality. Give the queer section a catchy title such as "We're Here! We're Queer! We're Banned Books!" By organizing this display, you'll help increase public awareness that censors are targeting not just books, but a specific group of people. You'll also send a message that you do not allow discrimination in your library. For extra impact, you might cover the titles of books in your display with brown paper. You'll certainly pique the curiosity of your teenaged patrons. You may even raise their awareness level so that they'll combat attempts at banning books in the future. Check out the American Library Association's Web site, www.ala.org, for promotional materials and other resources that you can use to supplement your display.

PRIDE MONTH DISPLAY

What You Will Need

- ▼ Exhibit materials that depict queer history and culture, such as pictures of queer icons or of historic moments such as the Stonewall riots
- ▼ Signage and exhibit materials such as banners, pictures, and lettering
- ▼ A rainbow flag or other queer symbols such as the upside-down pink triangle and the color lavender
- ▼ Paper, tape, glue, stapler, markers, pens, cut-out lettering, etc.
- ▼ Display space
- ▼ A well-balanced mix from your LGBTQ collection including both historical and present-day items; fiction and nonfiction; graphic novels; titles about movers and shakers in queer history; titles on queer culture and politics; periodicals; music; films; television shows

How to Make It Happen

June is Pride Month, a time during which queer communities nationwide celebrate by hosting parades, concerts, and conferences. It was in late June

1969 when queer folk stood up to police who were attempting to raid Stonewall, a gay bar in New York City's Greenwich Village. Known as the "Stonewall Riots," this incident jump-started the modern queer rights movement. The first Pride parade was held in New York a year later, and today queer communities worldwide hold celebrations each June to show their pride. In 2000, President Clinton officially designated June as Gay and Lesbian Pride Month. This is the one time of the year when your library should be able to celebrate the queer community with displays and events—just as it would celebrate Women's History Month and Black History Month.

In creating this display, look at the queer community as a whole: Think about its history, its newsmakers, triumphs and tragedies, celebrations, culture, queer icons, queer celebrities, queer everything! You can beef up your display with fiction titles from your YA collection as well as queer classics. Break out your Ellen DeGeneres biography and your David Sedaris memoirs, queer classics such as *Giovanni's Room*, and don't forget to include *GLBTQ: The Survival Guide for Queer and Questioning Teens*! You might also post flyers on how to set up a gay-straight alliance in a high school, or pamphlets from local queer community groups, as well as GLSEN and PFLAG. However you decide to commemorate Pride, just remember that this is an opportunity to make your library "go gay" for one month.

NATIONAL COMING OUT DAY DISPLAY

What You Will Need

▼ Books about coming out including fiction, nonfiction, biographies and memoirs, poetry, drama, and short stories
▼ Signage and exhibit materials such as banners, pictures, and lettering
▼ Paper, tape, glue, stapler, markers, pens, cut-out lettering, etc.
▼ Display space

Title Tie-Ins

▼ *Absolutely, Positively Not . . .*, by David LaRochelle*
▼ *The Bermudez Triangle*, by Maureen Johnson*
▼ *Deliver Us from Evie*, by M. E. Kerr*
▼ *Empress of the World*, by Sara Ryan*
▼ *The Full Spectrum*, ed. by David Levithan and Billy Merrell*

▼ *How I Learned to Snap*, by Kirk Read*

▼ *Keeping You a Secret*, by Julie Anne Peters*

▼ *Leave Myself Behind*, by Bart Yates*

▼ *Luna: A Novel,* by Julie Anne Peters*

▼ *Talking in the Dark: A Poetry Memoir*, by Billy Merrell*

▼ *Totally Joe*, by James Howe*

▼ *When I Knew*, ed. by Robert Trachtenberg*

How to Make It Happen

National Coming Out Day is October 11th. It commemorates a march on Washington in October 1987, when half a million queer people spoke out for equal rights. National Coming Out Day was first celebrated in 1988 and is now managed by the Human Rights Campaign's National Coming Out Project (Human Rights Campaign, 2005). Why not celebrate it in your library with a display of coming out stories, both fiction, nonfiction, biography, and memoirs? Choose titles that not only portray queer people coming out of the closet but also trace the evolution of coming out: in other words, books that show how coming out was a lot harder in the past than it is today. Of course, it still is hard for a lot of people, so you should choose titles that make this point, too. Be sure to include a mix of fiction and nonfiction titles, such as memoirs and biographies, and be sure to represent everyone in the queer family: lesbians, gays, bisexuals, and trans people. Remember, coming out is not about flaunting sexuality: It's about being honest about whom you love.

START YOUR OWN LGBTQ BOOK DISCUSSION GROUP

What You Will Need

▼ A table and chairs

▼ A discussion agenda, containing ice-breakers and open-ended questions

▼ Promotional flyers to advertise the date, time, and place of the discussion group

▼ LGBTQ-themed books

▼ Snacks (optional)

Title Tie-Ins

▼ *Bend, Don't Shatter*, ed. by T. Cole Rachel and Rita D. Costello*

▼ *From the Notebooks of Melanin Sun*, by Jacqueline Woodson*

▼ *Jack*, by A. M. Holmes*

▼ *Kissing Kate*, by Lauren Myracle*

▼ *Leave Myself Behind*, by Bart Yates*

▼ *The Perks of Being a Wallflower*, by Stephen Chbosky*

How to Make It Happen

For your first meeting, the only preliminary work you need to do is publicize your program, either through word of mouth, posting flyers, or listing it on your library's home page. If you want everyone in the group to read the same book, make sure that you already have multiple copies of the chosen title available before you begin promoting the group. That way, teens can arrive prepared. Alternatively, if everyone will be reading different books, you should prepare a list of suggested LGBTQ titles to help teens choose.

If you promote the discussion group with flyers, consider posting them at local community centers, schools, and other places where teenagers hang out. You might also call the librarians in your community's schools to ask if you can arrange to promote your programs and materials, including your LGBTQ book discussion group. Your library's teen advisory group will be another great resource to help spread the word. Ask them how they think you should promote their programs. Chances are, they will know someone, somewhere who will be interested. However you promote the group, be sure to mention that you don't have to be queer to read LGBTQ books.

It's up to you to decide where in your library to host the discussion. If you're concerned that other teens in the reading room will disturb your group, consider meeting in a more private space such as an office or conference room. That said, offering the LGBTQ discussion in an open environment where anyone can participate helps alleviate any embarrassment teens might feel about joining. Moreover, if people see that you're serving snacks, you'll attract more participants. Once everyone is sitting comfortably and eating, it's time begin. Ask who would like to start the introductions. Ice-breaker questions to start the discussion can be as simple as asking the participants' names, or as topic-specific as discussing favorite LGBTQ television shows and movies. You might find that some teens are so excited to be there that only a bare minimum of ice-breakers are necessary before the discussion takes on its own life—indeed, some teens have never had the opportunity to talk openly and in a safe space about LGBTQ topics. One question not to ask is how the group participants self-identify: You don't want to put them on the spot regarding their sexual orientation. If some kids choose to volunteer this information, make sure that they're protected from name-calling, taunts, and other forms of bullying. You want teens to feel that the library is a hate-free zone.

Don't be surprised if participants haven't chosen books to discuss for the first meeting. On your agenda you should make time to talk about how the teens would like to run the group: Would they prefer to read the same book together, or would each person like to read a different book? Teens often prefer the latter option and there are several reasons this approach is a good one. Teens value freedom of choice and letting them choose books individually will draw a broader audience. Allowing teens to choose their own books also lets other participants in the group see the range of titles available to them and thereby make a better decision about what to read next. When teens begin to recommend books to each other, that's the ultimate form of empowerment and participation in your library. And remember, whichever strategy you choose, you can always change it later.

When your group meets for the first time having selected their own books, it's also a good idea to bring a stack of titles that you can booktalk quickly in four or five sentences. Group members may respond by selecting titles that interest them and thus have something ready for the group's next meeting. In subsequent meetings, lead off with a discussion about a title that you've read recently and then go around the table and ask everyone to talk about the title they've chosen. This helps get the discussion going and spurs other participants to ask questions and voice their own opinions. The other advantage to booktalking is that it introduces group participants to the library's method of talking about books. After hearing a couple of booktalks, teens start to follow the same format on their own, which helps them feel more confident discussing literature.

If everyone arrives at the group having read the same book, it's up to you to prepare questions that specifically relate to the book and will spur conversation. If you've got a really dedicated audience, you can ask one or two of the kids if they'd like to prepare their own questions. Regardless of who moderates, try to make sure that each participant in the group gets a chance to speak at some point during the meeting. And at the end of the session, be sure to ask participants how you can improve things next time.

Discussing queer books differs little from discussing non-queer titles, but these books raise specific LGBTQ issues that you might want to touch upon in your discussion. To show you how, we've developed a handful of sample questions based on the novel *Boy Meets Boy*, by David Levithan.

▼ Can someone recap the plot of *Boy Meets Boy*?

▼ What part did you like the best/the least?

▼ Who was your favorite character and why?

▼ In the world of the book, how are queer people perceived?

▼ How does Paul and Noah's romance differ from the romances of heterosexual couples that you know? (If the teens can't come up with any reasons, that shows maybe this relationship isn't any different—but the process of teens working this idea through in their discussion is important.)

▼ Why is Tony different than all the other queer characters in the book?

▼ What other types of queer characters besides gay boys are there in the book?

▼ What other types of non-queer characters are there and how do they relate to the queer characters?

▼ What stereotypes can you find in *Boy Meets Boy* and how are they portrayed?

▼ What other books are similar to *Boy Meets Boy*?

▼ Do you think the book is realistic?

▼ What's up with the book's cover?

CREATE YOUR OWN QUEER BOOK SOUNDTRACK

What You Will Need

▼ An LGBTQ fiction or nonfiction title that's popular in your library

▼ A popular music CD collection

▼ An empty CD jewel case

▼ Supplies to decorate the jewel case including paper, markers, etc.

Title Tie-Ins

▼ *Dangerous Angels: The Weetzie Bat Books*, by Francesca Lia Block*

▼ *Far from Xanadu*, by Julie Anne Peters

▼ *Heart on My Sleeve*, by Ellen Wittlinger*

▼ *Nick & Norah's Infinite Playlist*, by David Levithan and Rachel Cohn*

▼ *Orphea Proud*, by Sharon Dennis Wyeth*

▼ *The Perks of Being a Wallflower*, by Stephen Chbosky*

How to Make It Happen

This program fuses the art of music with the craft of writing. Many novels, such as *Boy Meets Boy* and *Weetzie Bat*, already have a strong musical theme. For instance, many of the chapter headings in *Boy Meets Boy* are the titles of popular songs. With this in mind, along with the fact that many kids listen to music while they read, we invite you to try a new spin on a book discussion group: Ask kids to devise a list of popular songs that they feel capture the spirit, mood, and atmosphere of their favorite queer novel.

One way to limit the number of songs might be to restrict them to the number of chapters in the book: Each chapter gets one song that conveys the actions, events, and atmosphere within that chapter. For instance, in the first chapter of *Boy Meets Boy*, Paul, the protagonist, meets a boy named Noah and falls for him. At the time, Paul is visiting a bookstore where his friend Zeke is playing folk/hip-hop tunes in an open mike, but Paul has to leave so that he and his friend Joni can drive their friend Tony home before a midnight curfew. These images bring to mind any number of potential songs: a love ballad for Paul and Noah's meeting, such as "Transatlanticism" by Death Cab for Cutie; a Joni Mitchell song, maybe "Conversations," to characterize Paul's best friend, Joni; a song about driving such as "Drive My Car," by the Beatles, or "Fast Car," by Tracy Chapman; maybe a great gay hip-hop/folk song by Meshell N'degocello for Zeke's performance; a song about books, such as "Wrapped up in Books," by Belle and Sebastian, because much of the scene takes place in a bookstore. You get the idea. There are no limits to how you and your group build the mix CD. It's a great way to spark conversation about a book's characters, tone, plot, and symbols—especially since teens love to talk about music!

Once the mix is finished, your group should choose a name for it. Have them consider both the songs as well as the book that inspired them. Although copyright concerns prevent you from burning an actual mix CD, have your teens design CD covers, labels, and liner notes based on their song list. If you really want to knock the program out of the park, serve some snacks and play the songs they select in your library. Depending on your library's agreements with music distributors, you should have the right to play the songs in this setting without violating copyright law. Have your group explain to other teens in the YA room why they chose the songs they did.

CREATE YOUR OWN QUEER ZINE

What You Will Need

- ▼ Pens and pencils
- ▼ Writing pads and drawing paper
- ▼ Drawing utensils such as charcoal, colored pencils, markers, etc.
- ▼ Flyers for advertising

▼ Access to a photocopying machine

▼ Snacks (optional)

Title Tie-Ins

▼ *The Full Spectrum*, ed. by David Levithan and Billy Merrell*

▼ *Hard Love*, by Ellen Wittlinger*

▼ *How I Learned to Snap*, by Kirk Read*

▼ *Oasis*

▼ *Totally Joe*, by James Howe*

▼ *YGA*

How to Make It Happen

A zine is a great way for teens to get feelings and ideas out into the open. The process of creating a zine, moreover, helps teens improve their writing skills and gives them insight into how publishing operates. In a sense, this program is ideal for libraries because it allows writers and artists of all types—poets, novelists, short story writers, cartoon artists, etc.—to come together into one group, learn about each others' specializations, and work together in creating a cohesive project that the library can publish. Inviting an author to guide your kids through the process of writing makes a great twist on the program that can forge connections between your library and the wider community. The first step in conducting a zine workshop is to determine a schedule. We recommend a six- to eight-week program with meetings held on the same day and time each week. The bulk of the workshops will be group editing sessions, and these can occur as often as need be, but there are a few key steps that should take place at the start and conclusion of the entire program. Here is a sample lesson plan for how a seven-week workshop might run.

Pre-Session 1: Give yourself a few weeks before the workshop's first session to advertise the program. Writers are a dedicated bunch and will travel long distances if word gets out: particularly if they hear that your library will publish them. Be sure to post flyers in schools, local book stores, coffee shops, and wherever else teens hang out. If your community has a queer youth center, this is an obvious place to visit.

Session 1: Have everyone in the group introduce themselves by name, by their writing style, and by something quirky that maybe no one else knows about them as an icebreaker. Then, begin a discussion on the nature of their

LGBTQ zine, i.e., what subjects or themes the group wants to cover. Let your teens know that a zine is a very personal form of expression and they can feel free to choose emotions and issues with which they are familiar. Some ideas they might ponder:

▼ Coming out poetry or stories
▼ Love poetry or stories
▼ Queer science fiction and fantasy
▼ Queer comics, Manga, etc.
▼ Bisexuality
▼ Trans issues
▼ First same-sex kiss
▼ First same-sex confusion
▼ Straight-falls-for-queer stories
▼ Queer-falls-for-straight stories
▼ LGBTQ life at home and in school
▼ PDA (public displays of affection)

Assign tasks and ask everyone to return the following week with a rough draft of whatever topic they decide to pursue. The ideal is to get a variety of writing styles and ideas, but don't worry if your group is mainly composed of poets or short story writers because you can always ask teens to experiment later with a different genre.

Session 2: At the start of the second session, welcome everyone back to the group and thank them for persevering—let them know that now their zine is officially off the ground. Session 2 marks the first day of edits, but you might want to start with another icebreaker on this day, just to get everyone comfortable with one another—especially since they're about to read their works aloud and receive constructive criticism from other group members. You might consider offering snacks, although these often prove too distracting. Perhaps you, the librarian, should share something you've written to start the discussion. It doesn't have to be fantastic, just something to get everyone's minds going. Once you or another brave teen has taken the lead, hopefully the others will feel more at ease in reading their works aloud. Be sure that feedback steers clear of personal criticisms. Also, be sure to let the group know that writers can feel a little shy about reading their thoughts aloud to others. Hopefully, you'll create an inviting and safe environment in which teens know they can speak candidly. At the end of the session, ask the group to start revising their pieces and begin new ones.

Sessions 3 to 5: Continue much the same as the second session, encouraging your group to bring in new work along with earlier pieces they are revising. If you notice a decline in output, assign new topics. Some ideas to consider: Write a story exploring the theme "What if you were gay?" or, "What if your best friend were trans?" Or, write about why gay marriage should be legalized—or not. The point is to get teens to voice their opinions, explore new ideas, and reconsider old ones. Spontaneous writing exercises such as group poetry, magnetic poetry, and around-the-table-short-story writing are a great way to get their minds going. Continue these roundtable sessions until you or the group feels that you've compiled enough material for publication. You can meet for four days or you might meet for eight—it all depends on the cohesiveness of your group and their eagerness to write.

Session 6: In the final official session—day six, eight, etc.—have your group decide on the zine's title, cover art, table of contents, and how they want their bylines to appear. Collect the final drafts of their writings and compile them in their requested order. In true zine style, photocopy everything, collate the pages, and staple them together—you've got a zine!

Session 7: Host a party to celebrate publication of your zine. On the day of the party, set up a podium and/or microphone so that the zine authors can read their writings aloud for proud parents, friends, and librarians. Award each participant a few copies of the zine. Don't forget to keep copies for yourself and the library. If your teens are motivated, they might also post their zine online or distribute it for free in local bookstores and coffee shops.

CREATE YOUR OWN QUEER GRAPHIC NOVEL ANTHOLOGY

What You Will Need

▼ Art supplies such as pencils, markers, paper, paints, erasers, etc.

▼ A digital scanner, or funds to scan the artwork at a copy shop

▼ A software program that will allow you to manipulate artworks digitally

▼ A color printer, or funds to print at a copy shop

Title Tie-Ins

▼ Examples of queer graphic novels such as *Eerie Queerie**, *Stuck Rubber Baby*, *Shade the Changing Man*, *Enigma*, and the works of Ariel Schrag

▼ Fiction and nonfiction titles that would lend themselves easily to graphic novel format or inspire graphic novel–like artwork, such as *Bend, Don't Shatter**, *Clay's Way**, *Deliver Us from Evie**, *Luna**, *Orphea Proud**, *Weetzie Bat**, and *When I Knew**

How to Make It Happen

Calling all artists! Calling all graphic novel and Manga enthusiasts! Now is your chance to peruse graphic novels' pinker pages. This workshop asks participants to employ their artistic skills to create a collective anthology that will unite artists and ideas of all types. Participants can be of any sexual orientation, of course, but the idea is to produce a work that is queer-themed. All formats should be welcome in your anthology including painting, drawing, color, black and white, Manga, and collage. In the end, the artworks should be scanned into a single, final document to be reproduced and distributed to all participants—and added to your library's archives. We've outlined a schedule for how a graphic novel workshop might run. It stretches over seven sessions, but feel free to add or subtract days as necessary.

Sessions 1–3: During your first session, begin by having everyone in the group introduce themselves and describe what kinds of graphic novels they like and what they like to draw. To help explain the workshop's purpose, booktalk some queer-themed graphic novels from your library's collection. Afterward, get the group to talk about these books. Discussion questions might include:

▼ What different types of LGBTQ characters are represented?

▼ Can you describe the similarities and differences between LGBTQ graphic novels and straight ones?

▼ How does the design and look of the characters embody the LGBTQ experience?

▼ What scenarios can the group invent or relate that will lend themselves to the cartoon format?

▼ How can the group incorporate words or symbols that will express sound and characters' moods?

▼ How will dialog enhance the overall success of the graphic novel?

Next, have the group make a list of events they would like to chronicle in their own stories. If participants aren't inspired by the graphic novels you've already provided or by their own experiences, ask them to think about their favorite queer books or television programs and how they might incorporate ideas from those mediums. After these lists are finalized, discuss the length of the graphic novel with workshop participants. Should there be a limit on the number of pages that each participant can submit? Can the library afford to make full-color copies of the collective graphic novel for everyone? Do library funds dictate that the anthology be black and white, reproducible by regular photocopiers? These are all important questions that will help determine what artistic mediums may be used.

After your group has decided how long their project will be and what medium to use, have them begin drawing. Give each person a packet of paper that you've already marked up into cartoon-style frames or panels. Have the teens create a storyboard, i.e., write what they want to happen inside each frame. Once they've got their story plotted out, it should be easy to illustrate each frame according to the dialog. For artistic inspiration, have the group examine sample comics you provide. Depending on group members' individual experience levels, you might find yourself helping some teens more than others.

Sessions 4–5: Once the rough drafts are complete, take a break from the intensity of art creation and devote one entire workshop session to editing. Have each of the participants explain their submissions to the rest of the group and ask for feedback. Some questions to consider:

▼ How does their cartoon represent the queer community?

▼ What ways can they improve this representation?

▼ What artistic methods can they utilize to make the representation more clear and fully realized?

▼ Is the wording clear?

▼ Can other participants understand what the artist is trying to relate?

Be sure to start this conversation by saying that no one's feelings should be hurt by the editing session: Your critiques are intended as an exchange of ideas and helpful suggestions that, in the end, will help produce the best product possible. Following the first editing session, use the next session to implement suggestions and make any desired revisions—teens can also work on their submissions at home. Group members can work alone or you can assign them each a partner. You might also consider bringing in an artist from your community to help with the editing.

Session 6: For your last "official" workshop session, have each participant display his or her artwork and explain the process that went into creating it. Some questions you might have the teens answer:

▼ Why did they choose a particular LGBTQ experience?

▼ How did they choose to relate that experience through the comic format?

▼ What criticisms did they consider the most helpful from the group and how did they implement those criticisms?

▼ How do they feel about the final product?

Once the presentations are complete, begin making final publication decisions. Ask the group to think of a title for the anthology. Questions to consider:

▼ Do they want the title to include LGBTQ catchwords such as "out," "closet," "normal," "queer," etc.; a non-queer title; something clever?

▼ What title best represents their collection of artworks and collective mindset?

▼ What will go on the cover?

▼ Should someone design cover art?

▼ How do they want their names listed as authors? Do they want both first and last names; do they want to remain anonymous; use pen names; use first names only?

▼ How do they want their pieces to be arranged in the anthology: Whose piece goes first, whose goes last?

▼ Do they want to have dedications or bios included in the anthology?

After these questions are answered, have the artists give their submissions to you—it's time for you to put your publishing skills to work. The best way to format the anthology will be to scan each piece of art into a software program that will allow you to make each piece the same size and adjust image quality. Next, arrange the pieces in the desired order and save them as a single file ready for printing. If your library doesn't have a scanner or a color printer, you might take the artworks to a copy shop. If your budget doesn't allow for this, of course, use your library's regular photocopier.

Session 7: Celebrate the publication of your graphic novel collection by hosting a party in your library for the workshop participants, their friends, and families. Make the event as special as possible by saying a few congratulatory words to the participants, and call them to the front of the room to receive their graphic novel one-by-one so the audience can applaud. Explain the importance of the LGBTQ graphic novel and provide anecdotes about the creation of your group's own anthology. Have each participant sign a copy for the library.

HOST A QUEER TV NIGHT OR COFFEE HOUSE

What You Will Need

- ▼ A television monitor and DVD player
- ▼ Cable access (optional)
- ▼ Late library hours, or special permission from your director and/or security staff to stay open late for this program
- ▼ A suitable gathering space with comfortable chairs and tables
- ▼ Snacks

Title Tie-Ins

- ▼ *Buffy the Vampire Slayer**
- ▼ *Dawson's Creek*
- ▼ *My So-Called Life**
- ▼ *Queer Eye for the Straight Guy*
- ▼ *Will & Grace*

How to Make It Happen

If you are one of the lucky YA libraries to have your own television set, this no-brainer of a program is your chance to create a safe space for queer and queer-friendly teens alike. It goes without saying that watching TV is a popular pastime. Shy queer teens may come out of hiding to participate in this event, particularly since many libraries are generally quieter and less crowded during the evening hours. Queer staples *Will & Grace* and *Queer Eye for the Straight Guy* are already known to the mainstream American audience and thus, in most regions, are less likely to raise an eyebrow if teens gather at your library to watch them. You might also watch older shows that featured queer characters, such as *My So-Called Life*, *Dawson's Creek*, and *Buffy the Vampire Slayer*, if you can find them airing in syndication. If you have public performance rights for these shows, of course, you can watch them on DVD.

Whatever you decide to screen, reserve a suitable space in your library. You might need to get permission from your administrator and security personnel to keep the library open past its normal closing hours. Try to provide comfortable chairs or seating for the kids. Provide snacks and get ready for great conversations before, during, and after the show. All you need to do is turn on the television, pop the popcorn, pour the soda, pass the cookies, hand out napkins, and then sit back and relax—TV, our national babysitter, will take care of the rest! For a more interactive twist, you might institute a recurring queer-themed coffee house at your library. This open mike event could feature poetry readings, musicians, story tellers, sixties-style rap sessions, actors performing monologues, etc. You might also host a "gallery opening" to showcase art from your library's other LGBTQ programs. Again, the idea is to create a relaxed, safe space for kids to meet, make friends, and share ideas.

CREATE YOUR OWN LGBTQ WEB PAGE

What You Will Need

▼ Computers
▼ Web space, preferably on your library's server
▼ HTML or other Web design manuals
▼ LGBTQ book lists
▼ The URLs of queer resources available in your community

Title Tie-Ins

▼ *Geography Club*, by Brent Hartinger*
▼ *GLBTQ: The Survival Guide for Queer and Questioning Teens*, by Kelly Huegel*
▼ *Heart on My Sleeve*, by Ellen Wittlinger*
▼ *Luna: A Novel*, by Julie Anne Peters*
▼ *Rainbow Boys*, by Alex Sanchez*
▼ *A Tale of Two Summers*, by Brian Sloan*

How to Make It Happen

Many teenagers, regardless of their sexual orientation, are fascinated by technology. Teens use the Internet to connect and communicate with each other through e-mail, peer networking sites such as myspace.com, chat sessions and instant messaging, bulletin boards, podcasts, and blogs. No doubt they'll soon be connecting in ways we can only imagine. Teens visit each other's Web pages and blogs for miscellaneous thoughts, wisdom, gossip, and information of all sorts. The Internet is a teen's way of finding out what's going on in their own community and in the rest of the globe. In fact, the average teenager today spends more time surfing the Internet than watching television (Kroft, 2005). What better way to increase your library's Internet and LGBTQ awareness than by gathering teens to build a queer Web site for your library?

If you're inexperienced in Web design you'll need to do some homework before the program begins. For some basic pointers and library-specific tips, we recommend *Hooking Teens with the Net*, by Linda W. Braun. For a more general approach, try titles of the "Internet for Dummies" ilk. If you don't have the time to learn Web design yourself, consider buying software such as Adobe's Dreamweaver or Microsoft FrontPage, both of which make creating a Web pages nearly as simple as typing a Word document. To publish on your library's site you'll probably need clearance from your library's administrators—and you'll need the assistance of its IT department. If you're unable to publish on your library's Web site, you might instead work with teens to design a stand-alone site.

Depending on your programming skills and the amount of time that you and your teen team are willing to spend updating your site, the results of this activity can be as simple or as complicated as you like. Tech-savvy teens might be interested in creating bulletin boards or polls; or, if your group consists mostly of beginners, the site might be a strictly text-based page with information and few hyperlinks to additional resources. The goal is to create a visually appealing page with basic information about your library's LGBTQ offerings—such as a bibliography—and to get teens thinking about how they might build their own pages.

Have your workshop participants decide on an overall layout, taking into account background color, choice of icons, sidebars, font type, size, and color. Do they want to use a traditional queer symbol such as the rainbow flag or pink triangle for the site's background, or do they want a wash of pink—or something unrelated? After you and your group have settled on an overall design theme, hold a brainstorming session to figure out how to organize the site: how many pages it will include, where they want to post certain types of content, and how visitors will navigate through the site. Next, brainstorm content. A queer-themed library page might include any of the following:

▼ Lists of print and non-print materials. If you or your teens are technologically adept, hyperlink these lists to your library's online catalog so that teens will be able to see if the titles are currently available in your library. You could even link to authors' Web sites.

▼ Teen favorite lists. The best recommendations come from teenagers themselves. When your teens learn that they can post their own favorites on this site, they will tell their friends about it and this will spread the word about the site and your library.

▼ Teen reviews of LGBTQ materials. You can easily hyperlink the teens' favorites to actual teen reviews. It's a great way for teens to voice their opinions and boost their self-confidence. Their reviews are also an excellent tool for you, the librarian, to track what interests your patrons.

▼ Podcasts of LGBTQ teen experiences. Record your queer and queer-friendly teens sharing thoughts about their lives, their friends, families, hopes, and dreams and then post these conversations on the site. For more about how to create a podcast, see our "Create Your Own Coming Out Podcast" idea later in this chapter.

▼ A blogspot for musings from queer or queer-friendly teens. Blogging is hugely popular with teens—this will give them space to sound off. How about a special librarian blog where you talk about new queer materials and programs in the library?

▼ Online bulletin boards where LGBTQ and straight teens can explore queer and gender issues. We suggest that you assign members of your Web design team to moderate these online discussions. These chats can be great sounding boards for teens to share ideas and debate them with one another. Just be sure that your moderators are committed to monitoring the discussions regularly so they can alert you if there's any offensive language or materials. It's your job as the site's technical administrator to remove the offensive postings.

▼ Interviews, podcasts, and online chats with queer community members and authors of queer YA books.

▼ Hyperlinks to local queer community agencies and national groups.

BUILD A LIBRARY GAY-STRAIGHT ALLIANCE

What You Will Need

▼ Cooperation from library or school administrators
▼ A meeting place for the group to gather
▼ Flyers to advertise meetings
▼ An agenda for the meeting
▼ Plans for the future

Title Tie-Ins

▼ *Absolutely, Positively Not . . .*, by David LaRochelle*
▼ *Geography Club*, by Brent Hartinger*

▼ *The Misfits*, by James Howe

▼ *Rainbow Boys*, by Alex Sanchez*

How to Make It Happen

As its name suggests, a gay-straight alliance (GSA) brings queer and straight teens together with a shared purpose: to combat homophobia in all its forms. And homophobia, of course, comes in many forms. It can be in your face and confrontational, or it occurs in casual conversation when teens use the expression "that's so gay." The first GSAs emerged in the early 1990s. Although there are now more than 3,000 of them nationwide, only one in ten high schools has a GSA—in other words, most high schools don't have one (Cloud, 2005). Students' efforts to form new GSAs, in fact, often stir up sizeable controversies. Although it is illegal to discriminate against a GSA by preventing it and only it from meeting on school grounds, a number of local and state governments have simply chosen to ban all student groups—a scorched earth strategy that barely conceals its underlying bigotry. The *GLTBQ Survival Guide* has a great step-by-step guide for teens wishing to start GSAs in their schools. You should also visit the Gay, Lesbian and Straight Education Network's Web site, www.glsen.org, which features page after page of research, suggestions, and how-to kits designed specifically to combat homophobia in high schools. It also outlines the legality of and legal protections for GSAs. We specifically direct you to a report titled *The GLSEN Jump-Start: A How-To Guide for New and Established GSAs*. See our bibliography for the full URL.

Based on YALSA listserv chatter, we're aware of a few libraries around the country that are interested in starting GSAs based on teen requests: one in Toms River, New Jersey, and another in Oakland, California. The honor of starting the first library GSA, though, may go to Joseph Wilk, a YA librarian at the Pittsburgh Carnegie Library. In the winter of 2006, Wilk partnered with GLSEN and together they reached out to LGBTQ youth in Pittsburgh. When a critical mass had formed they formed a GSA that met at the library, watched a film together, and discussed LGBTQ issues (Martin, 2006). You might consider starting a GSA at your own library, or creating a gay-straight caucus within your teen advisory group. Start by talking to your patrons about this idea—or, as Wilk did, approach local community centers to find interested teens. Ask them what they know about GSAs and what they think about your library starting one. Who do they think would come to meetings? Would they support the group by bringing their own friends? If your teens don't seem particularly excited by a GSA, ask them if they know anyone else who might be interested.

Once you've gauged teens' interest level, initiate a conversation with your supervisors and administrators on the importance of forming a GSA. Talking points might include:

▼ the need to promote tolerance and combat homophobia in the school and library.

▼ the importance of recognition for all types of groups in the library or school.

▼ evidence that teens are asking for a GSA.

After you've received official support for the group, your next step might be to advertise it by posting flyers around your library or school, but there are different degrees of visibility for you to consider. For instance, instead of advertising the GSA before its first meeting, maybe your core group of queer and queer-friendly teens should hold the club in secret for a few sessions to boost participants' confidence levels. Then, when the time feels right, you can publicize it. Your core group of teens should help you make these decisions.

After you've advertised your first official meeting, formulate an agenda. Often, the best way to begin any meeting is simply to ask participants what they hope to accomplish. Another great way to get kids talking is through "icebreaker" introductions. Some icebreaker questions might include:

▼ What is your name?

▼ What is your favorite LGBTQ television show?

▼ What is your favorite LGBTQ book?

▼ What is your favorite LGBTQ film?

▼ How queer-friendly is the library or school atmosphere?

▼ What do you hope to accomplish by starting a GSA?

One question you should avoid asking, though, is how the teens self-identify. Queer or straight, everyone should be allowed to reveal this at their own choosing. Also keep in mind that this is your first meeting: Some people will be naturally shy, maybe petrified, others will be there with friends, and still others will be limelight seekers.

After the introductions have been made, let the real discussion begin. As the moderator, it's your job to ask open-ended questions and help keep the conversation moving. Talking points might include:

▼ What is the current mindset of other patrons concerning LGBTQ teens?

▼ What level of LGBTQ visibility can patrons achieve in your institution without becoming obvious targets for homophobia?

▼ Have there been specific instances of homophobia in your library?

▼ Do LGBTQ teens feel safe in your library?

▼ How can you prevent future acts of homophobia and increase teens' comfort?

▼ What resources are available to help you?

▼ How much support can you count on from administrators?

▼ What other activities or projects would the GSA like to accomplish?

Your GSA can be a liaison between your institution and local LGBTQ agencies. It can also host activities such as dances, poetry slams, and book discussions. Most important, your GSA gives your LGBTQ audience the kind of communal strength necessary to combat homophobia of all kinds. In terms of activities, you might suggest any and all of the following:

▼ Organize local observance of "No Name-Calling Week." This annual event is a joint project between GLSEN and Simon & Schuster. It was inspired by James Howe's YA novel *The Misfits*.

▼ Participate in GLSEN's "National Day of Silence," one day each year on which participants take a vow of silence to protest the discrimination and harassment that queer youth face.

▼ Design a Web site listing the LGBTQ resources in the library.

▼ Organize a night or weekend day for parents and family members to visit the library and see what resources are available for them.

▼ Hold a workshop about how to form a GSA at your high school.

▼ Hold a workshop about coming out.

▼ Teach straight kids how to dance. Really. In *Boy Meets Boy* the narrator Paul says that his school's GSA exists for a very specific, albeit gaytopian, purpose: "In sixth grade, Cody, Joni, a lesbian fourth grader named Laura, and I formed our elementary school's first gay-straight alliance. Quite honestly, we took one look around and figured the straight kids needed our help. For one thing, they were all wearing the same clothes. Also (and this was critical), they couldn't dance to save their lives" (Levithan, 2003:12).

QUEER EYE FOR THE STRAIGHT GUY . . . OR LIBRARIAN

What You Will Need

- ▼ Five queer teens with an interest in personal style
- ▼ A straight person, preferably with bad personal style . . . or a sense of humor and a willingness to be made over
- ▼ Magazines and/or catalogs containing both men's and women's fashion
- ▼ A professional stylist, if you can afford to hire one or if they're willing to volunteer
- ▼ Cosmetic, clothing, and hair product donations from department stores, salons, or boutiques in your community
- ▼ A laptop computer with Internet access and a screen projector (optional)

Title Tie-Ins

- ▼ *The Bermudez Triangle*, by Maureen Johnson*
- ▼ *Boy Meets Boy*, by David Levithan*
- ▼ *Getting It*, by Alex Sanchez
- ▼ *Queer Eye for the Straight Guy*
- ▼ *Out*
- ▼ *A Tale of Two Summers*, by Brian Sloan*

How to Make It Happen

This idea comes to us courtesy of Sheila Schofer, coordinator of young adult services at the Brooklyn Public Library. Makeover-themed reality television programs are wildly popular—a particular favorite is the cable show *Queer Eye for the Straight Guy*, in which the Fab Five turn a dumpy straight guy into a stylin' babe-magnet in less than one hour. What better way to celebrate Pride Month than to host your library's own "Queer Eye"? Since the television show is popular with both straight and queer audiences, this built-in comfort level should attract a diverse audience to your library. And, just like the TV show, this activity brings straight and queer folk together and provides opportunities to learn from one another. And you don't have to pick LGBTQ kids to be the fashion experts—any kid with an eye for style is welcome.

It may not seem like it, but this program can be designed to fit small and large budgets alike. In a low-tech version, it can be as simple as having a team of fashion-conscious teens develop a "style profile" for a straight person using clippings from fashion magazines and catalogs, or their personal opinions. Have the teens cut out clothes, hairstyles, and shades of make-up from photos and then paste these items onto storyboards that depict their makeover candidate. Get the group to think about how certain colors complement each other; what shoes say about someone's personality; and what types of outfits someone might wear to a job interview as opposed to a date or a trip to the supermarket. At the end of the program, have the stylists present the portfolio of storyboards to the makeover candidate.

If you have a bigger budget, or if community members are willing to donate time and materials, you can conduct a real makeover based on the all-knowing eyes of queer fashion experts. If you bring in an outside consultant, make sure this person is willing to coach your audience members by helping to turn their suggestions into a legitimate look appropriate for the straight guinea pig . . . er, makeover candidate. And remember, the candidate with bad fashion sense, straight or gay, could even be you! If you're in a school, perhaps the student body could nominate a faculty member to be made over—or the school principal. It all depends upon the willingness of your faculty and co-workers, and their ability to be good natured about fielding potentially dubious suggestions from your teens. If your library is in a really progressive community, this program could easily be adjusted to help teens "Discover Your Inner Drag Queen." Using costumes, make-up, and props, participants can go in drag as the opposite sex. They might even host their own cabaret show or karaoke night in your library.

To give you a better idea of how a big budget version of this program might run complete with an outside style expert and a "studio audience"—again, you can always trim it for a smaller budget!—we've outlined some instructions below:

Step 1: Select your library's "Fab Five" panel of teens with a good eye for style. Better yet, have your GSA or teen advisory group choose them. Like the TV show, each member of the team might have a specialty area such as clothes, hair, make-up, personal grooming, comportment, and culture. The teens can even select an expert in interior design to make over the YA reading room, your office, or a classroom.

Step 2: Identify a straight person who is willing to be made over. One way to find a makeover candidate is to have the teens nominate someone—but make sure that person is a good sport. This approach will probably improve the overall success of the program because this gives time to gather evidence that proves a makeover is necessary, including photos of recent fashion atrocities. Also, selecting someone ahead of time means your style gurus and audience alike will probably know the person and feel comfortable with him or her—comfortable enough to gently point out fashion faux pas.

Step 3: Find a professional style consultant. Good places to look include hair salons, make-up counters at department stores, fashion boutiques, and interior design firms. Be sure to explain the program's importance of bringing together queer and straight teen audiences in an activity that can promote tolerance. Ask a store manager if he or she can consider volunteering an employee's time and materials, or to make their services available at a discounted rate.

Step 4: Advertise your program with flyers, announcements, bulletin boards, etc., to draw as large an audience for the event as possible.

Step 5: Reserve a suitable space in your library to accommodate a crowd of potentially boisterous teens.

Step 6: Gather your Fab Five panel before the "air date" to go over how the event itself will run. Perhaps the professional stylist also might be willing to give them some pointers on how to help people find a personal style.

Step 7: On the day of the event, set up your teen area to look like a television studio. Make some chairs available for a "live studio audience." Also set up a table with chairs and water glasses for your Fab Five panel, and maybe a special podium for the professional stylist. Design a "Queer Eye" logo or banner to serve as a backdrop for the panel, and display your library's fashion periodicals so that the panel and audience can reference their style selections. And don't forget to save a chair for the makeover candidate!

Step 8: At the start of the event, introduce the panelist and stylist to the audience. Better yet, find a teen who's interested in hosting the event.

Step 9: Have your subject introduce himself or herself—or yourself—and explain what he or she wants the makeover to accomplish. This will help the Fab Five and professional stylist focus their efforts.

Step 10: After the introductions, have your host present the straight person's case: stylistic shortcomings, messy desk, disastrous office, inability to dance, mismatched ties, ugly shoes that look as though they belong in a nurse's office circa 1978, bad comb-overs, orange lipstick, you get the idea.

Step 11: Have the Fab Five panel collaborate with the professional stylist to formulate a new look for the makeover candidate. This process should be a discussion so that your audience can see and hear it in action. Have the panel ask the makeover candidate his or her opinion about clothes, fashion, make-up, workspaces, and living spaces. Have the panel show magazines, catalogs, or projections from Internet sites that might help the person gain a better sense of style. Let the makeover candidate select styles that he or she finds appealing.

Step 12: Have the professional stylist combine the opinions of the teen panel, the audience, and the makeover subject participant into a new look. Hopefully it's something that can be accomplished within the allotted time span of the event. If not, or if your budget does not allow for an actual makeover, have the team formulate a portfolio of storyboards that the makeover candidate can take home and ponder.

Step 13: Implement the makeover. Have the professional give your straight candidate a new haircut, make-up job, or help reorganize the messy office. Make sure he or she explains what's happening and why, i.e., how a certain haircut can better frame someone's face; why certain shades of make-up are suited for certain complexions; or the feng shui rationale for moving a desk into a different corner of the room. If you don't have time to do the makeover that same day, you could extend this program over two or three days. One session might consist of the style deliberations, the next might consist of the makeover, and the last one would be the dramatic "reveal."

Step 14: At the program's conclusion, thank the panel, the consultant, and the straight makeover candidate—be sure your audience cheers especially loudly for this person. Hand out "Queer Eye" certificates to the panel.

CREATE YOUR OWN COMING OUT PODCAST

What You Will Need

- ▼ A recording device with a built-in microphone, or an external microphone, and the necessary cables or devices to transfer sound from this device to a computer
- ▼ A software program to edit and mix the sound file
- ▼ Web space to store the files
- ▼ A computer with a CD burner (optional)
- ▼ Blank compact discs (optional)

Title Tie-Ins

- ▼ *Deliver Us from Evie*, by M. E. Kerr*
- ▼ *Empress of the World*, by Sara Ryan*
- ▼ *The Full Spectrum*, ed. by David Levithan and Billy Merrell*
- ▼ *How I Learned to Snap*, by Kirk Read*
- ▼ *Keeping You a Secret*, by Julie Anne Peters*

▼ *Luna: A Novel*, by Julie Anne Peters*
▼ *Totally Joe*, by James Howe*

How to Make It Happen

For LGBTQ teens, coming out can be the defining act of their teenage years. Coming out stories are as varied as the teens who tell them. Many are easy, happy, and heartwarming. Others are more complicated, and some are even terrible. Whatever the case, coming out stories are always heartfelt, intense, and worthy of sharing with friends, families, and others. At the same time, teens are always interested in the latest technological advances, everything from computers and gaming, to portable DVD players and iPods. This program unites teens' technological interests with their ability to tell a powerful story. For this program, ideally you might have a few LGBTQ teens, or family members of queer people, who are brave enough to share their own stories. But if there are no out teens in your library, instead just let teens riff on what it means to be queer in the world today. What matters most is giving teens a chance to share their stories and feelings—and, however you structure the program, be sure to tell teens they can remain anonymous.

This workshop can be as short or as long as necessary, but you will need at least two sessions to explain the concept and begin recording conversations, plus another couple of sessions to edit them and produce the show. Ideally, you should be able to upload the teens' coming out stories as a podcast available on your library's Web site—you could even make it available for subscription. This will show that your library supports queer teens and helps them contribute to the world beyond the library. We realize that this is not possible in every setting due to technical concerns as well as privacy issues, however, so another option is simply to burn CDs of the podcast for each teen. Whatever format you produce, ask your teens' permission to play the podcast in your library. For teens not involved in the project, this will be a great way to build awareness of queer people. Okay, that's the theory. Now for the step-by-step description of the program.

Step 1: For starters, what the heck is a podcast? The simplest description is that audio that's been digitized and made available for listening via the Internet, or for subscription-based download to an MP3 player. Do you need to know anything about radio production to make a podcast? No, but partnering with someone who does would certainly help make a better finished product. You might check with your local public radio station to see if they would be willing to help. Or, you might see if there is a local chapter of the National Lesbian & Gay Journalists Association in your area by visiting www.nlgja.org. Contact the chapter president to see if he or she can recommend a member with radio production skills. If neither of these options pan out, the free Web site www.transom.org offers basic tutorials in radio production.

Step 2: Next, choose your recording equipment and software. Any tape-recorder will do, but digital devices such as mini-disc recorders, digital audio-tape recorders, and flash memory recorders will give you better sound quality. Similarly, a professional microphone will give you better sound quality, but you can also use a computer's built-in microphone. Finally, if you can afford to purchase professional quality software, ProTools, by Avid, is the industry standard. A much cheaper option—it's free, in fact—is Audacity, by Source-Forge, which works on Windows-based machines as well as Macs. It's not as sophisticated as what the pros use, but it will do the trick. Download it from http://audacity.sourceforge.net. If you have a Mac, meanwhile, the Garage-Band software that comes bundled with your machine will also be fine.

Step 3: Publicize the workshop and reserve a quiet room where you can host it.

Step 4: On the first day of the workshop, be prepared with a few sample podcasts to play for the teens. Some LGBTQ examples include:

▼ OutLoud @ The Library, http://teenlink.nypl.org/turnitup.html
▼ OutLoud Radio, www.outloudradio.org

Some non-LGBTQ podcasts include:

▼ The Cheshire Public Library, www.cheshirelib.org/teens/cplpodcast.htm
▼ Emogirl, http://emogirltalkwp.podshow.com
▼ Generation PRX, www.generation.prx.org
▼ Hennepin County Library, www.hclib.org/teens/Podcasts.cfm
▼ Library Loft, www.libraryloft.org/podcasts.asp
▼ This East Oakland Life, www.eastoakland.libsyn.com
▼ Youth Radio, www.youthradio.org

After the teens listen to a few examples, get them to talk about what they liked or disliked in each one. Then, have them brainstorm how they'd like their podcast to sound. Questions to consider:

▼ Do they want the entire show to have a single theme, such as coming out, or should each segment be something different?
▼ Do they want each person in the group to share an individual story, or do they want to have dialog between two or more people?

▼ Do they want a variety of segments: stories, interviews, essays, etc.?

▼ Do they want things to be funny, serious, a variety of moods?

▼ How long should the podcast run?

▼ Do they want to have one or more hosts for the show?

Step 5: Start recording. To get good sound, keep the microphone as close to the person talking as possible, but make sure the recording volume isn't too "hot," i.e., too loud, because otherwise the sound will distort. At first, the teens might be a little shy of the microphone, so start the discussion with ice-breaker questions—your first name, your favorite book, etc.—and then do a few sample interviews. When doing a radio interview, the basic rule of thumb is to ask open-ended questions that cannot be answered with a simple yes or no. If your teens are reading essays, of course, this won't be a problem.

Step 6: Once the group feels that it's collected enough tape to make a show, begin sifting through everything. Listen for the most humorous, the most emotional, and the most revealing moments, then single these ones out for use in the show. Begin to build a story around them. Write a script for your hosts and have them record it.

Step 7: Load sound into your editing software and make any edits necessary. Assemble the podcast.

Step 8: Burn a CD of the finished product to play in your library and upload the files to your library's Web site. If one of the group members is artistic, have this person create a design for the CD cover. Hold a "listening party" to celebrate the show's completion.

CHECK OUT THE CIRCULATING QUEER

What You Will Need

▼ A study carrel, a conference room, or a table and chairs

▼ A queer person who is willing to talk about being queer

Title Tie-Ins

▼ *The Full Spectrum*, ed. by David Levithan and Billy Merrell*

▼ *Kings & Queens: Queers at the Prom*, by David Boyer*

▼ *When I Knew*, ed. by Robert Trachtenberg*

How to Make It Happen

Libraries in Denmark have decided that the best way to change social attitudes and defeat prejudice is to bring straight people face-to-face with LGBTQ folk. Called the "Living Library" project, it allows patrons to "check out" a queer for forty-five minutes of conversation. The project has since expanded to include members of other minority groups and has spread across Europe to Sweden, Norway, Holland, Hungary, and Portugal (Library Journal, 2005). It's not just queers who circulate. Journalists, animal rights activists, Muslim imams, drug addicts, asylum seekers, and even blind people are all available for check out. A librarian in Malmo, Sweden, explained that anyone, not just someone who's prejudiced, can reserve guests for a forty-five-minute conversation. "It could be that you're about to belong to one of these categories yourself, such as someone losing their eyesight. Or it could be someone who just found out their child is a lesbian. But then there are people who just want to unload a lot of anger. These people [who get borrowed] are ready for anything to happen" (Mattias, 2005).

Why not try something similar for teens at your library? We realize that a Living Library project would be impractical, even impossible to program in many U.S. communities. In some, it will raise concerns about so-called "homosexual recruiting." In others, it might smack of P. T. Barnum or Robert Ripley sensationalism. But this program is not about recruiting teens or about putting queer folk on display like zoo animals. It's about fostering understanding and respect. The word "prejudice" means to form a false opinion without any real knowledge of what something is like. This program can provide teens an excellent opportunity to meet someone who is comfortable being queer and ask that person frank questions. Armed with facts, potential homophobes will no longer be able to prejudge queers. And since fear is rooted in the unknown, this program might even help end homophobia. The circulating queer is also an excellent chance to provide your LGBTQ patrons with an out role model.

How would you go about finding an LGBTQ person brave enough to be the "circulating queer" at your library? In Europe, the librarians collaborate with local community groups. You might do the same. Start by seeing if there's a local chapter of GLSEN. Although your teens may not want to talk to a teacher—after all, they do it every day in school—teachers are a familiar part of life and so this fact will help reduce any exoticism associated with this program. Also, you're guaranteed that a teacher affiliated with GLSEN is a pro: someone able to talk comfortably with kids about what it's like to be queer. Finally, you might invite an openly queer YA author. Whoever you find, "check out" the person yourself first before your kids do. Chat about his or her experiences being queer. Make sure the person is comfortable talking with a group of kids and will have something valuable and educational to contribute. Next, decide if you want to have your guest made available for private conversations or a larger group. On the day of the event, establish some ground rules with your teens. These should include:

▼ A promise not to assault your guest physically. Warn the group that if someone does get violent, you'll call the police immediately and press charges.

▼ A promise not to assault or threaten the guest verbally with slurs or other intentionally offensive remarks. In Sweden, for instance, racist comments and "strong language" are not allowed (*Library Journal*, 2005).

While your teens should feel free to ask whatever they like—there are no stupid questions, particularly when it comes to being queer—you should set some reasonable parameters around the topic of sex, i.e., nothing too explicit.

After establishing the ground rules, give your teens an idea of what they might discuss with your guest. Since people might be shy at first, get the conversation going yourself. You could even prepare a handout listing some suggested questions. They might include:

▼ How do you self-identify?

▼ What words do you use to describe your community? (Queer, gay, etc.)

▼ Is it okay for straight people to call LGBTQ folk "queer"?

▼ How and when did you realize you weren't straight?

▼ How did you know it wasn't "just a phase"?

▼ Did you ever try to "go straight"?

▼ What's it like to go out on dates—is it any different?

▼ What does it mean to be "in the closet," and how does that feel?

▼ When did you come out to your friends and family— and what was that like?

▼ Were you out in school—what was high school like for you?

▼ What queer resources did you use when you were a teenager?

▼ Have you encountered homophobia and how does it make you feel?

▼ Do you feel respected by your community?

▼ Do you feel respected by your country?

▼ Are you religious and how do you reconcile religion with your sexual orientation?

▼ How do you feel about marriage for gays and lesbians?

▼ How do you think straight people can become more tolerant?

▼ What do you know about queer history?

▼ Do you have pride in being queer?

▼ Why are gay people always shoving their sexuality in straight people's faces? (Some straight people feel this way, so it's important that they get the chance to ask the question and get an answer.)

Afterward, be sure to thank your guest and your teens for their willingness to participate. Also, try to "debrief" with your guest and your teens. Perhaps you could prepare a brief exit survey to see if the group found this workshop helpful; how they might do it differently; and, most important, if it changed their perceptions of queer people.

HOST AN ANTI-PROM

What You Will Need

▼ A large open space, preferably a conference room or an auditorium

▼ Music: a boom box and mix CDs or, if you can afford it, a deejay

▼ Room decorations

▼ Refreshments, such as punch and chips, as well as napkins, plates, and cups

▼ Tables and chairs

▼ Crowns for the Anti-Prom King and Queen

▼ A disco ball (optional)

Title Tie-Ins

▼ *Hard Love*, by Ellen Wittlinger*

▼ *Kings & Queens: Queers at the Prom*, by David Boyer*

▼ *Rainbow High*, by Alex Sanchez*

▼ *A Really Nice Prom Mess*, by Brian Sloan*

How to Make It Happen

Why "Anti-Prom" and why the library? High school proms cost a lot of money and not every teenager can cough up a couple hundred bucks to attend. But, like all library services, Anti-Prom is free! Another reason for the Anti-Prom is that many queer teens feel nervous about bringing a same-sex date, or no date, to their high school's prom. With Anti-Prom, they have a prom all to themselves where they can hang out, dance together, and meet other people without fear of harassment. Similarly, many younger teens may not be allowed to attend their high school's prom, but your library's Anti-Prom should be open to them. And finally, teenagers have a subversive streak. What better way to tap into it than to offer them a prom where they can wear what they like, dress how they like, choose the music they like, and bring whomever they like? That's real empowerment.

Before you get started planning your Anti-Prom, you should decide how elaborate you want to make the event, which will depend largely on how much money you have available. Fortunately, regardless of what your budget allows, chances are the kids will have a great time dressing up, hanging out with their friends, learning about prom-related books, and listening to their favorite music. And, just as important, they will never again think of the library as a quiet, stodgy place where they're "shushed." They'll also have a lot more respect for you, the librarian and organizer, which means they won't hesitate to approach you at the information desk the next time they have a question about reading, research, or anything else.

A great resource for ideas about the Anti-Prom will be your library's own teen advisory group. If you don't have one, simply ask teens in your library to share their ideas—they'll no doubt have plenty. Divide your teen advisory group into committees for food, decorations, and music. Good planning is always key to any successful and well-attended event. You should begin at least three to five months ahead of time, particularly if you decide to have other programs that build up to the big event. For instance, you might invite a local make-up artist to offer "Personal Style" and "Prom Prep" workshops for the teens, teaching them etiquette in grooming, fashion, and dating.

If you can afford one, hire a deejay for the event. If not, enlist the help of your teens to create some mix CDs with music from your library's collection—but be aware that copyright laws permit you only to play these CDs in your library. (Things might get tricky with regard to copyright laws if kids are allowed to play their own CDs, so check with your library director.)

If you're expecting a large crowd, and your budget allows, you might also look into hiring a caterer for your Anti-Prom. Short of a caterer, most grocery stores sell sandwich platters and desserts in bulk. For less than $100 you and your teen advisory group should be able to whip up enough sandwiches and finger foods to feed a small army. For less than $50, chips, cookies, and soda will also do the trick. Whatever food you select for Anti-Prom, try to tie the items into the spirit of your prom theme. If your theme is "Blue Hawaii," for instance, serve blue-colored punch with small paper umbrellas. If you've got an older teen population in a progressive neighborhood, you might consider serving "mocktails": fruity, fun, nonalcoholic cocktails with crazy garnishes.

Finally, you'll need adult chaperones to make sure the teens don't get too wild and crazy. Invite other young adult librarians from your library system, bring in an author, or invite the leaders of local LGBTQ community groups. Not only will they help ease the staff's burden of crowd control, their presence in the library is a great opportunity for teens to interact with their favorite authors. You could even set up a table where the author can autograph books.

While the Anti-Prom is taking place, crown an Anti-Prom King and Queen. You might choose the boy and girl—or girl and girl, or boy and boy, or trans teen and trans teen—based on who has read the most prom-related books, or who has the best costumes, or who seems to be having the most fun. Your teen advisory group will be your best resource in helping determine selection criteria. If someone is a good photographer, ask if he or she would like to be the official Anti-Prom photographer; create a special "studio" by draping a sheet over the stacks and add a few decorative elements that match your Anti-Prom's theme. Afterward, if possible, e-mail pictures to participants, or post them on your YA room's Web page or an online sharing service such as flickr.com. For an interesting Anti-Prom display, your staff and event chaperones could even post photographs of themselves at their own proms!

BIBLIOGRAPHY

Abe, Debby. 2005a. "Controversial Book Will Return to Curtis High."
      News Tribune (Tacoma, Wash.), December 16. www.nexis.com
      (accessed January 23, 2006).
———. 2005b. "University Place District Bans Novel about Gay Teens."
      News Tribune (Tacoma, Wash.), November 20. www.nexis.com
      (accessed January 23, 2006).
The Advocate. 2006. "GenQ Poll." February 14:36.
ALA (American Library Association). 1948. "Library Bill of Rights,"
      amended 1996. Chicago: American Library Association. www.ala.
      org/ala/oif/statementspols/statementsif/librarybillofrights.pdf
      (accessed September 27, 2005).
———. 1951. "Labels and Rating Systems: An Interpretation of the
      Library Bill of Rights," amended 2005. Chicago: American Library
      Association. www.ala.org/ala/oif/statementspols/statementsif/
      interpretations/labelsratingsystems.pdf (accessed July 29, 2006).
———. 1972. "Free Access to Libraries for Minors: An Interpretation of
      the Library Bill of Rights," amended 2004. Chicago: American
      Library Association. www.ala.org/ala/oif/statementspols/statementsif/
      interpretations/freeaccesslibrariesminors.pdf (accessed September 27,
      2005).
———. 1973. "Restricted Access to Library Materials: An Interpretation
      of the Library Bill of Rights," amended 2004. Chicago: American
      Library Association. www.ala.org/ala/oif/statementspols/statementsif/
      interpretations/restrictedaccesslibrarymaterials.pdf (accessed
      September 27, 2005).
———. 1982. "Diversity in Collection Development: An Interpretation
      of the Library Bill of Rights," amended 1990. Chicago: American
      Library Association. www.ala.org/ala/oif/statementspols/statementsif/
      interpretations/diversitycollectiondevelopment.pdf (accessed
      September 27, 2005).
———. 1993. "Access to Library Resources and Services Regardless of
      Sex, Gender Identity, or Sexual Orientation: An Interpretation of the
      Library Bill of Rights," amended 2004. Chicago: American Library
      Association. www.ala.org/ala/oif/statementspols/statementsif/
      interpretations/accessgendersexorientation.pdf (accessed September
      27, 2005).

————. 2000. "The 100 Most Frequently Challenged Books of 1990–2000." Chicago: American Library Association. www.ala.org/ala/oif/bannedbooksweek/bbwlinks/top100.pdf (accessed September 27, 2005).

————. 2001. "OIF Censorship Database 1990–2000: Challenges by Type." Chicago: American Library Association. www.ala.org/ala/oif/bannedbooksweek/bbwlinks/challengesbytype19902000.pdf (accessed September 18, 2005).

————. 2004. "OIF Censorship Database 2000–2003: Challenges by Type." Chicago: American Library Association. www.ala.org/ala/oif/bannedbooksweek/bbwlinks/challengesbyyear20002003.pdf (accessed September 18, 2005).

————. 2005a. "Chocolate War Captures Top Spot on Most Challenged List." Press release. Chicago: American Library Association. www.ala.org/al_onlineTemplate.cfm?Section=february2005a&Template=/ContentManagement/ContentDisplay.cfm&ContentID=87991 (accessed July 29, 2006).

————. 2005b. "Resolution on Threats to Library Materials Related to Sex, Gender Identity, or Sexual Orientation." Chicago: American Library Association. www.ala.org/ala/oif/statementspols/ifresolutions/resolutionthreatslibrarymaterials.pdf (accessed September 27, 2005).

————. 2006. "@ your library: Attitudes toward Public Libraries Survey 2006." Chicago: American Library Association. www.ala.org/ala/ors/reports/2006KRCReport.pdf (accessed July 15, 2006).

————. Undated. "Challenged and Banned Books." Chicago: American Library Association. www.ala.org/ala/oif/bannedbooksweek/challengedbanned/challengedbanned.htm (accessed September 27, 2005).

Aldrich, Andrew. 2003. *How My Family Came to Be: Daddy, Papa, and Me*. Oakland, Calif.: New Family Press.

Alexander, Linda. 2005. "Gay Display Controversy: A Threat to Intellectual Freedom." *Florida Libraries* 48, no. 2 (Fall):24–27.

Ali, Anjuman. 2005. "Giving a Human Face to Prejudices." *Wisconsin State Journal*, September 18. www.nexis.com (accessed October 1, 2005).

Allison, Dorothy. 1993. *Bastard Out of Carolina*. New York: Plume.

American Civil Liberties Union Lesbian and Gay Rights Project. 2002. *Making Schools Safe: Anti-Harassment Training Program*, 2nd ed. New York: American Civil Liberties Union. www.aclu.org/images/asset_upload_file681_24003.pdf (accessed January 1, 2006).

American Libraries. 2003. "Topeka Library Settles Squabble with Employee." Vol. 8, no. 34. www.nexis.com (accessed July 15, 2006).

American Psychological Association. Undated. "Answers to Your Questions about Sexual Orientation and Homosexuality." Washington, D.C.: American Psychological Association. www.apa.org/topics/orientation.html (accessed July 29, 2006).

Angelou, Maya. 1983. *I Know Why the Caged Bird Sings*. New York: Bantam Books.

Associated Press. 2003. "Church Members Burn 'Harry Potter' Books, Book of Mormon." August 5, 2003. www.nexis.com (accessed, September 27, 2005).

———. 2004. "N.C. Elementary School Restricts Access to Book about Gay Prince." March 27, 2004. www.nexis.com (accessed July 15, 2006).

———. 2005. "Kanye West Calls for End to Gay Bashing." August 18. www.nexis.com (accessed July 28, 2006).

———. 2006. "Children's Book Moves to Nonfiction Section After Parents Complain." March 27, 2004. www.nexis.com (accessed July 15, 2006).

Atkins, Catherine. 2003. *Alt Ed*. New York: Putnam.

Baker, Jean M. 2002. *How Homophobia Hurts Children: Nurturing Diversity at Home, at School, and in the Community*. Binghamton, N.Y.: Harrington Park Press.

Baker, Michelle, and Stephen Tropiano, eds. 2005. *Queer Facts: The Greatest Gay and Lesbian Trivia Book Ever*. London: Sanctuary Press.

Baldwin, James. 2001. *Giovanni's Room*. New York: Modern Library.

Barack, Lauren. 2005. "AL Lawmaker to Ban Pro-Gay Books." *School Library Journal* 51, no. 1 (January):24.

Basso, Michael. 2003. *The Underground Guide to Teenage Sexuality*. Minneapolis: Fairview Press.

Bauer, Marion Dane, ed. 1994. *Am I Blue? Coming Out from the Silence*. New York: HarperCollins.

Bauer, Megan. 2001. "Anime, Manga, and Otaku Culture: A quick study guide for the uninitiated." *Voice of Youth Advocates* 24, no. 3 (August):186–87.

Beautiful Thing. 1996. DVD. Directed by Hettie MacDonald. Culver City, Calif.: Sony Pictures Classics, 2003.

Bell, Ruth. 1998. *Changing Bodies, Changing Lives: Expanded Third Edition: A Book for Teens on Sex and Relationships*. New York: Three Rivers Press.

Bernstein, Robert A. 2003. *Straight Parents, Gay Children: Keeping Families Together*. New York: Thunder's Mouth Press.

Blacker, Terrence. 2005. *Boy2Girl*. New York: Farrar, Straus & Giroux.

Block, Francesca Lia. 1991. *Weetzie Bat*. New York: Harper Keypoint.

———. 1998. *Dangerous Angels: The Weetzie Bat Books*. New York: Harper Trophy.

Blume, Judy. 1989. *Forever*. New York: Pocket Books.

Bono, Chastity. 1998. *Family Outing*. New York: Little, Brown.

Boock, Paula. 1999. *Dare, Truth, or Promise*. Boston: Houghton Mifflin.

Bott, C. J. 2000. "Fighting the Silence: How to Support Your Gay and Straight Students. *Voice of Youth Advocates* 23, no. 1:22–26.

Boys Don't Cry. 1999. DVD. Directed by Kimberly Peirce. Beverly Hills, Calif.: 20th Century Fox, 2000.

Boys Life 4: Four Play. 2003. DVD. Directed by Phillip J. Bartell, Alan Brown, Eric Mueller, and Brian Sloan. Santa Monica, Calif.: Strand Home Video.

Boyer, David. 2004. *Kings & Queens: Queers at the Prom*. Brooklyn, N.Y.: Soft Skull Press.

Braun, Linda W. 2003. *Hooking Teens with the Net*. New York: Neal-Schuman.

Brody, Jane E. 2006. "Children, Media and Sex: A Big Book of Blank Pages." *New York Times*, January 31. www.nexis.com (accessed July 15, 2006).

Brokeback Mountain. 2005. DVD. Directed by Ang Lee. Universal City, Calif.: Focus Features.

Brown, Rita Mae. 1983. *Rubyfruit Jungle*. New York: Bantam Books.

Bryant, Eric. 1995. "Pride and Prejudice," *Library Journal* 120, no. 12 (June 15):37–39.

Burroughs, Augusten. 2002. *Running with Scissors: A Memoir*. New York: St. Martin's Press.

Buffy the Vampire Slayer—The Complete Series. 1997. DVD. Directed by Joss Whedon et al. Beverly Hills, Calif.: 20th Century Fox, 2005.

But I'm a Cheerleader. 1999. DVD. Directed by Jamie Babbit. Universal City, Calif.: Universal Studios.

Cabot, Meg. 2001. *The Princess Diaries*. New York: Harper Trophy.

Caldwell, John. 2005. "Person of the Year: Kerry's Courage." *The Advocate*, December 20:38–44.

Carleo-Evangelist, Jordan. 2005. "These Bookmarks Would Offer a Warning." *Times Union* (Albany, N.Y.), June 2. www.nexis.com (accessed June 3, 2006).

Carmichael Jr., James V. 1998. "Homosexuality and United States Libraries: Land of the Free, but Not Home to the Gay." Paper presented at the 64th IFLA General Conference. The Hague: International Federation of Library Associations and Institutions. www.ifla.org/IV/ifla64/002-138e.htm (accessed July 15, 2006).

———. 2002. "Effects of the Gay Publishing Boom on Classes of Titles Retrieved under the Subject Headings 'Homosexuality,' 'Gay Men,' and 'Gays' in the OCLC WorldCat Database." *Journal of Homosexuality* 42, no. 3:65–89.

Carmichael Jr., James V., and Marilyn L. Shontz. 1996. "The Last Socially Acceptable Prejudice: Gay and Lesbian Issues, Social Responsibilities, and Coverage of These Topics in M.L.I.S./M.L.S. Programs." *Library Quarterly* 66, no. 1:21–58.

Cart, Michael. 1996a. *From Romance to Realism: 50 Years of Growth and Change in Young Adult Literature*. New York: HarperCollins.

———. 1996b. *My Father's Scar*. New York: Simon & Schuster.

Cart, Michael. 2003. "Boy Meets Boy." *Booklist.* August 1.
www.nexis.com (accessed July 29, 2006).

———, ed. 2003a. *Love & Sex: Ten Stories of Truth.* New York: Aladdin
Paperbacks.

———, ed. 2003b. *Necessary Noise: Stories about Our Families as They
Really Are.* New York: HarperCollins.

Cart, Michael, and Christine A. Jenkins. 2006. *The Heart Has Its
Reasons: Young Adult Literature with Gay/Lesbian/Queer Content,
1969–2004.* Scarecrow Studies in Young Adult Literature, No. 18,
Patty Campbell, series ed. Lantham, Md.: The Scarecrow Press.

The Celluloid Closet. 1996. DVD. Directed by Rob Epstein and Jeffrey
Friedman. Culver City, Calif.: Sony Pictures.

Cha, Kai-Ming. 2005. "Yaoi Manga: What Girls Like?" *Publishers
Weekly* 252, no. 10 (March 2):44–46.

Chambers, Aidan. 2002. *Postcards from No Man's Land.* New York:
Dutton.

Chandler, Kim. 2004. "Gay Book Ban Goal of State Lawmaker."
Birmingham News, December 1. www.nexis.com (accessed
September 27, 2005).

Chbosky, Stephen. 2004. *The Perks of Being a Wallflower.* New York:
Pocket Books.

Cho, Margaret. 2002. *I'm the One That I Want.* New York: Ballantine
Books.

———. 2005. *I Have Chosen to Stay and Fight.* New York: Riverhead
Books.

Cianciotto, Jason, and Sean Cahill. 2003. *Education Policy: Issues
Affecting Lesbian, Gay, Bisexual, and Transgender Youth.*
Washington, D.C.: National Gay and Lesbian Task Force Policy
Institute. www.thetaskforce.org/downloads/EducationPolicy.pdf
(accessed January 28, 2006).

Clamp. 2002. *Cardcaptor Sakura* series. Los Angeles: Tokyopop.

Cloud, John. 2005. "The Battle Over Gay Teens." *Time*, October 10:42–51.

Clyde, Laurel A. 2003. "School Libraries and Social Responsibility:
Support for Special Groups and Issues—The Case of Homosexuality."
Paper presented at the 69th IFLA General Conference. The Hague:
International Federation of Library Associations and Institutions.
www.ifla.org/IV/ifla69/papers/192e-Clyde.pdf (accessed July 15,
2006).

Clyde, Laurel A., and Marjorie Lobban. 2001. "A Door Half Open:
Young People's Access to Fiction Related to Homosexuality." *School
Libraries Worldwide* 7, no. 2 (July):17–30.

Cohn, Rachel. 2002. *Gingerbread.* New York: Simon & Schuster.

———. 2004. *Pop Princess.* New York: Simon & Schuster Books for
Young Readers.

———. 2005. *Shrimp.* New York: Simon & Schuster.

———. 2006. *Cupcake.* New York: Simon & Schuster.

Cohn, Rachel, and David Levithan. 2006. *Nick & Norah's Infinite Playlist*. New York: Knopf.

Cothran, Helen, ed. 2003. *Homosexuality*. Current Controversies series. Farmington Hills, Mich.: Greenhaven Press.

Crowther, Kitty. 2000. *Jack & Jim*. New York: Hyperion.

Crutcher, Chris. 1991. *Athletic Shorts*. New York: Greenwillow Books.

———. 1995. *Ironman*. New York: Greenwillow Books.

Cunningham, Michael. 1998. *The Hours*. New York: Farrar, Straus & Giroux.

Curry, Ann. 2005. "If I Ask, Will They Answer? Evaluating Public Library Reference Service to Gay and Lesbian Youth." *Reference & User Services Quarterly* 45, no. 1 (Fall):65–75.

Danky, James P. 2006. "The GLBT Community and the Right: The Role Libraries Can Play." *Counterpoise* 10, no. 1/2 (Winter/Spring):81–83.

Dawson's Creek—The Complete Fourth Season. 1998. DVD. Directed by Lou Antonio and Arvin Brown. Culver City, Calif.: Sony Pictures, 2004.

Day, Frances Ann. 2000. *Lesbian and Gay Voices: An Annotated Bibliography and Guide to Literature for Children and Young Adults*. Westport, Conn.: Greenwood Press.

De Haan, Linda, and Stern Nijland. 2002. *King & King*. Berkeley, Calif.: Tricycle Press.

De Oliveira, Eddie. 2004. *Lucky*. New York: PUSH.

DeGeneres, Ellen. 2003. *The Funny Thing Is*. New York: Simon & Schuster.

Desai Hidier, Tanuja. 2003. *Born Confused*. New York: PUSH.

Donague, Emma. 1996. *Kissing the Witch: Old Tales in New Skins*. New York: Joanna Cotler Books.

———. 2003. "The Welcome," in *Love & Sex: Ten Stories of Truth*, Michael Cart, ed. New York: Simon Pulse.

Donovan, John. 1969. *I'll Get There, It Better Be Worth the Trip*. New York: HaperCollins.

Doyle, Gerry and David Heinmann. "Protests Blast Cops on Book Burning." *Chicago Tribune*, June 21, 2006. www.nexis.com (accessed July 15, 2006).

Eberhart, George M. 2005. "Gay Pride Exhibit Leads to Countywide Ban." *American Libraries* 36, no. 7 (August):14–15.

Ebert, Roger. 1995. "Love Is Part of Greater Awakening for 'Two Girls'." *Chicago Sun-Times*, June 30. www.nexis.com (accessed January 27, 2006).

Edge of Seventeen. 1998. DVD. Directed by David Moreton. Santa Monica, Calif.: Strand Releasing.

Epstein, Robert. 2006. "Do Gays Have a Choice?" *Scientific American Mind* 17 no. 1 (February):50–57.

Ervin, Eric G. 2005. "'Symbolic' Books Shredded During Library Protest." *Houston Voice*, October 14. http://search.epnet.com (accessed July 15, 2006).

Escobar-Chaves, S. Liliana; Susan R. Tortolero; Christine M. Markham; Barbara J. Low; Patricia Eitel; and Patricia Thickstun. 2005. "Impact of the Media on Adolescent Sexual Attitudes and Behaviors." *Pediatrics* 116, no. 1 (July):303–326.

Ferber, Lawrence. 2005. "Yaoi Zowie." *Advocate*, November 22:84.

Ferris, Jean. 2000. *Eight Seconds*. New York: Harcourt.

Fierstein, Harvey. 2002. *The Sissy Duckling*. New York: Simon & Schuster.

Forbes, Keyona; Janes Gregoire; Miguel Tejada; and Patricia Thomas Rogers. 2003. "Teen Takes Case against Internet Filtering to Supreme Court." *New York Amsterdam News*, February 27–March 5:20.

Ford, Marcia. 2004. "From the Pulpit to the Bedroom." *Publishers Weekly* 251, no. 21 (May 24):8–11.

Forster, E.M. 2005. *Maurice*. Eastbourne, Great Britain: Gardners Books.

Frankowski, Barbara. 2004. "Sexual Orientation and Adolescents." *Pediatrics* 113, no. 6:1827–1832.

Freymann-Weyr, Garret. 2002. *My Heartbeat*. Boston: Houghton Mifflin.

Frost, Helen. 2003. *Keesha's House*. New York: Farrar, Straus & Giroux.

Garden, Nancy. 1992 *Annie on My Mind*. New York: Farrar, Straus & Giroux.

Garnar, Martin. 2001. "Changing Times: Information Destinations of the Lesbian, Gay, Bisexual, and Transgender Community in Denver, Colorado." *Information for Social Change* 12. http://libr.org/isc/articles/12-Garnar.html (accessed July 15, 2006).

Ginsberg, Allen. 1956. *Howl and Other Poems*. San Francisco: City Lights.

The GLBTQ Encyclopedia. Undated. Chicago: glbtq Inc. www.glbtq.com (accessed July 15, 2006).

GLSEN (Gay, Lesbian and Straight Education Network). 2001. *The GLSEN Jump-Start: A How-To Guide for New and Established GSAs*. New York: Gay, Lesbian and Straight Education Network. www.glsen.org/binary-data/GLSEN_ATTACHMENTS/file/182-2.pdf (accessed November 12, 2005).

———. 2003. *GLSEN Safe Space: A How-To Guide for Starting an Allies Program*. New York: Gay, Lesbian and Straight Education Network. www.glsen.org/binary-data/GLSEN_ATTACHMENTS/file/294-2.PDF (accessed November 12, 2005).

———. 2004. *State of the States 2004: A Policy Analysis of Lesbian, Gay, Bisexual and Transgender (LGBT) Safer Schools Issues*. New York: Gay, Lesbian and Straight Education Network. www.glsen.org/binary-data/GLSEN_ATTACHMENTS/file/338-3.PDF (accessed November 12, 2005).

———. 2005. *From Teasing to Torment: School Climate in America*. New York: Gay, Lesbian and Straight Education Network. www.glsen.org/binary-data/GLSEN_ATTACHMENTS/file/499-1.pdf (accessed November 12, 2005).

Goldberg, Beverly. 2006. "Oklahoma Bill Ties Funds to Gay-Free Kids' Collections." *American Libraries* 37, no. 4 (April):13.

Golderman, Gail, and Bruce Connolly. 2004. "We're Here, We're Queer: Gail Golderman & Bruce Connolly Rate the Women's, Gender, and Gay & Lesbian Studies Databases." *Library Journal netConnect*, (Summer):22–30.

Gosse, Douglas. 2005. "My Arts-Informed Narrative Inquiry into Homophobia in Elementary Schools as a Supply Teacher." *International Journal of Education & the Arts* 6, no. 7 (August 24):1–19.

Gottfriend, Ted. 1997. *James Baldwin: Voice From Harlem*. New York: Franklin Watts.

Greenberg, Jan, and Sandra Jordan. 2004. *Andy Warhol: Prince of Pop*. New York: Delacorte.

Greenblatt, Ellen. 2001. "Barriers to GLBT Library Service in the Electronic Age." *Information for Social Change* 12. http://libr.org/isc/articles/12-Greenblatt.html (accessed July 15, 2006).

———. 2005. "Exploring LGBTQ Online Resources." *Journal of Library Administration* 43, no. 3/4:85–101.

Griffeth, Nicola, ed. 1999. *Bending the Landscape: Original Gay and Lesbian Science Fiction*. New York: Overlook.

Grimsley, Jim. 1995. *Dream Boy*. Chapel Hill, N.C.: Algonquin Books.

Guy, Rosa. 2005. *Ruby*. East Orange, N.J.: Just Us Books.

Halprin, Brendan. 2004. *Donorboy*. New York: Villard.

Hamer, Judah S. 2003. "Coming-Out: Gay Males' Information Seeking." *School Libraries Worldwide* 9, no. 2 (July):73–89.

Hamilton College National Youth Polls. 2006. *Hot Button Issues Poll: Guns, Gays and Abortion*. Clinton, N.Y.: Hamilton College. www.hamilton.edu/news/polls/HotButtonFinalReport.pdf (accessed January 5, 2006).

Hammond, Harmony. 2006. "How to Change Vandalism into Art." *Gay & Lesbian Review Worldwide*, May–June:19.

Hart, Roger A. 1992. *Children's Participation: From Tokenism to Citizenship*. Innocenti Essays, no. 4. Florence, Italy: UNICEF International Child Development Centre.

Hartinger, Brent. 2003. *Geography Club*. New York: HarperTempest.

———. 2005. *The Order of the Poison Oak*. New York: HarperTempest.

———. 2007. *Split Screen: Attack of the Soul-Sucking Brain Zombies/Bride of the Soul-Sucking Brain Zombies*. New York: HarperTempest.

Hedwig and the Angry Inch. 2001. DVD. Directed by John Cameron Mitchell. Los Angeles: New Line Home Video.

Heims, Neil. 2005. *Allen Ginsberg*. Gay and Lesbian Writers series. New York: Chelsea House.

Hines, Sue. 2000. *Out of the Shadows*. New York: Avon Books.

Hix, Charles. 2001. "A New Generation Has Arrived." *Publishers Weekly* 248, no. 17 (April 23):30–31.

Hollinghurst, Alan. 1989. *The Swimming Pool Library*. New York: Vintage Books.

Holmes, A. M. 1989. *Jack*. New York: Macmillan.

Howe, James. 2003. *The Misfits*. New York: Aladdin Paperbacks.

————. 2005. *Totally Joe*. New York: Simon & Schuster.

Hudson Jr., David L. 2004. *Gay Rights*. Point/Counterpoint series. New York: Chelsea House.

Huegel, Kelly. 2003. *GLBTQ: The Survival Guide for Queer and Questioning Teens*. Minneapolis: Free Spirit.

Hughes-Hassell, Sandra and Alissa Hinckley. 2001. "Reaching Out to Lesbian, Gay, Bisexual, and Transgender Youth." *Journal of Youth Services in Libraries* 15, no.1 (Fall):39–41.

Human Rights Campaign. 2005. "A Chronology of Hate Crimes." Washington, D.C.: Human Rights Campaign. www.hrc.org/Template. cfm?Section=Home&Template=/ContentManagement/Content Display.cfm&ContentID=27103 (accessed November 12, 2005).

————. Undated. "In the Beginning, There Was a March: 1987." Washington, D.C.: Human Rights Campaign. www.hrc.org/Content/ NavigationMenu/Coming_Out/Get_Informed4/National_Coming_Out _Day/History/1987_In_the_Beginning.htm (accessed November 12, 2005).

Human Rights Watch. 2001. *Hatred in the Hallways: Violence and Discrimination against Lesbian, Gay, Bisexual and Transgendered Students in U.S. Schools*. New York: Human Rights Watch. www. hrw.org/reports/2001/uslgbt/toc.htm (accessed November 12, 2005).

Huntington, Geoffrey. 2002. *Sorcerers of the Nightwing*. Ravenscliff Series, no. 1. New York: Regan Books.

The Incredibly True Adventure of Two Girls in Love. 1995. DVD. Directed by Maria Maggenti. Los Angeles: New Line Home Video.

Intersex Society of North America. 2006. "What Is Intersex?" Rohnert Park, Calif.: Intersex Society of North America. www.isna.org/faq/ what_is_intersex (accessed July 27, 2006).

Jay, Karla, and Allen Young, eds. 1994. *Lavender Culture*. New York: New York University Press.

Jennings, Kevin. 2006. *Mama's Boy, Preacher's Son: A Memoir*. Boston: Beacon Press.

Jennings, Kevin, and Pat Shapiro, eds. 2003. *Always My Child: A Parent's Guide to Understanding Your Gay, Lesbian, Bisexual, Transgendered or Questioning Son or Daughter*. New York: Simon & Schuster.

Jo, Eun-Ha, and Park Sang Sun. 2004. *Les Bijoux* series. Los Angeles: Tokyopop.

Johnson, Bob. 2005a. "Allen Gets Muzzle Award for Bill to Ban Gay materials from Public Libraries." Associated Press, April 11. www.nexis.com (accessed September 27, 2005).

————. 2005b. "Gay Alabama Residents Ask Lawmakers: 'Why Do You Hate Us?'" Associated Press, April 20. www.nexis.com (accessed September 27, 2005).

Johnson, Maureen. 2004. *The Bermudez Triangle*. New York: Razorbill.

Jones, Jami L. 2003. "'I Build Resiliency': The Role of the School Media Specialist." *School Libraries Worldwide* 9, no. 2 (July):90–99.

———. 2004. "Beyond the Straight and Narrow: Librarians Can Give Gay Teens the Support They Need." *School Library Journal* 50, no. 5 (May): 45.

Jones, Patrick. 1998. *Connecting Young Adults and Libraries*, 2nd ed. New York: Neal-Schuman.

———. 2002a. *New Directions for Library Service to Young Adults*. Chicago: American Library Association.

———. 2002b. "New Directions for Serving Young Adults Means Building More Than Our Collections." *Journal of Youth Services in Libraries* 15, no. 3 (Spring):21–23.

Kaesar, Gigi, and Peggy Gillespie. 1999. *Love Makes a Family: Portraits of Lesbian, Gay, Bisexual, and Transgender Parents and Their Families*. Amherst, Mass.: University of Massachusetts Press.

Kaiser Family Foundation. 2002. "See No Evil: How Internet Filters Affect the Search for Online Health Information." Menlo Park, Calif.: The Henry J. Kaiser Family Foundation. www.kff.org/entmedia/upload/Chart-Pack.pdf (accessed January 27, 2006).

Kantrowitz, Arnie. 2005. *Walt Whitman*. Gay and Lesbian Writers series. New York: Chelsea House.

Kenan, Randall. 2005. *James Baldwin*. Gay and Lesbian Writers series. New York: Chelsea House.

Kerr, M. E. 1986. *Night Kites*. New York: Harper & Row.

———. 1994. *Deliver Us from Evie*. New York: Harper Trophy.

———. 1998. *"Hello," I Lied*. New York: Harper Trophy.

Kester, Norman G., ed. 1997. *Liberating Minds: The Stories and Professional Lives of Gay, Lesbian, and Bisexual Librarians and Their Advocates*. Jefferson, N.C.: McFarland.

Kissen, Rita M. 1996. *The Last Closet: The Real Lives of Lesbian and Gay Teachers*. Portsmouth, N.H.: Heinemann.

Kilpatrick, Thomas L. 1996. "A Critical Look at the Availability of Gay and Lesbian Periodical Literature in Libraries and Standard Indexing Services." *Serials Review* 22, no. 4 (Winter):71–82.

Knowles, John. 2003. *A Separate Peace*. New York: Scribner's.

Koertge, Ron. 2005. *The Arizona Kid*. Cambridge, Mass.: Candlewick.

Kosciw, Joseph G., ed. 2004. *The 2003 National School Climate Survey: The School-related Experiences of Our Nation's Lesbian, Gay, Bisexual and Transgender Youth*. New York: Gay, Lesbian and Straight Education Network. www.glsen.org/binary-data/GLSEN_ATTACHMENTS/file/300-3.PDF (accessed November 12, 2005).

Kroft, Steve. 2005. "Echo Boomers." *60 Minutes*, CBS, September 4. www.nexis.com (accessed September 21, 2005).

Kruse, Howard. 1995. *Stuck Rubber Baby*. New York: Paradox Press.

Kushner, Ellen. 1987. *Swordpoint*. New York: Arbor House.

The L Word—The Complete First Season. 2004. DVD. Directed by Ernest R. Dickerson and Tony Goldwyn. Los Angeles: Showtime Entertainment, 2004.

Lambda Legal. 2004. "Lambda Legal Sees Rise in Hostility toward Gay Youth Since Election, Expands Its Education Campaign to 'Hot Spots' in Missouri, Utah, Alabama, Iowa, Texas." Press release. New York: Lambda Legal Defense and Education Fund. www.lambda legal.org/cgi-bin/iowa/news/press.html?record=1584 (accessed November 12, 2005).

Lambda Legal and GLSEN. 2001. *A Guide to Effective Statewide Laws/Policies: Preventing Discrimination against LGBT Students in K-12 Schools.* New York: Lambda Legal Defense and Education Fund. www.lambdalegal.org/binary-data/LAMBDA_PDF/pdf/61.pdf (accessed November 12, 2005).

Langemack, Chapple. 2003. *The Booktalker's Bible: How to Talk about the Books You Love to Any Audience.* Westport, Conn.: Libraries Unlimited.

The Laramie Project. 2001. DVD. Directed by Moisés Kaufman. New York: HBO Home Video.

LaRochelle, David. 2005. *Absolutely, Positively Not. . .* New York: Arthur A. Levine Books.

Library Journal. 2005. "Lending 'People' at European Libraries." Vol. 130, no. 15 (September 15):13.

Lilies. 1996. DVD. Directed by John Greyson. San Jose, Calif.: Wolfe Video.

Levithan, David. 2003. *Boy Meets Boy.* New York: Knopf.

———. 2004a. *The Realm of Possibility.* New York: Knopf.

———. 2004b. "Supporting Gay Teen Literature: An Advocate Speaks Out for Representation on Library Shelves." *School Library Journal* 50, no. 10 (October):44–45.

———. 2006. *Wide Awake.* New York: Knopf.

Levithan, David, and Billy Merrell, eds. 2006. *The Full Spectrum: A New Generation of Writing about Gay, Lesbian, Bisexual, Transgender, Questioning, and Other Identities.* New York: Knopf.

Lewis, Johanna. 2003. "Boy Meets Boy." *School Library Journal* 49, no. 9 (September):216.

Linville, Darla. 2004. "Beyond Picket Fences: What Gay/Queer/LGBTQ Teens Want From the Library." *Voice of Youth Advocates* 27, no. 3 (August):183–186.

Loffreda, Beth. 2000. *Losing Matt Shepard: Life and Politics in the Aftermath of Anti-Gay Murder.* New York: Columbia University Press.

Lost Language of Cranes. 1991. VHS. Directed by Nigel Finch. London: BBC, 2002.

Lyon, George Ella. 2004. *Sonny's House of Spies.* New York: Atheneum Books for Young Readers.

Ma Vie En Rose. 1997. DVD. Directed by Alain Berliner. Culver City, Calif.: Sony Pictures, 1999.

MacPherson, Karen. 2005. "Attempted Book Bans Focus Now on Gays." *Pittsburgh Post-Gazette*, September 24. www.nexis.com (accessed September 27, 2005).

Marcus, Sharon. 2005. "Queer Theory for Everyone: A Review Essay." *Signs: Journal of Women in Culture & Society* 31, no. 1 (Autumn): 191–218.

Malloy, Brian. 2002. *The Year of Ice*. New York: St. Martin's Press.

Mannes, Marc; Eugene C. Roehlkepartain; and Peter L. Benson. 2005. "Unleashing the Power of Community to Strengthen the Well-Being of Children, Youth, and Families: An Asset-building Approach." *Child Welfare* 84, no. 2 (March/April):233–250.

Manning, Sarra. 2005. *Pretty Things*. New York: Dutton.

Martin, Hillias J. 2006. "A Library Outing: Serving Queer and Questioning Teens." *Young Adult Library Services* 4, no. 4:38–39.

Martin, Jack, and Anne Rouyer. 2003. "Practical Booktalking Tips." Unpublished pamphlet. New York: New York Public Library.

Mastbaum, Blair. 2004. *Clay's Way*. Los Angeles: Alyson Books.

Mastoon, Adam. 2001. *The Shared Heart*. New York: HarperTempest.

Matthews, Andrew. 2003. *The Flip Side*. New York: Delacorte.

Mattias, Karen. 2005. "Swedish Library to Let Visitors Borrow Living People in Campaign to Fight Prejudice." Associated Press, August 19. www.nexis.com (accessed September 27, 2005).

Maupin, Armistead. 1989. *Tales of the City*. New York: Harper Perennial.

McCafferty, Megan. 2001. *Sloppy Firsts*. New York: Three Rivers Press.

McCafferty, Megan, ed. 2004. *Sixteen: Stories about that Sweet and Bitter Birthday*. New York: Three Rivers Press.

McCloud, Scott. 1993. *Understanding Comics: The Invisible Art*. New York: Harper Perennial.

McKissack, Patricia C., and Frederick L. McKissack. 1998. *Young, Black and Determined: A Biography of Lorraine Hansberry*. New York: Holiday House.

Merrell, Billy. 2003. *Talking in the Dark: A Poetry Memoir*. New York: PUSH.

Merriam-Webster. 1988. *Webster's Ninth New Collegiate Dictionary*. Springfield, Mass.: Merriam-Webster.

Milligan, Peter. 1995. *Enigma*. New York: Vertigo.

———. 2003. *Shade the Changing Man*. New York: Vertigo.

Miltner, Katherine A. 2005. "Discriminatory Filtering: CIPA's Effect on Our Nation's Youth and Why the Supreme Court Erred in Upholding the Constitutionality of the Children's Internet Protection Act." *Federal Communications Law Journal*, May 1. www.nexis.com (accessed July 15, 2005).

Murdock, James. 2004a. "A Brave Post-Gay World." *Voice of Youth Advocates* 27, no. 3 (August):187–188.

———. 2004b. "David Levithan's Teen Gaytopia: An Author's Works Create a World of 'Possibility.'" *New York Blade*, August 6:15.

———. 2004c. "The New Teen Literature Market." *Marketplace*, American Public Media, September 8. http://marketplace.publicradio. org/shows/2004/09/08_mpp.html (accessed July 29, 2006).

———. 2006. "Branching Out: Los Angeles and Other Cities Are Encouraging Greater Diversity in the Design of Branch Libraries and Restoring a Sense of Civic Pride in These Buildings." *Architectural Record* 194, no. 5 (May):145–148.

My So-Called Life. 1994. DVD. Directed by Victor Du Bois and Michael Engler. New York: BMG Special Products, 2002.

Myracle, Lauren. 2003. *Kissing Kate.* New York: Dutton.

National Adoption Information Clearinghouse. 2000. "Gay and Lesbian Adoptive Parents: Resources for Professionals and Parents." Washington, D.C.: National Adoption Information Clearinghouse. www.childwelfare.gov/pubs/f_gay/f_gay.cfm (accessed July 27, 2006).

National Mental Health Association. 2002. *What Does Gay Mean? TeenEXCEL Survey.* Alexandria, Va.: National Mental Health Association. www.nmha.org/whatdoesgaymean/WhatDoesGayMean TeenSurvey.pdf (accessed January 23, 2006).

National School Boards Association. 2004. *Dealing with Legal Matters Surrounding Students' Sexual Orientation and Gender Identity.* Alexandria, Va.: National School Boards Association. www.nsba.org/ site/docs/34600/34527.pdf (accessed October 2, 2005).

Newman, Leslea. 2000. *Heather Has Two Mommies*, Tenth Anniversary ed. Los Angeles: Alyson Books.

No Name-Calling Week Coalition. Undated. "The History of the No Name-Calling Week Project." New York: No Name-Calling Week Coalition. www.nonamecallingweek.org/cgi-bin/iowa/all/about/ index.html (accessed November 12, 2005).

Noel, Josh. 2006a. "Gays Glad Book Fire Not about Prejudice." *Chicago Tribune*, June 23, 2006. www.nexis.com (accessed July 15, 2006).

———. 2006b. "Library Fire Not Linked to Anti-Gay Sentiment." *Chicago Tribune*, June 22, 2006. www.nexis.com (accessed July 15, 2006).

Nunokawa, Jeff. 2005. *Oscar Wilde.* Gay and Lesbian Writers series. New York: Chelsea House.

Oates, Joyce Carol. 2005. *Sexy.* New York: HarperTempest.

Parker, Gretchen. 2005. "Librarians Find Fault in Gay Pride Stance," *Tampa Tribune*, July 7. www.nexis.com (accessed September 27, 2005).

Parnell, Peter. 2005. *And Tango Makes Three.* New York: Simon & Schuster.

Pavao, Kate. 2003. "Out of the Closet." *Publishers Weekly* 250, no. 48 (December 1):23–25.

Pecoskie, Jennifer L., and Pamela J. McKenzie. 2004. "Canadian Census Data as a Tool for Evaluating Public Library Holdings of Award-Winning Lesbian Fiction." *Canadian Journal of Information and Library Science* 28, no. 2 (June):3–23.

Peters, Julie Anne. 2003. *Keeping You a Secret.* New York: Little, Brown.

———. 2004. *Luna: A Novel.* New York: Little, Brown.

———. 2005. *Far from Xanadu.* New York: Little, Brown.

———. 2006. *Between Mom and Jo.* New York: Little, Brown.

Plum-Ucci, Carol. 2004. *What Happened to Lani Garver?* New York: Harcourt Paperbacks.

Ponton, Lynn. 2002. *"What Does Gay Mean?": How to Talk with Kids About Sexual Orientation and Prejudice.* Alexandria, Va.: National Mental Health Association. www.nmha.org/whatdoesgaymean/what DoesGayMean.pdf (accessed January 23, 2006).

Queer As Folk—The Complete First Season. 2000. DVD. Directed by Alex Chapple and Michael DeCarlo. Los Angeles: Showtime Entertainment, 2002.

Queer Eye for the Straight Guy—The Fab Five Collection. 2003. DVD. Directed by Brendon Carter and Stephen Kijak. Del Mar, Calif.: Genius Entertainment, 2005.

Rachel, T. Cole, and Rita D. Costello, eds. 2004. *Bend, Don't Shatter: Poets on the Beginning of Desire.* New York: Soft Skull Press.

Read, Kirk. 2001. *How I Learned to Snap: A Small-Town Coming-of-Age Coming-Out Story.* Athens, Ga.: Hill Street Press.

Reference and User Services Association. 2004. "Guidelines for Behavioral Performance of Reference and Information Service Providers." Chicago: American Library Association. www.ala.org/ala/ rusa/rusaprotools/referenceguide/guidelinesbehavioral.htm (accessed September 27, 2005).

Reichman, Henry. 1993. *Censorship and Selection: Issues and Answers for Schools.* Chicago: American Library Association; Arlington, Va.: American Association of School Administrators.

Reynolds, David S. 2005. *Walt Whitman: Lives and Legacies.* New York: Oxford University Press.

Rich, Jason. 2002. *Growing Up Gay in America: Informative and Practical Advice for Teen Guys Questioning Their Sexuality and Growing Up Gay.* Portland, Ore.: Franklin Street Books.

Rooney, Francis. 2004. *Hear Me Out: True Stories of Teens Educating and Confronting Homophobia.* Toronto: Second Story Press.

Rothbauer, Paulette. 2004. "The Internet in the Reading Accounts of Lesbian and Queer Young Women: Failed Searches and Unsanctioned Reading." *Canadian Journal of Information and Library Science* 28, no. 4 (December):89–110.

Ryan, Sara. 2001. *Empress of the World.* New York: Viking.

Safe Schools Coalition. 2004. "GLBT Civil & Human Rights in Brief in Schools & Families." Seattle, Wash: Safe Schools Coalition. www.safeschoolscoalition.org/GLBTCivilHumanRightsinSchoolsin Brief.pdf (accessed January 28, 2006).

Safren, Steven A. and Richard A. Heimberg. 1999. "Depression, Hopelessness, Suicidality, and Related Factors in Sexual Minority and Heterosexual Adolescents." *Journal of Consulting & Clinical Psychology* 67, no. 6 (December):859–867.

Sanchez, Alex. 2001. *Rainbow Boys*. New York: Simon & Schuster.

———. 2003. *Rainbow High*. New York: Simon & Schuster.

———. 2004. *So Hard to Say*. New York: Simon & Schuster.

———. 2005. *Rainbow Road*. New York: Simon & Schuster.

———. 2006. *Getting It*. New York: Simon & Schuster.

Savage, Dawn. 2004. "Homosexual Themes, Issues, and Characters in Young Adult Literature: An Overview." *Indiana Libraries* 23, no. 2 (July):29–33.

Savin-Williams, Ritch C. 2005. *The New Gay Teenager*. Cambridge, Mass.: Harvard University Press.

Scoppettone, Sandra. 1991. *Trying Hard to Hear You*. Los Angeles: Alyson Books.

Schrag, Ariel. 1997. *Definition*. San Jose, Calif.: SLG Publishing.

———. 1999. *Awkward*. San Jose, Calif.: SLG Publishing.

———. 2000. *Potential*. San Jose, Calif.: SLG Publishing.

Sedaris, David. 1998. *Naked*. Boston: Back Bay Books.

Sell, Randall L; James A. Wells; and David Wypij. 1995. "The Prevalence of Homosexual Behavior and Attraction in the United States, the United Kingdom and France: Results of National Population-based Samples." *Archives of Sexual Behavior* 24, no. 3 (June):235–248.

Shaw, Tucker. 2005. *The Hookup Artist*. New York: HarperCollins.

Shiozu, Shuri. 2004. *Eerie Queerie*. Los Angeles: Tokyopop.

Sickles, Amy. 2005. *Adrienne Rich*. Gay and Lesbian Writers series. New York: Chelsea House.

Singer, Bennett L., ed. 1994. *Growing Up Gay and Lesbian: A Literary Anthology*. New York: New Press.

Sloan, Brian. 2005. *A Really Nice Prom Mess*. New York: Simon & Schuster.

———. 2006. *A Tale of Two Summers*. New York: Simon & Schuster.

Smith, Alison. 2004. *Name All the Animals: A Memoir*. New York: Scribner's.

Snow, Judith E., ed. 2004. *How It Feels to Have a Gay or Lesbian Parent: A Book By Kids for Kids of All Ages*. San Francisco: Harrington Park Press.

Snyder, Jane McIntosh. 2005. *Sappho*. Gay and Lesbian Writers series. New York: Chelsea House.

Soehnlein, K.M. 2000. *The World of Normal Boys*. New York: Kensington Books.

Sones, Sonya. 2004. *One of Those Hideous Books Where the Mother Dies*. New York: Simon & Schuster.

Sonnie, Amy, ed. 2000. *Revolutionary Voices: A Multicultural Queer Youth Anthology*. Los Angeles: Alyson Books.

Spence, Alex. 2000. "Controversial Books in the Public Library: A Comparative Survey of Holdings of Gay-Related Children's Picture Books." *Library Quarterly* 70, no. 3:335–379.

Stevenson, Michael R., and Cogan, Jeanine C. 2003. *Everyday Activism: A Handbook for Lesbian, Gay, and Bisexual People and Their Allies.* Oxford: Routledge.

Stines, Joe. 2005. "A Management Issue." *Florida Libraries* 48, no. 2 (Fall):25–27.

Stone, Irving. 1987. *The Agony and the Ecstasy.* New York: Signet.

Summer, Jane, ed. 2004. *Not the Only One: Lesbian and Gay Fiction for Teens.* Los Angeles: Alyson Books.

Takeuchi, Naoko. 1998. *Sailor Moon.* Los Angeles: Mixx Entertainment.

Thompson, Chad W. 2004. *Loving Homosexuals as Jesus Would: A Fresh Christian Approach.* Grand Rapids, Mich.: Brazos Press.

The Times of Harvey Milk. 1983. DVD. Directed by Rob Epstein. New York: New Yorker Films, 2004.

Tobias, Andrew, and John Reid. 1993. *The Best Little Boy in the World.* New York: Ballantine Books.

Toronto Star. 2005. "Lesbians on Loan." August 27. www.nexis.com (accessed October 1, 2005).

Trachtenberg, Robert, ed. 2005. *When I Knew.* New York: Regan Books.

Tripp, C.A. 2005. *The Intimate World of Abraham Lincoln.* New York: Simon & Schuster.

Trujillo, Carla. 2003. *What Night Brings.* Willimantic, Conn.: Curbstone Press.

Valentine, Johnny. 2004. *One Dad, Two Dads, Brown Dads, Blue Dads.* Los Angeles: Alyson Books.

Vaillancourt, Renée J. 2000. *Bare Bones Young Adult Services: Tips for Public Library Generalists.* Chicago: American Library Association.

Vare, Jonatha W., and Terry L. Norton. 1998. "Understanding Gay and Lesbian Youth: Sticks, Stones, and Silence." *The Clearing House.* www.nexis.com (accessed January 23, 2006).

Vidal, Gore. 2003. *The City and the Pillar.* New York: Vintage Books.

Von Ziegesar, Cecily. 2002–2006. *Gossip Girl.* Series. New York: Little, Brown.

Walker, Alice. 2003. *The Color Purple.* New York: Harvest Books.

Walker, Kate. 1993. *Peter.* Boston: Houghton Mifflin.

Warren, Patricia Nell. 1996. *The Front Runner.* Beverly Hills, Calif.: Wildcat Press.

Weiner, Stephen. 2002. "Beyond Superheroes: Comics Get Serious." *Library Journal* 127, no. 2 (February):55–62.

Whelan, Debra Lau. 2006. "Out and Ignored: Why Are So Many School Libraries Reluctant to Embrace Gay Teens?" *School Library Journal* 52, no. 1 (January):46–50.

White, Edmund. 2002. *A Boy's Own Story.* New York: Modern Library.

White, Jocelyn, and Marissa Martinez. 1997. *The Lesbian Health Book: Caring For Ourselves*. Emeryville, Calif.: Seal Press.

Whitman, Walt. 2005. *Leaves of Grass: First and "Death Bed" Editions*, Karen Karbiener, ed. New York: Barnes & Noble Classics.

Wild Reeds. 1995. DVD. Directed by André Téchiné. Beverly Hills, Calif.: 20th Century Fox.

Wilde, Oscar. 1998. *The Picture of Dorian Gray*. New York: Modern Library.

Wilhoite, Michael. 1991. *Daddy's Roommate*. Los Angeles: Alyson Books.

Will & Grace—Season One. 1998. DVD. Directed by James Burrows. Santa Monica, Calif.: Lions Gate, 2003.

Windmeyer, Shane L. 2006. *The Advocate College Guide for LGBT Students*. Los Angeles: Alyson Publications.

Winick, Judd. 2003. *Green Lantern: Brother's Keeper*. New York: DC Comics.

———. 2000. *Pedro and Me: Friendship, Loss, and What I Learned*. New York: Henry Holt.

Wittlinger, Ellen. 1999. *Hard Love*. New York: Simon & Schuster.

———. 2004. *Heart on My Sleeve*. New York: Simon & Schuster.

Wolfe, Virginia Euwer. 2001. *True Believer*. New York: Atheneum Books.

Woodson, Jacqueline. 1997. *From the Notebooks of Melanin Sun*. New York: Scholastic Paperbacks.

———. 2003. *The House You Pass on the Way*. New York: Speak.

———. 2004. *The Dear One*. New York: Speak.

Wright, Bil. 2000. *Sunday You Learn How To Box*. New York: Touchstone.

Wyeth, Sharon Dennis. 2004. *Orphea Proud*. New York: Delacorte.

YALSA (Young Adult Library Services Association). 2003a. "Adolescent Development/Developmental Assets: Moment of Truth Rap." *SUS III Handbook*. Chicago: Young Adult Library Services Association. www. ala.org/ala/yalsa/yalsamemonly/yalsamounder/yalsamotopics/rap.pdf (accessed July 29, 2006).

———. 2003b. "Adolescent Development/Developmental Assets: Seven Developmental Needs of YAs." *SUS III Handbook*. Chicago: Young Adult Library Services Association. www.ala.org/ala/yalsa/yalsamemonly/yalsamounder/yalsamotopics/sevenneeds.pdf (accessed February 5, 2006).

———. 2006. *Gay Lesbian Bi-Sexual Transgendered Questioning: Books, Websites, and Other Resources for Teens and Their Advocates*. Pamphlet distributed at the 2006 Annual Conference, New Orleans, June 26, 2006. Chicago: Young Adult Library Services Association.

Yamanaka, Lois Ann. 2000. *Name Me Nobody*. New York: Hyperion.

Yates, Bart. 2003. *Leave Myself Behind*. New York: Kensington Books.

Young, Cathy, ed. 2003. *One Hot Second: Stories of Desire*. New York: Knopf.

INDEX

ABOUT THE AUTHORS

Hillias J. ("Jack") Martin, Jr., has worked in public libraries since the age of twelve: first as a volunteer for the library in the rural county of Georgia where he grew up, and now as assistant coordinator of young adult services for The New York Public Library. Jack earned a B.A. in English and Drama from the University of Georgia, then an M.L.I.S. from Pratt Institute. After moving to New York City by way of Providence, R.I., he became a young adult librarian at NYPL's Teen Central in the Donnell Library Center. He was promoted to his current position in 2005. Jack is a member of the American Library Association, the Young Adult Library Services Association, and the New York Library Association. In addition to serving on YALSA's Quick Picks for Reluctant Young Adult Readers committee, Jack is a certified YALSA Serving the Underserved trainer. He is a board member of *Voice of Youth Advocates*, and he also reviews books for *School Library Journal* and *Kirkus Reviews*.

James Murdock is a freelance journalist. He received an A.B. from Brown University in architectural history and urban studies, then later an M.S. from the Columbia University Graduate School of Journalism. His first full-time job was for a newspaper in southern Rhode Island, where he was a general assignment reporter. James later served as associate editor of the real estate journal *Commercial Property News*. As a freelancer, his work appears in a variety of publications, including *Architectural Record*, ArtInfo.com, *New York Blade*, and *VOYA*. James also reports stories for public radio, where his work can be heard on American Public Media's *Marketplace*. James is a member of the National Lesbian & Gay Journalists Association.

Jack and James met at the Providence Public Library in 1999 and have been together ever since. Currently, they live in New York with their two hyperactive cats. This is their first book.